"Never has the delicate balance of life and death been
so beautifully expressed. Kristoffer speaks both clearly
and powerfully about experiences that we all will go
through, demonstrating how spiritual, emotional, and
physical truths combine to allow us to move forward."

Cat Treadwell, Druid priest and
author of *Facing the Darkness*

the Journey into Spirit

ABOUT THE AUTHOR

Kristoffer Hughes is a certified anatomical pathology technologist who has worked professionally in service to Her Majesty's coroner at morgues throughout the United Kingdom for the past twenty-five years. He is an experienced professional funeral celebrant and officiator who frequently presents workshops, lectures, and courses that explore the function of mortuary ritual and practice as well as death customs and philosophy. He is a priest of the Druid tradition and is the current head of the Anglesey Druid Order. He lives on the Isle of Anglesey, off the coast of North Wales. Visit his website at:

WWW.KRISTOFFERHUGHES.CO.UK

the *Journey into Spirit*

A PAGAN'S PERSPECTIVE ON DEATH, DYING & BEREAVEMENT

KRISTOFFER HUGHES

Llewellyn Publications
WOODBURY, MINNESOTA

FIRST EDITION
First Printing, 2014

Book design and edit: Rebecca Zins
Cover design: Kevin R. Brown
Cover photo: Shutterstock/3597920/Jill Battaglia
Interior floral illustrations from *Ornamental Flowers, Buds and Leaves*
by V. Ruprich-Robert (Dover Publications, 2010); line illustrations
on pages 6, 89, and 117 by Llewellyn Art Department

Llewellyn Publications is a registered trademark of Llewellyn Worldwide Ltd.

Library of Congress Cataloging-in-Publication Data
Hughes, Kristoffer, 1971–
The journey into spirit : a pagan's perspective on death, dying & bereavement
/ Kristoffer Hughes.—First edition.
    pages cm
Includes bibliographical references.
ISBN 978-0-7387-4075-1
1. Death—Religious aspects—Neopaganism. 2. Death—Religious aspects—
Paganism. I. Title.
BF1572.D43H84 2014
299′.94—dc23

2014016200

Llewellyn Publications
A Division of Llewellyn Worldwide Ltd.
2143 Wooddale Drive
Woodbury, MN 55125-2989
www.llewellyn.com
Printed in the United States of America

THIS BOOK IS DEDICATED TO THE DEAD WHOSE TALES LIE WITHIN

My grandmother
MARGARET BERYL ROBERTS

My friend
HAYDN THOMAS FRANKLYN

My father
ALAN JOHN HUGHES

My teacher and dearest friend
MYFANWY DAVIES

My sister
RACHEL ANN DAVIES

My feline companion
MILLIE

A fellow Druid
PETER DODD

You will always be remembered.

CONTENTS

AUTHOR'S NOTE

In the United Kingdom, the common term for a morgue is *mortuary*. However, in the USA and Canada, *mortuary* is the common term used to describe a funeral home. For ease of reference, I have chosen to use the term *morgue* to describe a public facility for the examination of the dead as instructed or governed by a coroner or medical examiner.

INTRODUCTION

What happens to us when we die?

Death initiates the unfathomable separation of body and spirit. The vessel of experience and expression—the human body—is our primary point of reference; it lives, it breathes, it loves, it cries, and then suddenly it ceases to be. The force or energy that drives it leaves, and body and spirit veer in different directions. But what then—what happens to us at that point of separation? Where do *we* go?

Human beings have never ceased in their attempt to understand the function of death and the mystery it holds; it has power, and all too often it is a devastating force that shatters lives and tears at the heart. At times death comes as a friend, offering respite and release, and yet questions may still remain. Where have they gone? How can all that energy, all those memories, simply cease to exist?

In truth, they don't; nature does not waste anything. Our memories and experience of being human are not annihilated at the point of death; something remains, and yet the answers offered here may differ from what you have previously encountered. Within the Pagan traditions, the commonly held belief is that upon death we enter another world, which is perceived as a place of perpetual summer or feasting—a place of rest before reentry into the world by the process of reincarnation. This book serves to challenge that theory and to offer another way of thinking about death.

But how do I know this—who am I to sit here and type these words of comfort and offer hope to the hearts of the bereaved and the inquiring mind?

Death has been my life; I have lived in its shadow since my teenage years. It has been my constant companion, my security, and my mentor. For over twenty years I have worked as an autopsy technologist in morgues throughout the United Kingdom, serving and protecting the dead. In my spiritual life I have developed into a priest of the dead, a walker between the worlds, a psychopomp.

It is the living of a life in death that causes me to pen these words; it is living in the kingdom of the dead that has taught me so much about death. I serve the reaper of spirits, and by proxy I walk hand in hand with the dead, yet my relationship with death has been perplexing. I have learned, seen, and witnessed the effects of death and the process that occurs during that transition, but I have also been pained by it. My faithfulness to the reaper has bought me no credit and offered me no favors, for it has taken my loved ones also. I have knelt before the altar of grief and cried my heart into a red mist, and I have learned much; this is what I share with you in the pages that follow.

I must stress: I am not a medium. I do not hear the dead, and very rarely do I see echoes of them reaching from beyond the realms of life. The most adequate word to describe my abilities is clairsentient; I feel and sense images and messages, information and data that flow from the quantum machinery of spirit and soul to sink into the fluidness of my mind. I do not offer anecdotes of conversations with the dead or personal messages that are pertinent to a single individual. I share with you a knowing that comes from having lived with the dead, of being privileged to share their world and glean a deeper understanding of the process of crossing over.

Through death I have learned the meaning of life, and I am comforted by my understanding and experience of the hereafter.

If you are reading this book, chances are you have lost someone close to you. You may be recently bereaved, a seeker on the path of spirit, or a grove, solitary, coven, or group member who seeks to explore the function of death in modern Paganism. Whatever your motives for reading my words, my intention is that I convey to you a message of hope that arises from experience, and that after reading this your relationship with death may be different. I do not have all the answers, but those that I do offer are of immense comfort to me, and I hope that they will be beneficial to you. Bear in mind that some of the concepts I portray here may assist to transport you beyond what is comfortable or familiar, but I hope that what you will sense is the sincerity of the words that I share by having lived so closely to death.

In the following pages I lay open my heart to you; some of these words have not been easy for me to pen, and throughout you will find me recalling my personal encounters with death and grief. I write these stories in honor of those whom I have loved and lost, and what I have learned from the process of bereavement. I conclude each personal section with a brief discourse that explores what I have learned from my encounters with a loved one's death.

Death is never easy, even to those who are in conviction of faith; we are still torn by the loss. I do not offer sensationalism; my intention is to evoke emotion rather than to shock. Indeed, within these pages some paragraphs may offer descriptive insights into the world behind the morgue doors, but I do so out of reflection, not out of a need to sensationalize or appear morbid. To understand my journey and the conclusions I have arrived at, it is necessary to peer into my world. Some of the images and scenes I portray may be disturbing to you, or you may find them upsetting. However, I feel this is necessary for you to understand the journey. I hope that by presenting you with a glimpse into the physical world of the dead, you will be comforted in the knowledge that those who serve them do so because they care.

Eventually the journey will move on to matters of the spirit. This book follows my own sequential journey with death and spirit, but it does so in tune with my own spiritual practice.

Humanity has always developed coping mechanisms to deal with the realities of life and death, and this book will provide a glimpse of the emotional and physical responses of one man's journey into the shadowy world of the unknown. I do this to satisfy some deep need within me to explore my own coping mechanisms and to share with my audience that journey in the hope that some of the mysteries of death are transmitted from my experience and amalgamated into yours.

IN THE REAPER'S SERVICE

Throughout this book I refer to an ambiguous figure that I call the reaper. I do not use this term flippantly, nor do I utilize it out of provocation or a sense of the dramatic. It is the word I use to refer to the force of death, or the energy or the personification of death, that humans have connected with for millennia.

I use this term in reference to a neutral energy whose primary function is to sever the ties of life. It does not perform this function out of malice; instead, it acts as a psychopomp, escorting the individual from this life to the beyond. Over the years, I have developed a reverence and deep respect for this energy, the initiator of the process of death. My own attempt to personify this energy is, of course, deeply indicative of my own coping mechanisms; I consciously give it an anthropomorphic persona simply because I need to. It allows me to identify with the energy that I have devoted my life to serve.

THE THREE REALMS OF EXISTENCE

Spiritually I am a priest in the Celtic Druid tradition, which has long claimed the immortality of the human spirit. This living with death has enriched my spiritual quest; in fact, it has informed many aspects of it. However, one does not need to be a follower of the Celtic or Druidic tradition to find this book useful, for the information within it is applicable to many systems and traditions and to those who do not identify with any belief system. The framework I use is Celtic in nature simply because that is the tradition I embrace, but even within my own tradition very little is written of death. Therefore, the material herein is based mostly on experience and yet tied to the Celtic culture by means of language and symbols.

Within the modern Pagan Celtic worldview is the principle of the three realms of existence, which forms the central pattern of this book. This concept is taken mostly from the works of Iolo Morganwg and his pioneering body of literature titled *Barddas*. This material was compiled at the end of the eighteenth century and has inspired much of the modern Celtic tradition.

This worldview is beautiful in its simplicity; it provides a sense of place, of sequence and mystery. Its teachings are deeply profound and applicable beyond the shores of the Celtic nations. It is based on the principle of three concentric circles, each one indicative of a state of being. As the energy dissolves from one, it transfers to the other, bringing elements of the previous realm with it; therefore, all three realms, although they appear separate, are inexorably connected. They can be demonstrated thus:

The first three parts of this book correspond to the three realms, and I offer you this brief introduction to them. Further exploration will be provided within each individual section.

PART 1: THE CIRCLE OF ABRED—
THE REALM OF NECESSITY

This is the physical world, the here and now, living in the moment. It is the earthly plane; it is hard, real, tangible, and stable. In this part you will be introduced to the physical nature of death and my relationship with it—what I have learned from that process and how it acts as key to the spirit. It is the first point of reference; it is necessary. This is the cold face of death and the dissolution of the corpse. The body is honored here during life and after death. In the Celtic tongue this realm is called Abred (pronounced AH-bred).

PART 2: THE CIRCLE OF GWYNVYD—
THE REALM OF SPIRIT

This is the dimension of spirit—the spirit world, if you like; it is that place which is hidden from our mortal eyes by a gossamer-thin veil. Occasionally we may catch a glimpse of its mystery, and some have the ability to clearly perceive it and convey messages from those who occupy that space. It is our location after the death of the physical body, yet we are in constant contact with it while we are in Abred. It is a place that we sense and feel. In this section I explore questions of emotions, grief, and the spirit. In the Celtic tongue this realm is known as Gwynvyd (goo-IN-vid), meaning the "pure world."

PART 3: THE CIRCLE OF CEUGANT—
THE REALM OF INFINITY

This is the realm of the soul, of singularity; it is from this place that all things originate, and it is to this place that all things return. It is the first point of being and the final destination; it is the source. We originate here. This is our true home. In this section I delve into the dizzy realms of infinity and of the ultimate destination and function of the soul. In the Celtic tongue this realm is called Ceugant (KAY-gant).

The above concepts are not limited to the worldview of the Celts. Parallels can be seen in the majority of spiritual systems where threefold divisions are common.

Part 4 of this book explores ritual and practice pertinent to the experience of death and bereavement.

All I am in life is in response to what I have learned from death. As a consequence I became aware of the spiritual, and I looked to my own culture to make sense of this. My findings mold the material for this book. In essence, the Pagan tradition is a life-affirming path; very little focus is placed on death, which is considered merely a transitory stage and is not feared. By means of the life that I have lived, I have learned a few things along the way, and it is these findings combined with the magic of my spiritual tradition that I offer to you in the pages that follow. So I ask that you join me on a journey into faith, belief, love, loss, hope, and experience.

I live knowing that death is not the end, and neither is it the beginning; it is one step along a perpetual, never-ending road of being.

Kristoffer Hughes
Isle of Anglesey
AUTUMN 2013

A LIGHT IN THE DARKNESS

Mad from life's history, glad to death's mystery,
Swift to be hurled—anywhere, anywhere out of the world!

THOMAS HOOD

The inky black darkness is torn apart by the shards of light that emanate from the lighthouse; silently her lamp turns, comforting those who traverse the seas in search of land. The darkness, however, screams at the intrusion, and only the pealing laughter of the seals seems unaffected by the blinding light that perpetually shines from the beacon. I snuggle deeper in the black wool of the cloak that clings to my body, as if even it attempts to hide from the searing, blinding light. I can see nothing of the sea somewhere beyond the rocks; I am only aware of the subtle thudding of waves as they make contact with the island.

Breathing deeply, I slowly rise to my feet. My backside is sore from the hard wooden bench I have been sitting on for the last two hours. The lighthouse continues to shine, blinding me from this angle; I turn my face sharply away from the glare and quickly move to the edge of the cliff, finding a way down, away from the relentless light.

My feet feel moisture. The cold caress of the Celtic Sea seeps into my boots as I near the water's edge. It is better down here. The light is high above me, moving through the cloudless sky; the dark is less threatened here—it has crevices and coves in which to bask. I breathe more easily and sense the tension escaping my body, allowing it to fall into the dark sea and be carried away to some distant shore.

Memories of laughter and good company slowly swim into my mind of the people I have left behind at the house, a mile and a half from here. I turn towards the direction of warmth, thinking of good food and mead, of fireplaces and beds, but I see nothing other than light streaking across inky blackness. There is no electricity on this island, no cars, no mobile phone signal, and no warm, comforting glows whispering from windows—only darkness and the lighthouse.

I am on the island of Bardsey, just beyond the tip of the Llyn Peninsula in North Wales. This tiny island holds a magic that is difficult to articulate; it has a special kind of stillness that is unheard of in the "civilized" world of technology and stuff that permeates life on the mainland. This is a wild place of weather and nature, of contemplation and reflection. People come here to get away from it all, yet ironically they cannot get away from themselves; perhaps that is what draws people here—to be immersed in self with little or no distractions.

Gazing out to the west with the moist breeze against my skin, I breathe in tune with my life, feeling the pull of it. And yet I am aware of the significance of the west to my ancestors and to ancient civilizations across the globe: it is the direction of the dead. To the west our ships ultimately sail on that final, solitary voyage beyond the gates of life and into the halls of the dead. My Celtic forefathers spoke of the otherworld and of the land of the dead being across the western sea. The Egyptians revered the west as the resting place of their dead and the domain of the setting sun and the spirits of their tribe. Tradition and heritage sing from this place, and eventually that song will consume us as the last breath rises from our lips and joins death's song.

A few weeks ago I was diagnosed with a tumor that has invaded my thyroid; I can feel it there, an alien presence within my own body, yet nonetheless a part of me. Luckily it is not invasive, and neither will it destroy my body nor lead to my own death. I am unfortunate to have a tumor but fortunate to have this type of tumor. A relatively straightforward surgical procedure will harmlessly remove it and any threat it poses to my well-being. That my father died of cancer only two years past is a poignant reminder to my subconscious of my own frailty. I am not invincible; one day, a presently unknown something will come and take my life. And here upon this shore, in the no man's land where the tide meets the rugged shoreline, I contemplate the million and one situations and circumstances that brought me to this place. In solitude, facing the west, I surrender to that most primal and feared of all things, the promise of death. It is these few hours of quiet contemplation that cause me to write these words, to share with you a world behind the doors of death, that place of mystery and taboo.

I trained as a morgue/autopsy technologist. The morgue has become my second home: a place of security and surety, a place where life feels so near and yet death so apparent. It is a world of tears, of deep grief that rips the heart apart in a cloud of red splinters; it is a place of laughter and rejoicing, of living in the moment. It is a place of investigation, of justice, of research and expansion. But above all it is the house of the dead. This is their domain, their realm; we serve them, those who have gone before us. We are the guardians of the dead.

The reaper of spirits has no presence here; its billowing black cloak and scythe have fulfilled their duty elsewhere. It is only the cold, hard face of death that lives here with the tears of those left behind. And yet life surges within the heart of the morgue, within the bodies of those who call this place home for thirty-seven hours or more a week. It is a place of paradox, contradictions, silence, and reflection; for many it is the end of a long journey, while to others like myself it is a vital part of that journey, reaching forwards in time, stretching out to feel the fingertips of death that beckon us all onwards and closer to the grave.

But what exactly happens to us when we die?

the *Realm of Necessity*

PART 1

THE CIRCLE OF ABRED

IN WHICH ARE ALL CORPORAL AND DEAD EXISTENCES

From the earth is the flesh
From the water, the blood
From the air, the breath
From the hardness, the bones
From the salt is the feeling
From the sun is light and agitation
From the truth is understanding
From the Great Spirit is the Soul.

ADAPTED FROM *THE BARDDAS OF IOLO MORGANWG*

The three principal calamities of Abred: necessity, forgetfulness, and death.

The physical form carries the experience of living, of being present in the world. The body, a genius of evolution and biology, is a perfect, harmonious combination of molecules that form tissue and organs that bring function to a machine that contains the spirit. The separation of body and spirit after death has a devastating effect on those who are inevitably left behind to grieve.

In an attempt to alleviate the pain of death, many will denounce the importance of the body, claiming that after death it serves no purpose. In the Celtic tradition the body is honored as a vessel that expressed life; it is not denounced but instead treated with utmost respect and dignity before being returned to the elements from which it came. Separation of body and spirit is acknowledged, but this fact does not negate the respect one has for the corpse. Prehistorically, grave goods affirm this notion that the dead were treated with respect, reflecting spiritual concepts or beliefs.

In the realm of necessity, Abred, we learn what it is to be human; we are immersed in life, yet paradoxically we are subjected to death. It is the only realm of existence where death has a function, and as the name of the realm suggests, this function is necessary. In order for the continuation of life to perpetuate on the physical plane, all things must die. The circle of Abred is the circle of repetition; all things are governed by the cycle of birth, life, death, and rebirth.

We may abhor the power of death, yet when we look to nature we see the beauty and magic that hides within it. The deep green leaves of an oak in late summer give way to the ochre of autumn foliage; these in turn die and fall to the ground beneath the shadow of the tree. From their decomposition the earth is enriched, and new life is nurtured to rise majestically in the spring. All things die, and from their graves grow future generations of plant, animal, and human. Without death, there would be no life.

Human beings are a part of nature; human nature is nature. There is no separation. The carbon atoms of our bodies were forged by the deaths of stars. In the incomprehensible heat of a burning sun, elements compressed and gave rise to atoms that brought form and shape to the physical universe. When our sun dies and consumes the planets of our solar system, the pattern will be repeated. Our bodies, broken down to their constituent atoms, will be recycled to bring new and different shapes to the universe. Nothing is truly lost; the power of nature is too great, too wondrous. She is the ultimate recycler. The function of death in the realm of necessity is to transform; it does not seek to destroy, for nothing in nature can be truly destroyed—instead, it simply changes its form.

Cast your eyes from the pages of this book and look at the back of your left hand. Know that the carbon molecules that make up your skin and the blood that flows in the veins beneath are not new; they have existed before the joining of your spirit and body. Your spirit has lived a million times before in a million different shapes. This is but one step along the journey of the universe—a vast, wondrous universe that sings in praise of itself—and its voice right now, at this very moment, is you. You bring to the universe something exquisitely unique: the experience of being you.

One day the force that holds your body and spirit in unison will fail, and separation will occur. Your human body will perish, and nature will at once attempt to break it down, returning it to its original state of molecules and atoms that dance in search of a new form. Whether by process of disease or accident, the dying of the body causes massive shifts in the lives of those left behind. We are bereaved; we grieve the loss of touch, of caress, of the deliciousness of human interaction. In life we are constantly in the midst of death.

Our individual journeys through the realm of necessity are unique, and they do not occur independently of the world, for we are a part of this planet. Nothing exists in a vacuum. Our lives affect the world; however minutely, we matter. We are an integral part of the great song of the universe, and every single second of our lives counts; they mean something—in good times and bad, through exhilaration and despair, we are constantly contributing to the great song.

The following chapters are a discourse in my own journey through necessity and my introduction and assimilation into the mysteries of death. They are the first tantalizing steps of a roller coaster journey into the fabric of the spirit.

THE CALL OF THE REAPER

My shroud of white, stuck all with yew, O prepare it!
My part of death, no one so true did share it.

SHAKESPEARE, *TWELFTH NIGHT*

I watched a man die today.

The automatic doors swept aside with a graceful hiss, and for a second we stood face to face, inches apart, two strangers about to meet at the point of death. The sounds of the busy ferry terminal faded into nowhere as my eyes met his. The vacant windows to his spirit emptied further as I watched his pupils dilate like the lens of a camera and witnessed the snapshot of death as it severed the ties of life. My breath caught momentarily somewhere in the center of my being as my brain feebly attempted to assimilate this experience into my own neural database. I had no point of reference, no comparable encounter to help articulate what I was observing, yet somehow, somewhere deep within the core of my spirit, I knew that I was a privileged onlooker to witness the actual moment of death.

His body crumpled like newspaper casually thrown to the ground; I recall flinching at the hollow thud as his head crashed onto the cold marble flooring. A dull echo resounded through the busy shipping terminal that was a hive of activity: people rushing here and there, old friends reuniting, the tears of lovers parting, the public announcement system bellowing information for the weary or excited traveler. The echoing thud of human skull against marble and the ensuing silence felt like an intrusion, an abnormal interruption to the relentless humdrum of the terminal and of normality. In that brief moment it was as if every soul in that building felt the breath of Death and the chill of its cloak as it passed through a place of such vibrancy, of so much life. In pursuit of its victim, its presence instilled a gasp into the lungs of those present; by unknown means, every individual sensed the awesome power of Death.

The man's body assumed a supine position on the cold floor, his hands slapping onto the polished surface as if gently appreciating the smoothness of the marble. His head turned to one side, his mouth a gaping cavern, and in that moment our eyes met again. I felt his empty gaze sear my own spirit, reaching into my heart, which leapt empathically at the termination of another life.

After the involuntary silence that befell the terminal, the volume increased once more with voices of concern and people running towards the fallen man—some out of genuine concern but, alas, many out of sheer curiosity, victims of the human condition. Perhaps to witness the suffering of another momentarily relieves the pain within damaged hearts, providing temporary relief and the sense of "oh well, I'm still here, that's good, thank God it wasn't me."

Time itself seemed affected—drawn or sucked into the unfolding event. The seemingly delayed scream of anguish that rose from the gentleman's wife seemed overdue and oddly out of place, yet her cry had the ability to shock time back into its normal course. She fell to her knees beside her husband, as did a colleague and I, who were merely feet away. My colleague instinctively initiated CPR, calling out instructions, yelling for someone to call an ambulance, but it was too late.

The last breath to leave the man's chest seemed labored, broken, and crackly, leading finally into a deep sigh. Looking into his eyes, I saw no fear, no terror as I somehow had expected, but rather a contented surrender to the journey ahead. As his pupils dilated fully to let in the light of the day—light that would shine uselessly onto dead nerves—I sensed his life end and witnessed his body falling away from the spark of life, falling out of his spirit, which expanded to encompass the universe.

He was dead, just a cooling, dense amalgamation of matter, of flesh rendered useless. Yet something inexplicable was shifting in the very air that we breathed; I could not fathom nor make sense of it at the time. Something was missing, yet the atmosphere seemed to crackle with some energy that to my teenage mind was too great, too vast for me to fathom.

Our first encounters with death can shock us into unfamiliar territory. We may be accustomed to images of death and dying on TV and in the violent world of many video games. But when Death visits in person, it can leave us feeling discombobulated and somewhat beside ourselves. My first encounter, as described above, came with no warning—life and death collided in an instant in a public place. There was no time for preparation, and yet those few moments in the company of a fellow human being's death deeply affected my life.

Consider, if you will, your experience with someone's death.

Stop for a minute, take a deep breath, and cast your mind to your first encounter with death. At what point in your life did that happen, if it has happened at all? How did it make you feel, and what effect did it have on you? Perhaps you have yet to experience someone's death; do you recall seeing it on TV? If so, how did that affect your life or leave a lasting impression? Our first encounter with death, particularly in childhood, can have lasting impressions that mold our future relationship with it. If you are able, recall the thoughts and feelings that were initiated by your encounter with death. Were they the same then as they are now? How has your relationship and understanding of death changed since that first encounter? Jot these thoughts down in a notepad so that you may look at them again in the future.

A CHILD'S CALLING

I had sensed the reaper's calling, the sublime whisper and the chill wind of the scythe as it fell. Something about the situation felt familiar, as if I had witnessed it a million times before. It was as if a voice was calling me from somewhere beyond the visible world. I had heard it before, years previously, during childhood.

It was the music that stuck in my head, causing me to hum it continuously; the actual content of the program had not imprinted on me, or so I thought. I was painfully young—how young I fail to recall—but young enough and susceptible enough to be affected by something on a deeply subconscious level. Music has that ability to haunt us and remind us of deep-set memories, of places and people long believed to have been forgotten. I doubt that we actually forget anything; they are simply stored away in some dark corner of the mind for possible future use.

The music that haunted me was to the popular '70s American drama *Quincy, M.E.* I may well have observed morgue scenes before this time, maybe a drama or play that took its characters into the shadowy world of the morgue. However, this particular program demanded my attention; my heart quickened its rhythm and my eyes were dazzled by the images of pristine white walls and the silence of steel. I recall asking family members questions that referred to the dead—where they were stored, why they were there, what had happened to them, where was my local morgue?

The overwhelming memory I have of this time of questioning is the uncomfortable response I invoked. The awkward fidgeting of adults confronted with a question they did not want to explore, the twitching of eyes that disbelieved the sight of a child eagerly lost in questions of death. The residual memory I have is not one of having asked something inappropriate but rather the fact that I was fascinated by their awkwardness. I perceived their fear, and this intrigued me further, for fear was something that I certainly did not feel, but why did they? The sense of being dismissed only stirred the calling further; I developed into a deeply thinking child, immersed in thoughts and concepts, quietly observing the mundane world about me.

The recollection of me as a child enveloped in a room of ghastly 1970s wallpaper and totally immersed in televised images seems, in hindsight, to have been the point of initial stirring, the first calling of the reaper. I do not use the term *calling* flippantly; I do so to describe a deep sense of attachment to a concept that previously had not affected my life. Career choices bear little relevance to young children who are mostly lost in the rapture and magic of youthful innocence, and this fact applied to me, as it does to every child. Yet something within me changed at this point. I became aware of a deeper aspect to life and that somehow I was different from my peers. It was something that lay beyond my ability to articulate at the time, yet I cannot deny that I felt something move and ignite within the center of my being.

It was at this point that the morgue doors creaked open and a sliver of light appeared beyond its threshold, tantalizingly bright yet continuously clinging onto its secrets. I was not yet permitted entry, however, and the calling grew ever louder.

DEATH'S DESIGN

Some people find themselves in the death business by chance, accident, or necessity; others are born into it, molded by parents or peers and directed into the industry. I believe I differ, as many others do, in that I sensed a calling—I knew that deep down, it was something I could do and do well. It was not an accident that stirred my interest or attraction, and neither was it a morbid fascination; I would argue to this day that I am not morbidly fascinated. The *Oxford English Dictionary* defines a calling as a vocation and further describes a vocation as "a strong belief that one ought to pursue a particular career or occupation."

The term *calling* is perhaps familiar to you in reference to a member of a church, convent, or monastery, but is that sense of calling only limited to duty of religion? I would argue that it can be heard in many walks of life and that it whispers to us at an early age, when we are impressionable enough for it to inspire our life choices. The formation of my own life choices was made, I believe, in response to the calling that I sensed—a calling to leave behind the security and, to an extent, the blissful ignorance of the ordinary world and embark on a journey into the land betwixt and between the living and the dead.

To feel that one is called into the service of something comes with responsibility and also the ability to respond to that calling, and this was no easy task for a teenager in the Welsh schooling system of the 1980s. Generally those who sense a calling express it at a cost, for one of the prices we pay is that of disdainful ridicule. I felt this ridicule, lined with disgust, during my later school years with the mournful approach of Career Day.

Summoned to a windowless room, each child would sit before the judging eyes of the career officer and present before them a notion that would secure their place in the world of responsible adults. I felt a degree of excitement anticipating that help was at hand—that this guru of career choices would grace me with the valuable information I needed to enter the world of the morgue.

I was not an ignorant child; I had studied what I deemed important and immersed myself in subjects that somehow accessorized the calling I felt. Biology and human sciences became subjects that enthralled me; the workings of the remarkable human machine and the process of disease would sing to me. When I knocked on the careers office door that fateful day in February, I approached that portal armed with the knowledge that I knew what my calling was. I knew what was required of me and what I needed to secure to permit me entry beyond the morgue doors.

The disbelief was obvious; she made no attempt to hide her disdain as both her eyes engorged themselves against their lids, pushing them back to reveal the horrified glare of a person repelled. I recognized the speechless stance of a person without the ability to respond to what was, in my mind, a perfectly ordinary question. I had seen the same uncomfortable look on the faces of my family.

I sighed as she swung from one buttock to the other, bracing herself to deal with what she felt was an unhinged child. Something within me terminated the experience; I realized that no assistance was to be had here. I felt my eyes glaze over; my dejected mind shut itself off. I politely nodded and smiled as she advised me to think of other subjects that would be less damaging—something a little healthier perhaps? I had obviously watched far too many horror movies and needed to check in with reality and put these fanciful yet disturbing thoughts behind me. I held my school bag against my chest, clutching it to me as if attempting to shield myself from her negativity. I gave her nothing in return; I smiled politely, thanked her for her help, and slipped quietly out of the room.

The complete dismissal of my ambitions and sense of calling had been dashed. I felt a welling in the back of my eyes, a silent cry in my throat, and tears forced themselves to the edges of my eyes. My calling—I had to respond to it, I had a responsibility to it. At that point I clearly saw two paths before me, a fork in the road of my life. One took me to a place of tears and utter rejection, giving up on my dreams and taking a "normal" route into adulthood. The other was the sweeping touch of my fabric sleeve as I wiped the tears away in sheer determination to succeed. I chose the latter, with a hard swallow; I decided to take matters into my own hands. I would wipe that disdainful smirk off Mrs. Career Officer's face. I was not about to allow one person's inability and compromised coping mechanisms to change my life's course.

The formation of my life happened at that pivotal point, in direct contrast to the encouragement my fellow pupils received; I possessed only my own sense of determination in light of discouragement. Even then I would take to writing, putting pen to paper and expressing thoughts and emotions; I was fascinated by the response I had invoked. This calling, arising from the song of death, did something to people; it stirred the cauldron of their fears in a manner that intrigued me immensely. I would explore the facets of the human spirit and of my own spirit in relation to death.

I must stress at this point that I was not a particularly unusual child, at least not on the surface. I interacted with my peers, played, and partook in mischief and frivolity just the same as any other child in my age group. I shared similar concerns and felt the same pressures to fit in, be popular, and be good at various things. My background is as diverse as my interests; a loving family cared for me, siblings and various adults with different careers influenced my studies and hobbies and helped me to find my place in the world, to see direction.

There is perhaps a misconception that one who consciously chooses to live with death must have been damaged as a child or have been somewhat out of the ordinary. Alas, to that camp of thought, my childhood was nothing of the sort: it was extraordinarily ordinary. Not a single member of my immediate family had any spiritual or religious leanings; my early years were devoid of any influence in that realm. I was to draw my own conclusions and be guided into an exploration of the spirit by other means, a fact that continues to baffle my family.

A KINDRED SPIRIT

It was a knowing smile that instilled within me the sense of possibility and potential, a chance meeting with another who served the reaper. After several inquiries into the profession, I met with a future colleague, and we approached each other on a windswept day, the smell of brine singing of the sea that crashed onto the nearby shore. I immediately sensed his knowing; he could tell that I was no ordinary teenager—that the light burning in my eyes expressed the calling that he himself had heard decades before. My colleagues will concur that we can simply tell by some unknown means whether or not an individual is suitable for entry into the profession. I doubt we could articulate or describe this process fully, but we do have the ability to know who can or cannot perform the task required of us. As we left the tumultuous coastline and entered the sanctuary of the nearby park, sheltered by trees and amidst the haze and headiness of a sea of bluebells, this man, whom I had never met before, sensed that I had the spark; the hand of the reaper was on my shoulder.

I have heard it said that individuals come into our lives when we least expect them. They bring something to us that we need and take us on journeys of exploration and learning. Perhaps we are led to those who help us to grow and develop, and maybe in return we assist them in their own growth. I am not entirely sure if I believe this concept or not, but I cannot deny that the right people at the right time uncannily appeared in my life, took me by the hand, and guided me in the direction that I intrinsically knew my life would take. As I have discovered on the course of this extraordinary life, there is more to heaven and earth than first meets the eye, and if I have learned anything, it is to suspend disbelief and observe the passing of life with an open, receptive gaze.

It was this receptiveness that permitted my entry into the world that I now inhabit. New connections and new experiences and perhaps my own ability to articulate my wanting to enter the profession eventually led to admission. This was not a straightforward task; the process was intense and required some preparation.

AT DEATH'S DOOR

On a stormy October day in 1991 it transpired that an apprentice position in a neighboring morgue was to be advertised. It was my new "morgue friend" who had informed me of this and started the process of my preparation. He took me under his wing and spoke to me of the world I wanted to enter; he was to become my guide, the person that to this day I look up to and have aspired to imitate, to be as good as I perceived him to be. The position was in a morgue in the next county; if I was to be successful, I would have to move from home—a daunting prospect for an insular young man.

My parents shared my excitement when I informed them that a position was soon to be made available and that I would apply. I was to be given a tour of my local morgue the following day, my first introduction to this new world. I may have had expectations—if I did, I do not recall them—but I can clearly remember how I felt that somehow my life was about to take the course it was designed to. My hands shook as I dressed the following morning, my mother having to knot the tie that my hands could not fathom. I can still see the reflection in the mirror, locked into my mind's eye, of a fresh, excited-looking young man—with substantially more hair—on the verge of a new adventure.

The world sped past as the bus took me on the journey into my future—ceremoniously, it seemed—disembarking me on the pavement outside the large general hospital that housed my local morgue. Following the signs, I arrived at the solid wooden doors that separated the outside world from a place of mystery that lay only inches beyond. My finger did not waver as it reached forward and pushed the bell.

It was the friendliness that struck me first. As the doors opened I was faced with a tidy, nondescript foyer and the smiling faces of three men. My guide was there, of course, his gentle features and subtle smile reassuring me that all was well and that I was welcome. He beckoned me in. As I stepped over the threshold, I felt the embrace of the three men beyond, who seemed pleased that I was entering their world. They seemed eager to share the secrets that I was sure hid just beyond what I could visibly see. Their faces were kindly, their eyes smiled as well as their lips; they appeared compassionate and friendly, warm and accommodating. In the back of my mind I believe I expected some form of rebuke or defensive response of someone who felt I was an intrusion; in actuality it was the opposite. It seemed I was welcome here.

It was the smell that next reached my senses; it was not in any way repellent or repulsive but yet immensely unique and indicative of the environment. The entire air smelled clean, sanitized, as if the very molecules of oxygen and nitrogen had been scrubbed with disinfectant. A cacophony of chitchat reached my ears as my eyes attempted to take in all that was before me, which in hindsight was very little other than closed doors and a desk. I heard one of the men state that he would make us all tea while my guide would give me the grand tour. The voices seemed distant, as if I was hearing them through a gelatinous barrier that I could not see. I could hardly believe where I was, that I was actually standing in a morgue. Suddenly the sounds clarified, and I could hear the distant hum of machinery and fans.

My guide gestured for me to follow him into a stark room, its pale beige walls serving only to highlight the emptiness of the space. Only a large, oblong trolley occupied the floor, standing alone, a silent sentinel to a task I was yet to identify. My eyes were drawn to the opposite wall, which seemed to consist of several doors, ten in total. They were white, with a large steel handle placed directly in the middle and to the side of each one. A humming sound arose from the direction of the doors, which I suddenly realized were the refrigerators in which lay the bodies of the dead.

I had expected to be greeted by individual square doors, each one opening onto its own cavernous space, which is what I had seen on the television. In reality it was quite different. My guide glided over to one of the doors and, while explaining the function of the refrigerator, he opened one of them. Instead of the typical Americanized storage units I had seen on TV, this unit disguised a single space, in front of which stood several doors. Each door presented a shelving system expertly fitted into the space that held four steel trays.

Each tray contained a bundle covered in a white sheet.

Four bodies lay before me. Although my view was limited, I could see the shape and forms of the corpses that lay beneath the sheets. I felt no shock at this sight; I recall only feeling humbled to have been given the opportunity to see the resting place of the recently departed. From my perspective, they had no features, no names—they existed only as bundles wrapped in cloth, yet they were people. Their final form as human beings lay before me on cold steel. The door closed, gently hiding them from my view; my guide continued his explanation of the morgue's function and purpose as he gestured for me to follow him. We left the fridge room, as they are commonly called, and reentered the main vestibule of the morgue. From here he took me through another door that bore the ominous sign POSTMORTEM ROOM upon its veneered surface.

Whatever expectations I had were quickly eliminated as we entered a pristine room of polished floors, white walls, and banks of shining steel. Running down the center of the room stood the postmortem tables, robust chunks of steel that hissed as air was drawn through them by some invisible force, their surfaces reflecting the powerful lights that shone from above. They seemed practical, functional, yet were not unpleasant to look at; their design was elegant even if their purpose was quite the opposite. I listened intently to my guides' commentary of the room's functionality and how it operated on a daily basis. I was fascinated. A part of me had expected carnage, to see evidence of the tasks that this room harbored, yet it was impeccably clean and organized; these men evidently took pride in their place of work. I was surprised to hear that only an hour previously four postmortem examinations had taken place in this room, yet nothing remained to suggest what had recently occurred.

Much of what I heard I had previously read in pursuit of research into the profession, so the content of my guide's speech came as no surprise; it was the environment that surprised me. There were no shadows, no dark corners, no black-painted walls or overhead lighting that shone only a pale beam in circles onto the floor. There were no drapes of deep purple or the sound of organ music, no grim-faced tall men with hunchbacks who patronized the bereaved. The entire department was floodlit in brilliant light, corners were sharp and clean, the floors polished to within an inch of their lives. The staff dressed in shirts with bright ties and emitted an air of quiet professionalism. As I entered the staff room, a cheery disposition hung in the air; comfortable chairs invited me to be seated as a mug of steaming tea was thrust into my hands. It was normal, ordinary, yet paradoxically extraordinary!

Subsequently I have witnessed the discomfort some people suffer within a morgue environment; their entire bodies seem to twitch, their disposition expressing their need to leave this place of the dead. I felt nothing of that nature. I felt at home, comfortable in the company of those who shared a commonality; they too were in the reaper's service. I felt relaxed in their company; although they were significantly older than me, the years between us seemed irrelevant. I finally felt that someone in the world was not repelled by my wish to work with the dead. The conversation ceased as a loud bell rang; the men muttered something to each other and gestured for me to follow them. With reassuring smiles they led me back to the fridge room.

A funeral director had arrived to collect one of the morgue's temporary residents. He was a jolly man, his red cheeks belying the years spent in cold cemeteries in all weathers; he smiled kindly at me as my guide explained who I was and what I was doing there. He shook my hand, and I recall him saying enthusiastically to me, "Welcome to our world!" The sound of metal against metal alerted me to movement; I turned to witness a tray, along with its occupant, sliding gracefully yet noisily from the cavernous refrigerator. One of the morgue men casually yet respectfully removed the sheets that served to hide the person beneath it. The men spoke to each other normally, one calling out the name of the deceased whilst the funeral director confirmed the name and the address. My guide explained the process of collection and the paperwork required to ensure that the process was accurate and efficient.

It was an elderly man who lay on the tray before me. I walked slowly to the side of the tray as the funeral director positioned a pale wooden coffin against the opposite side. The gentleman's head lay on a white painted wooden block that had a half-moon depression cut into it; this held his head to prevent it rolling to one side. My guide explained the process of identification as he lifted the gentleman's arm and revealed the name tag that encircled his wrist. A pale shroud made of soft fabric hung loosely about the man's shoulders; its sleeves seemed a little baggy for his thin frame. He had a kindly face; his mouth was relaxed yet had a hint of a smile to it. His skin was tinged with a pale yellow color and looked like the surface of a church candle, like tallow.

The funeral director sighed heavily beside me and reached forward to pass his fingers through the gentleman's white hair.

"No more pain, eh, Bob? No more pain. Let's get you back to the village," he muttered quietly. His comment was directed at the deceased man; it was not for our benefit. I smiled at him. He turned and said, "Bob was popular round the village; everybody knew Bob. He had it tough, been ill for such a long time: cancer. Terrible thing, terrible! But he was a fighter, old Bob; he fought till he could fight no more. He'll be missed."

"Was he a friend of yours?" I asked him.

"Aye, he was indeed, a good friend, a very good friend. Now all I can do is give him a good sendoff. He'd like that," he replied.

The morgue men stood silently beside us, and at a signal from the funeral director, they reached forward and gently lifted the man's body from the tray and placed him carefully into his coffin. The lid slid into place, and in moments the coffin was loaded into the back of a hearse that stood patiently outside the morgue's private entrance.

I never found anything out about Bob; I saw only his body and the manner in which the morgue staff treated him. Bob had been the first morgue body I had seen, and although it was my first experience, it was not alien; it seemed normal. I was comfortable in this environment and happy to pursue a life in this profession.

My heart thumped against my sternum as I stood at the bottom of the stairs. I had heard the arrival of the postman and the anticipated thud of envelopes thrust through the letterbox. I could see a small brown envelope with my name upon it; my mother pushed it eagerly into my hands, and with shaking fingers I opened it.

I had been shortlisted for the morgue position in the neighboring county. I had prepared for every possible question they could ask. I had studied long and hard the systems of the body and the legalities of morgue procedures and practice. I was naturally nervous but quietly confident; for some inexplicable reason, I knew deep down that

I would win the job. The process itself is still a blur in my memory—almost like a dream, its edges seem hazy and unclear; even the subsequent tour of the morgue has a subtle quality to it, as if enveloped in fog. And yet overriding the entire experience was a sense of knowing. Everything felt right. I knew that I was standing in a location where I would spend the next several years of my life.

I did not wait long for an answer. The following morning the piercing ring of the telephone pealed through the house. The female voice on the other side informed me that I had been appointed; I was stunned into silence, barely able to acknowledge her. She congratulated me, and the line went dead. It was real. I had waited a few years for this moment to happen and, finally, here it was.

At last I was permitted entry into the halls of the dead.

FIRST LOSS

The term *nain*, pronounced exactly as the number nine in English, is the Welsh term for grandmother. I adored my nain; she was perfect in every way, the epitome of what a grandmother should be: loving, kind, compassionate, wise, and very funny. She had always been there and loved me so much, which filled my heart with warmth and comfort, knowing that no matter what I did or where I went, my nain loved me without condition. She was a constant, unchanging thing in my life, and wherever my journey took me, eventually it would bring me back to her; she was always there, sitting in her large, comfortable chair, engrossed in the latest movie or soap opera and yet always wanting to hear of my latest adventure and tales. I would sit next to her for hours chatting about any such nonsense, anything just to be there in her presence; somehow it made me feel safe.

In my younger years I was in sufferance of sinusitis, a ghastly business that brought me so much pain and discomfort. Analgesia did much to ease the pressure in my forehead, but it was Nain who was the real magic. She would occasionally come to my room, sit on the bed next to me, and wipe the tears of pain from my eyes and stroke her hand against my forehead. She would pull the covers up tightly about my shoulders and tuck them under me, always whispering the almost untranslatable Welsh words *swatia rwan*, meaning something on the lines of "snuggle up now." There was magic in those two words and in her actions, something that no drug could mimic. It was the magical quality that only a nain could possess.

I recall so vividly being informed that my nain was terminally ill. She had been diagnosed with chronic obstructive pulmonary disease and would not get better. This intrusion to the status quo was unacceptable; my mind could barely cope with the information, and my heart thumped painfully against my ribcage, causing my breath to arise in gasps. This would change my world, and it was a world I did not fancy. I cried myself to sleep that night in fear of losing my nain, but it would be ten years later that the condition took her life.

Nain's health deteriorated to the point where she could no longer breathe with ease; every movement, every step caused her to gasp for air that would not enter her bloodstream. It was devastating to watch. Ultimately she was hospitalized and placed in an austere room to await the coming of the reaper. It was within this room that her life would end and mine would change. I had become accustomed to death—had spent over a decade dealing with the dead and the bereaved—and yet I had never ventured to the other side of the fence, as it were. Grief and personal encounters with death had not thus far crossed my path. That was about to change.

There was a cruelty to my nain's death in that the drugs the hospital administered caused her to gasp rapidly in an attempt to force oxygen into the blood, and it served only to heighten her suffering. Her family stood about her, helplessly watching her grab at air in a futile attempt to breathe. She was dying, and there was nothing anyone could do to prevent that, and yet in those last long hours the hospital, in its attempt to work ethically, inadvertently prolonged her suffering.

I had no point of reference in my life to deal with this situation; my emotions felt trapped in the top of my chest, unable to make it past the gullet and form into a scream. It was at that point that something happened; my nain pulled the oxygen mask from her face and gasped, "I can't take this anymore!" Up until that point in time, her will to live had been as strong as an ox, and then all at once something gave way and she longed for peace, for the suffering to end. Her fight for life was over. She had fought and battled for ten long years; her body and mind could take no more. For years I had willed her to live, to keep fighting to remain alive; I could not fathom a world without Nain in it, I did not want that world, I would not accept it. And then suddenly I was willing for her to die, to take that leap into the unknown and take her place as an ancestor, to be away from the pain. My brain seemed to burn under the glare of the situation; there was nothing to prepare any of us for what was happening.

Her treatment was stopped and the room dimmed. A serene sleepiness came over her countenance, and she lay as if deep in slumber; her chest barely betrayed the soft breath that no longer functioned to keep her brain saturated in precious oxygen. So many of us stood in that room—a vigil, waiting for the moment to arrive when she left this life. Her fingernails tinged with blue, her skin cooled—her soft skin that I loved so much and that smelled of her favorite perfume, skin that felt like warm dough beneath my fingers, now cooled and prepared itself for death. I loved her so much; how could she leave? Why? What would my life be without her? She was serene at this moment; surely she could be brought back to wakefulness and all would be well; why had I been willing her to die only an hour before? Nothing made sense; all I knew was that I was about to lose something precious.

It was dark outside, and yet I could see the outline of the Snowdonia mountain range that she had lived within for so many years of her life. The room was too silent, too still, even though a dozen people stood there waiting, watching. I moved towards my nain and took her hand. Sweeping my hand against her forehead, I gently tugged at the sheet, pulling it higher onto her shoulders. "Nain," I called gently. Her eyes flickered and opened. She looked directly at me, into the windows of my spirit. "Nain, *swatia rwan*," I told her, words that she had spoken to me so many times in the past, now aimed at her in the hope that she would feel safe and assured. Her eyelids closed slowly, her breath shallower, slower, until at last it stopped completely.

I was lost in immanent loss, and yet abruptly an intrusive thought entered my mind: I found myself thinking of my great-great-grandmother who had died before I was a year old. My nain adored her; she had spent most of her youth in her company, and for some reason she came into my mind at that moment. Something changed in the room— the very air shifted as if to accommodate something unfathomable. I distinctly recall sensing what I can only describe as a sigh that was felt rather than heard. At that moment, the nurse who had been sitting next to Nain with her fingers discreetly upon her pulse turned to the family and said, "She's gone."

My heart exploded into sharp red splinters, each one flying out of me in a futile searching, hoping that the tears would be powerful enough to bring her back. But she was gone; all that remained was a dense, cooling corpse. Whatever it was that drove it, that thing that animated it, had just departed; it was obvious by its very absence. In the days that followed and the further descent into grief, it became obvious to me that I was ill-equipped to deal with or understand the process, and in time I would realize that all the people I dealt with every day were also equally ill-equipped.

Perhaps the worst symptom of bereavement is potential isolation. I certainly felt this after my nain's death. It felt as if her passing meant nothing to the world—it didn't care, she was just a grandmother, and it wasn't as if I had lost a parent. I sensed that for many there was a hierarchical tier that defined how important someone's death was; siblings, parents, and partners sat relatively high up on that imaginary tier, whereas grandparents and friends did not. And while this is an unfair assumption, in the throes of grief it feels all too tangible and real. I believe that it arises from the fact that generally people just don't know what to say. But having been there, if you encounter somebody—a friend, a relative, a colleague—who has experienced the death of someone they loved, just be there. Words are not necessary, but knowing that someone cares about how you feel is priceless.

As a consequence of Nain's death, I found myself questioning my own spiritual path. Where was she? Where had she actually gone? Was she the same? I had all these damned questions and yet nobody could give me an answer that made any sense. Other folk from different traditions attempted to tell me that she was being prepared for reincarnation, but this made no sense to me—none whatsoever! I kept thinking that only a hundred years ago there had been a billion people on this planet, and now there are over six billion, so where did the new five billion or so spirits come from? Where were they prior to coming here? If we were being continuously recycled into new bodies, then surely the number would remain the same? I could make no sense of the matter; it all seemed too convoluted and too convenient. The lack of death philosophy in my own tradition was the thing that would ultimately teach me the nature of death and the spirit. I was looking in all the wrong places.

Questions of the spirit arose together with questions of mortality. Unlike my grandmother, who had been diagnosed with terminal chronic obstructive pulmonary disorder, I delighted in the illusion of youthful invincibility. Actively thinking about one's own death seemed loathsome to a young person in the midst of living. However, the loss of a loved one brings the fragility of mortality crashing to the fore.

Three months before my grandmother's passing, I had attended an end-of-life conference in England where one of the speakers was a forty-five-year-old woman with terminal cancer. I half expected to see a sick person, whereas the individual who stepped to the podium was radiant with life. I had never seen someone be so alive! Her demeanor was vibrant and powerful, her countenance bright and jovial—hardly stereotypical of someone at death's door. The concept of time and what we do with it is radically different to someone who is dying—but aren't we all dying, just at different velocities? My grandmother had eleven years to prepare for her death; the lady who exuded so much life in the shadow of death had merely a year.

My experiences with these two women, a loving grandmother and a stranger, changed me. I was complacent, but I don't think that's necessarily a bad thing, just normal. We go through daily life and its routine with barely a thought that it could be over at any moment. We all have dreams and aspirations, stuff that we would love to accomplish or do before we die. Invariably we don't, and then when death comes knocking we may be filled with regret. My grandmother and the stranger taught me something invaluable: just do it; *live!* From that point onwards, I changed my life. I started to do what felt important to me. Responsibilities are one thing, but it is surprising what else you can fit into life.

Consider that tomorrow you are given a terminal diagnosis. You have twelve months to live. What would you do with that time? How would you live? Write it down in a notepad or journal; really think about it. When you are done, ask yourself this question:

What is stopping me from doing some of these things now?

APPROACHING THE HALLS
OF THE DEAD

*Death cancels everything but truth, and strips a
man of everything but genius and virtue.*

WILLIAM HAZLITT

I knew that the following few years were to be challenging, an adventure in learning, but little did I realize that they would also be an intense journey into the core of my own being—an exploration of "self," if you like. And as I approached the morgue doors that fateful December morning, I had no idea how my life was about to change, how this experience would mold more than just my professional life.

In stark contrast to the cold winter outside, the morgue was warm and welcoming, I had previously met the staff and immediately liked them; I felt certain that I would fit in. I was beckoned into the bright, warm office and shown to what would be my desk, my own little corner in the kingdom of the dead. For what seemed like an age I stared down at the old brown desk, its surface scratched and etched by tools and pens and anything sharp. It had its own story of movement within this place, of the comings and goings of staff members over the years. I was dumbstruck that this was to be my corner, the place that identified my position as a member of the staff. I felt proud.

The morgue stood beyond the public facade of the hospital that housed it, its large entrance standing prominently under a canopy of steel upon which was emblazoned the word MORTUARY in large black lettering. The atmosphere inside reflected the disposition of those who worked there: jovially respectful. People tend to form images in their heads of the stereotypical morgue; in reality, they do not conform to the media-influenced image that we may imagine. My first morgue was as bright as the daylight outside its large frosted windows. Its airy corridors invoked a clinical rather than a morbid feel, and its decor was ordinary pale colors that reflected the light. I had always imagined that morgues would be out of sight—and, indeed, some of them are—however, this one was not. It did not hide its face from the public; it did not seek to disguise the fact that it existed. Signs directed visitors and staff to its doors; it held no shame.

I was shown to my own changing room, a little room at the far end of the postmortem room. It was simple yet comfortable; I had a shower, a mirror by which to make myself presentable to those who would visit, and, perhaps most importantly, it served as space that was private. A pair of surgical scrubs in my size lay draped over a chair, and my uniform hung by a hanger near the door. All these things had been made in preparation for my arrival. I felt honored to be here, to have been accepted as part of an exclusive team. Surgical slippers and boots stood neatly by the sink, waiting for my feet. These things were all mine—simple material goods that also heralded the beginning of my journey.

My colleague was also to be my teacher, and it would be her role to prepare and instruct me in the duties of a busy morgue. I may have had some theoretical understanding of this process but no practical comprehension. She was also responsible for training me in the fine details of postmortem examinations. I was soon to discover that morgues are complex places where various systems are in place to ensure the safety of those who work there and to protect the dead until their release. On the surface, this all seemed rather straightforward; in reality, it proved to be a little more involved.

I quickly learned that when we die, a vast operational system is initiated behind the scenes. It happens silently and subtly; it serves to lessen the burden of the bereaved and ensure a professional, effective service that cares for the dead and is conscious of the living. It is a world that only a few are privileged to see.

The modern morgue process has been a century and a half in the making since its inception in the latter half of the nineteenth century. Other than advances in equipment, standard operational procedures, and matters of health and safety, the primary directive of any morgue remains the same: to house and protect the dead. It is a place that is surprisingly alive with activity, yet the main users of the service can no longer be given the term *alive*. Amidst death there is always life, and in the morgue environment that life is expressed in the energy and vitality of those who make this place home for the majority of their working lives.

The types of morgues that I have occupied have been of the coronal variety, or places of investigation. The primary function of these morgues is to examine the body after death; this process is called the autopsy, meaning "to see oneself," or postmortem examination. Postmortem—meaning "after death"—is the term that is generally used to describe the process of examining a body after it has died to establish cause of death. I was yet to be introduced to this aspect of the work and had no real concept of whether I would cope with it or not. In hindsight I imagined that it would be several days, perhaps weeks, before I was permitted entry into the postmortem room. I was quite incorrect.

My experience of the morgue is deeply personal, yet we are all familiar with these repositories of the dead in one way or another. It may well be that you have visited one to view or identify a deceased individual, or there is a good chance that you have seen them dramatically portrayed on TV. But let's explore your perception of these places a little deeper.

Stop for a moment, take a deep breath, relax, and consider the following. Words have power, and some are compelling in the fact that they are immensely emotive. Words associated with death can spark the imagination and our morbid curiosity. Consider the word morgue; *what does it invoke? What images instantly come to mind when you are confronted with that word? Televised images of morgues tend to portray gloomy, shadowy rooms filled with machinery and tools that in themselves compel us to fear them. They have the ability to send shivers down the spine, but why? In reality these places are well lit and consist mostly of rather corporate-looking offices. Many fear these places. Do you? If so, why?*

Fear of these places is not ingrained in us; it is by no means instinctive. We have been programmed by our culture and society to imbue these places with fearful meanings. They have become places that reflect our fear of death.

Consider your perceptions of morgues, mortuaries, and other places associated with the dead and whether they have any basis in reality. Jot down your thoughts.

AUTOPSY: SEEING ONESELF

My initiation was to be the following day, and although my role within that space would be ancillary for some time, it was imperative that I immediately be subjected to that environment. Scheduled for examination that morning was an elderly lady. I admit that my hands trembled somewhat as I tied the plastic apron about my middle and awkwardly stepped into my surgical boots. The gloves would not embrace my hands as they ought to, and I felt out of place enveloped in plastic protective equipment.

By the time I stepped into the postmortem room itself, I felt a little vulnerable and quite discombobulated by the forthcoming encounter; after all, the next hour or so was to make or break my career. My colleague stood by; she was gracious, kind, and gentle, and her smile reassured me that I was in good hands—that her eye would be upon me throughout the entire procedure.

I recall the light in the room. The brilliance of sunshine streamed in through the large windows; albeit frosted, they still allowed enough radiant light to bathe the room with an ethereal radiance. The rays sparkled off the metal and somehow only seemed to highlight the paleness of the lady who occupied the postmortem table that I approached. My colleague's voice drifted into my mind—words of advice. I nodded in response to her commands and my heart quickened as I heard the words, "Nobody likes a martyr. There is no shame in feeling poorly or queasy. Just leave the room if you are struggling." They affected me; I didn't want to have to leave—I had not come this far to be defeated by my incapacity to deal with this! A movement to her right and the pathologist entered the room. He nodded at me and smiled. I think he spoke to me; alas, the words have not been retained.

She lifted the patient's arm and checked the identity bracelet that embraced the lady's thin wrist. She looked at the pathologist, who confirmed the patient's identity and that the details tallied with the information provided by the coroner's office. I noticed the deceased's golden wedding band glistening against her naked skin and felt my breath quicken in my chest—this was not just a body, a corpse; it used to be a person. My imagination ran wildly at that point, envisioning her life; this had not been a static body for any great length of time. Only yesterday she had been a living, breathing individual who had no concept that that very evening she would make her appointment with the reaper. This was someone who had fallen as a child and grazed her knee, someone who had learned to ride a bike, who may have struggled at math, and who ran free in the hills around her home. She had fallen in love, perhaps even had her heart broken along the way. From the information we had received, I knew that she had mothered three children, all of whom had given her grandchildren in return. Someone loved this woman; she was not just a corpse, she was more than that: she was a human being.

My journey into the life of this lady was broken by words that filtered from my colleague's mouth to reach my numb ears.

"What we do here isn't nice. It is necessary, but it's not pleasant. You need to learn right now that these are people, not just things; never lose sight of the fact that they are still deserving of our respect. We always treat them with as much dignity as is possible under the circumstances." I nodded at her. Something within me understood how important it was that we never lose sight of their humanity. That we treat them well and with consideration, without compromising our own emotional capabilities, was and continues to be a vital component of living this life with death.

The room fell silent again as my colleague took her knife and made a long incision from the patient's collarbone to just above the pubic line. I had expected blood, a torrent of blood, yet to my surprise there was none—only the pale yellow of subcutaneous fat and the pinkish red of muscle lay hidden beneath the skin. A whispering part of me half expected a piercing scream to rise from the lady's lips in protest at this invasion of her mortal remains, yet she remained forever still, the grip of death having silenced her voice. Still, her body harbored a tale, and this procedure was, in essence, the process of eviscerating not only her internal organs but also the story of her last minutes, hours, and days. I flinched as the sternum was removed with a surgical saw, the motion causing her body to rock slightly; its lifting revealed the compartment wherein lie the lungs and the heart, the center of a person.

To observe this act is to be surrounded by paradox and contradiction; one can conceive of the legalities involved and the necessary aspect of the examination. The function of the autopsy as a procedure that has fundamentally caused the progression of medicine and anatomical knowledge cannot be disputed. But something also happens to a person who witnesses this act for the first time. The mind can barely comprehend that it is witnessing the seemingly painful evisceration of another human being. As organs are lifted from the frame of a person to reveal an empty carcass devoid of its machinery, the brain screams in protest. This is the breaking point, the border at which the majority would fall and succumb to nausea or the overwhelming urge to faint. I was still standing, my mind reeling by the amount of information my brain was receiving and desperately trying to make sense of. Something within me had been hardwired to accept the images and emotional data and store it without cracking the shell of my sanity.

My entire conscious being seemed to float in and out of the postmortem room; there were times during the procedure where I literally felt beside myself. At other moments I had immense clarity of vision and sound, where everything within the room—the sights, the colors, the noises that rose from the air filtration system, the taps that vomited hot, steaming water—seemed intensely vivid. My brain was beginning to engage with something other than the horror I was witnessing.

I am suddenly aware of the provocation of words here and ask that you humor my tangent. I do not use the word *horror* lightly, for I believe that to the majority, the actions that happen within this most secretive of environments is tantamount to the true meaning of the word. Derived from the Latin *horrere,* meaning "to shudder" and implying a state of shock, fear, or disgust, it adequately articulates the feeling that most ordinary people would encounter in this place. I do not use this word to denigrate my profession but to express the true nature of what we encounter. Death may come as a peaceful visitor, but for many it does not; there are times when the mortal shell is left in states that would test the most strongly willed mind or the toughest of stomachs.

It is indeed horror, but for reasons left to explore, some of us within society have a built-in capacity to deal with continuous subjection to horror. Does it alter us? Yes, I believe it does. What I wish to express in this tangential diversion from the narrative is that I do not use these words for shock value or to sensationalize the situation. I do so for I feel they express a very real and tangible quality to this work.

Returning to the body of the old lady on the table, I noticed that my engagement was not focused on getting used to a dead body being laid open before me; instead, I was fascinated by its workings. The intricacy of the organs and their very design fascinated me; it all had a purpose, a function, and it had kept this individual alive and well for the majority of her life. Considering that actual anatomy bears little semblance to the illustrations in textbooks, I could not identify the majority of organs and tissue that my colleague severed from their ties. Everything from the floor of the mouth to the reproductive system lay before me in a single mass stained purplish-red. The sheer complexities of the body's systems were apparent to me at that point. How on earth did all that stuff know what to do?

She carried the organs to the dissection bench a few feet from the main postmortem table and laid them carefully upon a white plastic cutting board. The pathologist thanked her and proceeded with his dissection. The torso lay empty, a hollow shell that once contained the necessary components to make this vehicle work. The pathologist summoned me to his side. In his gloved hands he held the lady's heart. Admittedly, I had to be told what it was; to my eyes it was just a mass of reddish tissue. He explained the anatomy of the organ, pointing to the vessels that enter and leave it, pumping life-giving blood to the rest of the body. It sat in his palm and seemed so small, so unassuming. I recall being fascinated by its size, yet I was acutely aware of the metaphorical emphasis we humans place on the heart. Its stereotypical shape bears little resemblance to the actual organ itself, and the majority of people would not necessarily know how its chambers work, and yet we refer to it often as a metaphor. It plays such a vital role in our use of language, allegory, and attributions. Looking at the heart that lay before me, watching the pathologist insert scissors into its vessels and cut it open along the flow path, my mind wandered again.

We use the word *heart* so often, without giving it much thought. He has a big heart, she is heartless, it broke my heart, my heart bled for them—common phrases that we slip into everyday conversation. Do they refer to the actual organ, this slippery, dense configuration of powerful muscles? Or do they refer to something more metaphysical? Seemingly the heart's position in our language is reflective of its placement in the body as the beating core of a person; it is the sound, the pulsing feeling of life relentlessly pounding against our chests. Within the postmortem room, gazing at a real heart that had once beaten so strongly, I wondered if this lady had had her heart broken or if it had lifted her to the soaring heights of elation through joy or pleasure. I wondered if those feelings had anything to do in actuality with this organ; did this chunk of muscle actually seat an emotion? I had no further thoughts at the time that concerned or attempted to articulate questions of emotion and spirit, but my curiosity into our state of being had been initiated.

"You see this?" remarked the pathologist, pointing with the tip of his scalpel to a tube-like structure that seemed occluded by something I could not identify. "This is the left anterior descending coronary artery. It's completely blocked. A buildup of material, cholesterol and the like, causes the arteries to fur up; they can eventually block up completely. When that happens, the heart is starved of blood; it fails, and the person dies." I nodded, partially understanding what he said but not completely comprehending the process. It seemed simple, too simple, that this tiny little vessel's blockage had caused this woman to die, and it all seemed so drastic, so final! My mind did not at that time have the capacity to make sense of that, to conceptualize the finite nature of our bodies and the fragility of life. Mostly we rush headlong through life with very little appreciation for the fragile state that we call life.

Stop for a minute and take a deep breath. Do you have an actual appreciation of the finite nature of your body? Have you confronted situations in your own life that have highlighted its fragility through illness, an accident, etc.? There are times in life when we exude invincibility, perhaps in the blooming vitality of youth believing ourselves to be untouchable, beyond the reaches of death. Have you experienced this carefree invincibility in your own life? In the vitality of youthfulness, death seems impossible—something that happens to someone else. Is this a defensive strategy that ensures our total immersion in life and living or is it indicative of our attempts to ignore the inevitable? If you have been faced by the fragile nature of your own finite nature, how has this colored your life?

The old lady on the postmortem table had been entirely eviscerated, a task that I realized I would be conducting myself in the future. The quiet, empty shell before me existed as testament to the silence that has surrounded this profession and its priests since time immemorial. I felt at this point that I was witnessing and becoming a part of something unique, something that I could be proud of. Partly this arose to the fact that I knew I could do this; I had not been affected to my detriment, and the deep knowing I had felt for so many years had finally been confirmed. This was to be the greatest part of my life, something that would seep into my blood and eventually mold and define the person I was later to become.

POST POSTMORTEM

The air of the outside world seemed too normal! People went about their ordinary business, chatting and laughing, contemplating their evenings ahead, yet I had been privy to a day that was far from what these folk would consider normal. A part of me wanted to call out, to shout, to tell them what I had seen, what I felt, what I been through— to gain some reaction from the world that another realm existed beyond the ordinary veneer. The proclamation never came; a silence was being born within me, a silence that would persist until the tapping of these words on a keyboard.

As I returned to my new home that evening, I felt something was changing; I felt the imminent abandonment of the carefree young man that I had been until this day. I listened to the inner stirrings of myself "growing up" and having to grow up in order to develop the capacity to deal with the life that I was choosing. I had been given a golden opportunity, above so many other applicants, but it came with a price. The carefree young man would transform as a consequence; into what, at that time I had no idea. I was about to immerse myself in a world that continuously dealt with the most terrifying, mysterious, and scariest part of human existence.

For the duration of my training I would be housed in health service accommodation, comprised of an old building that sat on the side of a wooded hill. The old hospital across the way looked like a country house together with landscaped gardens and ornamental trees. The building in which I lived (along with some forty or so other folk) lay in a hollow surrounded by mature trees. At night the vixens would call their mates with their spine-tingling cries, and the clashing of antlers echoed over the hill as deer rutted. The location and the beauty of the place and the friendships one forges in these environments helped to ease the discomfort of leaving home. It acted as a sanctuary where I could engage in my studies and digest the impact my new life was having on me.

It was within this place that I started to make sense of my new life—words of articulation that expressed movement within me were dampened by new experiences, new friends. Yet as I fell towards sleep, my mind would wander about the stirrings of growth that whispered from the depth of my mind. Primarily this arose in reply to the responsibility of the work I had chosen; I was learning how to respond to being in service to the dead and the bereaved. I was barely out of my teens and yet thrust into a tremendously adult environment where maturity was expected but without the complete loss of innocence. I realized that the essentialness of frivolity and joyousness—perhaps accentuated in stark contrast to the horror I witnessed as each day carried me into my own future—were vital qualities of an individual in my position.

The world around me became an ever-increasingly beautiful and wondrous place. I saw the magic and spark of life in everything that surrounded me. My joy came from the act of living—yet this sense of joy and awe arose from my living with death. It would be years before I was to make sense of this and realize that my life was turning new corners with every passing day. My training was a wonderful and special part of my life; I think on it fondly. The course of training in this profession is remarkably different from the majority of career paths. It mostly involved on-the-job training and the direct experience of the morgue's everyday operations. In addition, we attended school in a distant county for two weeks at a time, where we were immersed in the theoretical aspects of the profession. This was a process of molding; it was here that we trained the mind to retain information and learn about the making of the body, the process of disease, and the complexities of the law. This place made sense of the necessity of morgues and our role within them.

KNIFE'S EDGE

I swallowed hard, hoping that this would prevent my hand from shaking; the hiss of the air conditioning system and a dripping tap seemed to mock my hesitancy. I took a breath; it seemed overtly pronounced and I felt the insecurity of being judged by watching eyes, but when I looked into them they were kind and reassuring. They had been in this position themselves. Months had passed before I arrived at the left-hand side of the postmortem table, my hand clasped tightly around a steel handle. The handle extended some six inches, and from its terminus extended another four inches of intensely sharp steel. I knew this moment would arrive, my appointment with the blade, and yet it was not exclusively my appointment. Someone else was involved in this process who only sixteen hours previously had been blissfully unaware of his fate. As he bid farewell to his wife that evening, his football kit flung about his shoulder, little did he know, perhaps mercifully, that the next person to pay him significant attention would be me.

A part of my mind looked beyond the blade and at the man that lay beneath it—a handsome man, his hair graying slightly at the temples. His broad shoulders and stocky build exuded health, not death. I wondered for a minute why a fit man in his forties would suddenly die. A discreet cough from my colleague brought my attention back to the task at hand.

"Are you ready?" she asked. "He has a story to tell, Kris, and he can tell us what it is. We can help give his family the answers that they desperately need."

Her words made sense; this man had just died without warning or obvious cause. His destiny had not been to return home that evening; instead, his next appointment was with the reaper. I muttered an apology to him for some reason, afraid that somehow I was going to hurt him. My colleague's instructions seemed distant, yet I absorbed them, responding with the appropriate nods of comprehension. I knew what

I had to do, but I had nothing to prepare me for the actuality of pressing an impossibly sharp blade into the flesh of another human being. The wound I would inflict would be immense, brutal almost. I had watched this procedure a hundred times or more, which I assumed was adequate preparation for the task itself; alas, I was wrong. I still had no idea of pressure, of the feel of resistance—steel against flesh.

Another sharp intake of breath and the blade performed its task. I felt the skin at the base of his neck give a slight click as the blade sliced into it, the sense of bone pressed against the knife as the incision widened before it, a wake of incised skin cascaded behind it. A slight sound, indescribable, arose from the wound as the blade severed the hair upon his chest, which parted unwillingly against the steel. I avoided glancing at his face, perhaps afraid that his eyes would penetrate my spirit and question my harming him. I dismissed the thought and, as instructed, released the pressure as the blade swept over his abdomen. Then suddenly something changed.

The room came back into sharp focus, voices clear; my head reeled at the amount of information that exploded into the forefront of my consciousness. I was naming structures in my head as I watched them appear from the curtain of skin and muscle. My colleague prompted me to name organs and tissue, to tell her which muscles my knife dissected and what lay beneath them. I had acknowledged the man's humanity, and now the makings of his machine became the focus of our attention.

Beads of sweat appeared on my forehead as I lifted his sternum free from his ribcage; beneath lay the lungs and the heart. I immediately noticed the blue tinge to the sack that contained his heart and realized it to be abnormal. We were closer to finding the cause of his death. My meticulous training and hours of study were being put to the test. My knife flayed at connecting tissue and viscera, responding to the fire of instruction that my colleague voiced. Eventually I lifted his organs free of his body and carried them to the dissecting bench where the pathologist waited patiently. He smiled at me kindly. "You did well," he said.

As I left the morgue that evening, with the setting sun casting long shadows, I sensed that something fundamental had changed within me. I felt like another channel of feeling, of sensing, had been opened deep in some unfathomable part of my being. I could find no words that would adequately articulate what I felt, but something was quite different; something was happening to me. I was changing. The very fabric of the world—my own perception of reality—was shifting. I was becoming something other than the innocent young man who had entered that morgue all those months before.

VISCERAL INSULATION

Over twenty years have subsequently passed. Today I am more than accustomed to life behind the morgue doors, yet further revelations and new thoughts have continuously teased my mind as I moved deeper into the service of the dead. Of all the things I have learned on this journey, there is one particular concept that disturbs me and is indicative of the human condition and its relationship with death. For years I had only a vague sense of what this was until I happened across a book by one of England's most respected archaeologists. In his book *The Buried Soul: How Humans Invented Death*, Timothy Taylor identifies a concept that has served to protect the living from all that is morbid and deathlike, and he identifies a group of people who serve this concept: he calls them "visceral insulators," and they serve to insulate the general populace from all that is visceral (Taylor 273–288).

I am one of these people; inadvertently I stepped onto the path of a successive lineage of priests who have served humanity since the dawning of our species. From the morgue temples of ancient Egypt to the Neolithic burial mounds and chambers of Europe, visceral insulators have always existed to protect the living from the dead. Over time, the distance between the living world and that of the dead has widened, and today we live in a world where the dead are kept under institutional control. People are screened from the presumed morbidity of it all; the blood, the trauma, and the stench of death and decay are hidden behind shields of professionalism and serve to keep the living in blissful ignorance of the cold reality of corporeality. The modern world assumes that the bereaved are too vulnerable to deal with the dead, and that they should be guided away from these houses of the dead and from caring for the body. Society behaves in a manner that belies its fears of death; by protecting the masses and keeping them away from death, we hope to prevent the mind from ever having to deal with the painful notion of our own inevitable mortality. However, nothing is truly hidden or disguised; eventually death finds us—and those we love.

Visceral insulation is a symptom of humanity's fear, and it has increasingly strengthened its grip. A symptom of this can be seen reflected in the intense morbid curiosity that occupies so many imaginations, as many are drawn to images of death and murder. The Western world has become obsessively fascinated by fictional images of death and horror, yet paradoxically we are distanced from the dead. There was a time only a few decades past when the family would care for their own dead. Now we hand those whom we loved into the care of strangers—into the hands of the visceral insulators. We trust them, take them at their word, and do as they ask—anything to avoid dealing with the cold reality of a dead body. And yet within the ranks of the visceral insulators there are those who feel, who serve the dead with spiritual empathy, who honor the vessels they prepare and guard as a house for the spirit.

All visceral insulators serve the dead with dignity and respect, but the spiritual has mostly been replaced by a clinical professionalism; bodies are processed in readiness for examination or funerals rather than in readiness for their departure from this world. This is largely a symptom of visceral insulation, but things are slowly changing. There are those who choose to speak out against the austere and evasive power of visceral insulation, myself included, and seek to educate and empower people to approach death with different eyes. As Mr. Taylor explains in his book, the process of visceral insulation has created a series of comfort zones wherein we can insulate ourselves from death itself. Within these zones we neutralize its power over us and attempt to remove death from the cycle of life; we ignore it in the desperate hope that we will never have to deal with it. The process of insulation is perpetuated not so much because we fear the death of others but rather that we fear our own.

Stop for a minute and consider the following. Are there situations in your life that you tend to avoid, either subconsciously or consciously? Situations that may well be compelling in their potential uncontrollability? To what extent does visceral insulation affect your life? Consider tasks in life that others perform so that you don't have to. While the focus here is on death, visceral insulation encompasses all things that are inherently disturbing: childbirth screams, grief, slaughterhouses, capital punishment. Consider your food's source and the insulating factor that may gloss the fact that a life was taken to provide you with that chicken salad. On initial examination, visceral insulation may not be immediately apparent; therefore, consider it consciously. Take time to draw a list of the occupations and roles that people around you assume that insulate you from the grim and the ghastly. None of us exist in a vacuum. Perhaps you have become habituated to an unpleasant task so that someone else does not have to do it. Consider these threads of insulation in your life and in the lives of others, and try, if you can, to gain a better appreciation of its implications.

DYING EVERY SECOND, DYING EVERY DAY

Our fear of death causes us to avoid it at all costs—to attempt to run to the hills of life in the hope that the valleys of death never pull us into their gloom. We may encourage visceral insulators to take responsibility for the corpse lest we get our hands dirty and touch the cold face of death. We avoid death, yet oddly (and, to some, surprisingly) we need death in order to survive. We believe ourselves to be a body, a machine, a conglomeration of cells and tissue, organs and liquids that make up a human being. It trudges through life, growing and changing its shape, until all at once it stops, falls to the ground, and slowly dissolves into nonexistence, dead. And yet the thing we fear the most is continuously present within us, and were we to stop and think on this for a while—to sense the continuous presence of death within us—I believe it would serve to teach us its purpose and meaning and, by proxy, decrease our fear of it.

Every single part of our body is governed by a peculiar process called apoptosis. This word comes to us from the Greek, meaning "the dropping off of petals or leaves," and it is a term that is used in medicine to describe programmed cell death, or PCD. Its etymology in the Greek language relays a profound teaching: the leaves and petals of flowers and trees must drop off and die in order for new growth to develop and evolve; without this dropping off, life would become stagnant.

The process of apoptosis causes every single cell in our bodies to commit suicide, and it does so for a single purpose: to enable new, healthy cells to develop. A messenger is released from the brain and directed towards a cell that is either damaged or nearing the end of its natural cycle of living. The messenger attaches itself to the cell and, in simple terms, commands it to die. The cell immediately responds. Its systems are switched off and it dies; its remains are cleaned up by other cells, then transported to the spleen and removed from the body. New cells are created to replace it that, in turn, will be called upon to die when their allocated time has lapsed or they are damaged in the throes of their work. Without this programmed death of cells, the entire body would cease to operate, and it would die. In truth, in order for us to live, we must continuously die. Your entire body is renewed by the process of apoptosis; almost every single physical particle within you is dying in order for you to live.

There are times, however, when cells refuse to respond to the command of programmed cell death, and they flee from the messengers of death. Their unwillingness to die causes immense damage to the body. These rogue cells are the basis for disease and cancers; their rebellion can cause the death of the whole. Programmed cell death is essential, and each cell is aware of its purpose and dies selflessly, programmed to respond to a greater plan: the plan of life, which is inexorably interwoven with death. The selfish response of a cell and its unwillingness to die causes destruction that goes against the harmonious pattern of life and death. Nobody knows why a cell responds in this way; one could hypothesize that it does so out of fear or trepidation, but that would imply that it feels or is conscious on a level that may make us uncomfortable, knowing that another pattern of consciousness lives within us. For if a cell has consciousness and yet our entire cellular makeup is continuously renewed, where does our consciousness reside? This can be a tricky question to contemplate and perhaps one that we pay little heed to, but let's consider it for a moment.

> *Stop for a minute and take a deep breath and consider the following. What is the nature of consciousness as you understand it? Where is it located? Consider your body as a whole. Is there a particular part of it that you equate with housing the consciousness, and is this concept of consciousness the same as that of the spirit? Do you consider them to be one and the same? If not, why? Is your consciousness "you"? Consider*

whether your consciousness resides within your body or whether your
body resides in consciousness?

Do you consider consciousness to be a facet of sentient beings only,
or do inhabitants of the plant and mineral kingdoms also express con-
sciousness? Jot your thoughts in a notepad or journal.

Apoptosis brings an awareness of the essential nature of death, but it also raises more questions than it answers. For within it we glean a sense of the spirit, of a force that is beyond the mere makeup of the body and its component parts that are in a constant state of flux, locked within the cycles of birth, life, death, and rebirth. We may be continuously dying but yet something remains unchanged, implying that it is not subject to the same physical laws as our cells are. We may consider ourselves to be the sum total of our bodies, but apoptosis tells us that we are not—that, in fact, the only constant, the individuality or the spirit, is not bound to the cells, or it too would be governed by it. Instead it observes and experiences the body from another place, untouched by apoptosis, until the process of programmed cell death takes its ultimate stand and the entire body falls from life and spirit.

Apoptosis serves to teach us a valuable lesson: to look at death from the inside. Primarily we see death happening out there, on the evening news, to other people; it's terrible and tragic, sad and upsetting, scary! It's always happening somewhere else. Apoptosis teaches us that it's also happening right here, right now—that the message of death is life, and that life is utterly dependent on death. This reciprocation teaches us that death is necessary and normal and it is happening all the time. To become aware of the process of programmed cell death within you is to become aware of the constant that is unaffected by it, and this awareness alleviates some of the fear we hold on to.

As a Pagan, I find this notion affirms the animistic nature of the universe. We may perceive that all things are a habitation of the divine spark of life, and yet that concept is perhaps not readily internalized. To the Pagan, apoptosis provides a window to observe and sense the plethora of other "lives" that exist within your own, seemingly independent of your consciousness. Attempting to ascend to the lofty realms of the spirit can be a fickle and difficult process. But by descending inward through matter into the complexity of our physical bodies, we can encounter mystery in a less ethereal manner. We are the embodiment of mystery; it resides within us.

In order to sense the constant that is unaffected by apoptosis, we must attempt to still our thoughts and shut off the constant chitchat that floods the mind. Meditation is the most effective method of connecting to the unchanging constant. You may have been led to believe that meditation is difficult or time consuming, but nothing can be further from the truth. Simply focus on your breathing and the rise and fall of your chest; breathe in through your nose and out through your mouth. Imagine that your body becomes lighter and lighter, as light as a feather.

Focus on your body as a whole and recall to mind an image of outer space from a popular science fiction program, magazine, or book. Imagine that the cells and molecules of your body resemble these images. Galaxies and nebula swim within the fabric of your body. Consider that within your body exists a vast and unknowable system of life; it is a world within a world.

Imagine that at the center of your body, just beneath your sternum, is a darkness that is infinitely darker than what surrounds it. Take your awareness to this place. The galaxies of cells and structures within your body expand to fill all of space. Descend further into the inky blackness at your center. Imagine your inner space expanding to become all of space; within you is the vast unknowable universe. It is not out there. You are it.

Become the nothingness that contains all things. Become the constant. Watch any thoughts that arise as if on a cinema screen; be impartial to them. Watch words and sentences dissolve into nothing. Descend into the constant that is unaffected by your body. Stop.

Remain in this space for as long as you are able, until thoughts intrude and the body intervenes. Our awareness of the constant arises from not-being, not-thinking. Descend into this void when you have need to sense the constant that is unaffected by living.

DANCING WITH DEATH

We may avoid thoughts of our own death and turn our faces away from the inevitable shedding of our mortal shell. To die is completely unavoidable and, as we have seen, a continuous and essential process whether we are aware of it or not. We all succumb to its power to take us from this world. But then what? Before we embark on questions of the spirit, let us contemplate what is left behind.

Your body has been a vessel for the spirit and the very thing that contained the experience of living; death is the termination of the machine that enables us to be a part of this world. Its falling away from the living world, from the constant interaction with its surroundings, is arguably devastating to the majority of those left behind, but what of the body itself? It is so easy to conform to society's expectations and simply dispose of it without thought of honoring it for the life it lived. How we choose to dispose of our remains can express the life that we lived and the way we saw the world and our place in it.

My Celtic ancestors honored the bodies of the dead, and this can be seen reflected in the plethora of grave goods from the Iron Age. Dead bodies were not simply cast aside but were moved to a place specifically designated as being separate from the world of the living. In many cases, mounds would be erected above graves; such was the case of the best-preserved Celtic grave in Europe, at Hochdorf in Germany.

A Celtic chieftain was placed in an exquisite grave on a bronze couch; a cauldron that held over 100 gallons of mead sat at his feet, and place settings for nine meals together with nine drinking horns adorned the grave walls. This display of grave goods may not necessarily be indicative of a belief in an afterlife per se, but it certainly demonstrates a deep sense of honor and respect for the dead. Some scholars have claimed that the placement of personal belongings indicated that the goods were somehow tainted by death and could not be used by the living tribe. They may have been gifts to the gods, or possibly the spiritual energy of the items accompanied the deceased to the otherworld (Green 68–69). We will never truly know what they believed, but we can fathom that the dead were treated honorably.

Consider your own death—not the process itself but rather the aftermath, the cold silence of the corpse. Contemplate the following:

What would you like to happen to your body once it is dead?
How does this reflect your life or spiritual tradition?

Do you wish to be buried or cremated?

Are your wishes clear? Have you ensured that your next of kin and loved ones are aware of your desires?

What kind of funeral service or eulogy would you like?
Have you given it much thought?

Are your affairs in order to save your relatives distress when you are not around to inform them of details?

Consider that the earth has provided for you all your life.
What gift can you give it in return after your death?

If you have chosen to be buried, have you chosen the location?
Have you considered ecological or green alternatives such as
woodland burial grounds?

What impact will the disposal of your dead body have on the
environment?

How will the disposal of your dead body reflect your life as a Pagan?

Contemplate each of the above questions in turn, allowing each one to sink into your mind, then write your thoughts in a journal or diary. By preparing the mind with questions of this nature, you are empowering yourself and your family and preparing for your own death with clarity and focus.

Far too often families are left stumbling in the dark, the grief of bereavement made even more difficult by not knowing what the deceased's wishes were. We can prevent this with a little foresight and planning. Have you ever attended a funeral? The majority, it is sad to say, are poor, inadequate ceremonies of farewell that normally conform to a standard system of religion that the deceased may well have had no interest in. I have attended many funerals over the years; most amount to twenty-five minutes of readings from a standard funeral service book designed by the Anglican Church. I have witnessed the bereaved sit in bafflement at a sudden influx of religious doctrine that they are unfamiliar with—why? The answer is simple: we have become distanced from death and the dead, and we turn to what is easier, not necessarily what is honorable. Things do not have to be this way; there is always another way. A little foresight and the adjustment of our own perception of death can radically change the manner in which we deal with death and our own inevitable demise.

Prior to moving on to the spirit, let's take a moment to discover who you have been in this life thus far.

You will need a journal, paper, or diary for this exercise. Consider that three hours ago you died; in this hypothetical exercise, the circumstances of that death are unimportant. Tomorrow an obituary will appear in your local newspaper, but rather than being compiled by those left behind, this one will be written by you. Take to pen and paper and compose your own obituary. Who have you been; what have you been? What are your relationships, and to whom do you connect? Consider sitting between lives and reading your own obituary as it would appear in the hand of another, and then consider how you would have done it differently.

Allow the words to fall easily from your mind onto paper; there are no limitations to the amount of words, simply let them come. By all means, read it back to yourself. Is it an adequate description of you and your life or is it how you would like others to remember you? Fold the obituary up and secure it somewhere safe. Do not read it again until one whole year has passed.

When you have finished reading this book and taken on board some of its theories and hypotheses, reread your obituary when the year has passed. Is it different? How has your own perception of "you" changed?

WHEN LIFE IS TOO MUCH TO BEAR

Golden sands shimmer beneath a noonday sun. A little boy squeals in delight and sheer abandonment as he scampers, naked to the elements, towards what calls him: the sea. With skin as brown as toast and hair that reflects the warm summer sunshine, a child and the briny sea meet in praise of each other. His little brother runs behind him, eager to share in the playful delights of a day at the beach. To live by the sea is to love it, to want it, to need it. At every opportunity, tasks and chores are heartily abandoned with joyful surrender in favor of an impromptu beach bag, packed for fun and frolics, cast hastily into the car.

Haydn and his brother are lost in the blissfulness of sand and sea and the wonder of their youthfulness. Their mother and I sit against the rocky headland of the little bay that we know so well, smiling at the joyful innocence of children. We have done this so often it is almost a ritual; the bay is comfortable, deeply familiar, and safe. Here we can rest awhile and put worldly matters to right, then abandon such concerns for the delights of play that even adults should occasionally partake of. Long, warm summer months of play and enjoyment, our spirits caressed by the waves of the Celtic Sea, have enriched our lives, bringing to them a sense of place and awe.

I recall so clearly the childish squeals as Haydn would splash his mother and me with cold seawater as we hesitantly stepped into the shallows, those squeals transforming to triumphant cries as we dove into the waves. We would play for hours, four spirits lost in the joys of nature. But there is one day that I see clearer than any other.

The warm sun had called us back to shore to soak up those precious rays and regain our breaths; a quick swig from a warm bottle of soda and a well-deserved cigarette satisfyingly rewarded our exhaustive efforts in the water. I had turned onto my back, propped up on my elbows, my face worshiping the sun above me, when my gaze caught Haydn and his brother at the edge of the waves. They played at that point where sea meets land, a place between places, a time between times. Haydn looked over to where his mother and I sat, and it was then I saw it. There was something otherworldly about this boy; a spark shone in his eyes that declared he was somehow not of this world, at least not entirely. He had the feel of the Fey, the fair folk, about him, a magical quality that could neither be articulated nor expressed by words alone. I was not alone in my observations; his parents felt it too, a certain depth of soul that their child held.

Those days of youthful surrender and play were precious, and the memories rise to this day, even when I consider them fastened down by the bonds of time. Haydn was not related by blood; he was my best friend's firstborn, and I knew him from an early age. The passage of time brought changes to him and to me; we grew at different paces, he into the tumultuous years of adolescence and I into my own experience. Yet from the wings I watched and smiled; he grew quickly, it seemed, the years passing with frightening speed. Before long he had arrived in adulthood and to his own series of life choices and paths. Most teenagers encounter problems; perhaps they are a requirement of growth, maybe they define the adult who strives to emerge? Haydn was not immune to this, and there were times when he needed things that those who loved him could no longer provide. His own two feet and that sense of adult responsibility eventually took his life in surprising directions.

Cooking was his passion; I would watch him in his teenage years pondering over recipe books and smile at his enthusiasm. His path took him away from his homeland and to new experiences—some of them good, while others served only to frustrate his spirit. It was the city of Sheffield that finally called him with the promise of new work, new opportunities, and direction. In hindsight it is easy to recall that sense of the otherworld that I perceived about him, and that somehow that would prevail and eventually seep into his life. The tumultuous, hormone-driven teenager calmed, but another form of frustration arose, one that, alas, nobody could truly understand. The little boy in the water had changed into an adult capable of many things, full of potential, but who are we to judge the potential in another and make decisions on their behalf? Perhaps we may think we know what is best for another, but ultimately we can only realistically be responsible for ourselves. On a fateful September day, the call of the otherworld grew too strong, and for reasons known only to him, Haydn purposefully turned his face from this world and took his own life.

It was the silence at the other end of the phone that alerted me to what had taken place, then the sheer outpouring of grief as his mother attempted to explain. I was 300 miles away, unable to leap in the car and drive to my friend to offer some solace, some familiarity in the darkest hour of a mother's life. Instead I took the train from London to Sheffield and we would meet there. It had not struck me at that point that I would be seeing Haydn at a morgue, a place deeply familiar to me, yet not under these circumstances.

A nod from my friend and her husband told me to enter the viewing room first; I knew that my opinion counted, that for me to inform them that it was okay would somehow make the experience more tolerable. Yet it was quite intolerable to walk into that room and see the body of someone I had known and loved for so many years. He lay upon a standard morgue viewing trolley, a heavy cotton velvet pall draped over his form; a shroud lay about his neck in a feeble attempt to hide the mark that caused his death. His face had the familiar pallor of death, somewhere between pale beige yet tinged with the hue of tallow; his mouth gaped open enough for me to see the whiteness of his teeth. My mind invoked memories of when I had seen that very mouth curl into smiles and laughter; now it lay cold and empty. I had no sense of Haydn being in this shell that lay before me. The scene, however, was painfully familiar. I attempted to fathom how many people I had presented in the same fashion, dressed in the same manner, but personal connection prevented further mindless debate.

I saw only the child I knew from years previously, the innocent boy who played in the sea. The otherworld had called him, the pull of that place was too strong for him to resist, and as a consequence here he lay. I flinched at the touch of his skin as my fingers caressed his cheek. The unnatural coldness shocked me, yet surely I knew that that would be the case. My patients are always artificially cold. But this was not a patient, this was someone I cared for, and the whimpering cries of his parents from the waiting room told me how painful this was. I turned my back to him, and with a single tear that stung my eye I nodded to his parents. I felt rather than saw them pass me into the chamber wherein lay their son.

It was the guttural cries, the howling screams of utter horror that tore at my heart, shattering it into a million sharp splinters that hung in the air like a specter, then slowly fell to the ground. Emptiness, cold emptiness like that of the morgue refrigerator took the place of where my heart should be. The pain of my friends rose behind me like an emotional tsunami that crashed through the fabric of the morgue walls. I could not begin to comprehend their despair, this newfound sense of utter helplessness and desolation. Their child lay dead before them; how would they begin to make sense of that?

His spirit danced on rope's end, caressed in the branches of a parkland tree; above him clouds moved silently in the blue skies, the sun shining its radiance. About him creatures continued their existence while birdsong filled the park with music. I fancifully imagine that at the moment of his departing, nature held her breath—that the park fell silent in empathy. Perhaps the tree that he chose for his rope enveloped his ailing spirit and made easier his passing. In my musings I like to think that the world takes note of our suffering, of our choices, and that it reacts to them, and that in our moments of utter surrender or despair it holds our consciousness in its arms. It comforts me to know that Haydn did not die alone; he left this world in the arms of nature, with the flowers and berries of autumn surrounding him, with the bark of tree and birdsong. We may equate company and connection only with fellow humans, but we are also creatures of nature; it too is our kin. I take comfort from that fact, and that at the end of Haydn's earthly life it was there to soothe his body's passing. In truth we will never understand those final moments, the emotion or the surrender to the calling of death.

How do we make sense of such tragedy and despair? Do we judge those who take their own lives too harshly?

What initiates that sense of wanting to kill oneself? In the majority of cases that I have dealt with at the morgue, it is commonly the result of a deep and insurmountable sense of alienation and isolation, of utter hopelessness. I have lost count of the amount of suicide notes that I have read over the years, and they mostly share a common thread: they arise from a sense of feeling powerless to change or move beyond a given situation. One can glean a sense of isolation that cuts the individual to the core, even if they may have been surrounded by family and friends. One can feel alone even in a crowd. This sense of alienation and isolation escalates, frustrates; the loss of control and myriad other conflicting emotionally charged responses kick in to push the individual further into a suicidal spiral. Eventually a deep sense of helplessness arises from that despair. It is at that point of helplessness that suicide invariably occurs.

In many cases suicide comes as an unexpected shock—one often hears people claim that they recognized no clues, there were no warnings. Suicide is the determined destruction of the self, but the motives for suicide can be as complex as the individual. Some sociologists claim that the definition of this is unclear, that one can display destructive or suicidal behavior through lifestyle, smoking, alcoholism, narcotic abuse, etc. And yet the deaths caused by these lifestyle choices do not carry the same stigma as someone who intentionally chooses to shoot themselves. What of those who choose to end their lives to maintain a sense of dignity, to be in control of their own deaths rather than at the mercy of a terminal illness? The lines of definition are blurred.

The internal emotional mechanism that drives the suicidal tendency is not necessarily externally apparent. Seeing signs of hopelessness and helplessness may allow one to move closer to the individual and offer support, but this is not always the case. Cries for help are common, but they are not necessarily the norm. It stands to reason that the conflicting, paradoxical emotional maelstrom of suicide and its arbitrary impact gives rise to feelings of guilt and helplessness in the bereaved. And it is also true that those bereaved by suicide may suffer prolonged periods of grief and encounter feelings of shame and rejection. The collateral damage as a result of suicide can be immense. So what do we do—how do we tend to the emotional fallout of a friend or a coven or grove member that encounters bereavement by suicide?

Primarily it is safe space that is important; words can be tricky, but be truthful with your words, however silly you may think they sound. Be sure to visit the bereaved and attempt as best as you can to discourage any feelings of guilt while encouraging the expression of grief. Guilt is a natural product of bereavement, but it's also one that can severely exacerbate the situation. But if you don't have words, just be there; a hand, a hug, and a shoulder to cry on is worth more than treasure.

But what happens when we lose someone to suicide? It is difficult to honor a decision that brings pain and that results in such loss, but perhaps the most honorable action is to be accepting of the choice that that individual made, however difficult that may be. When we accept that a person is entirely responsible for his own life and all the decisions and choices he makes, then perhaps we must also accept that he may ultimately be responsible in ending that life. The pain never goes away, but it does find a home somewhere within you. Honoring the individual's decision is not an easy task and may take years to achieve, but one does not need to fully understand why they killed themselves in order to honor that choice.

the *Realm of Spirit*

PART 2

THE CIRCLE OF GWYNVYD

IN WHICH ARE ALL ANIMATED
AND IMMORTAL BEINGS

In the spirit is the mind,
And in the mind is the Soul.
Without end, and blessed is he,
Who rightly exercises the faculties
That Great Spirit endued him
In order to attain endless Gwynvyd
Forever and ever.

ADAPTED FROM *THE BARDDAS OF IOLO MORGANWG*

The three primaries of Gwynvyd: the cessation of evil, the cessation of want, and the cessation of perishing.

The body has fallen from the spirit, and the ethereal senses open onto the second realm of existence, that of the subtle, that of spirit. No journey is implied or necessary; we originate from here and we return here to the welcoming company of the immortals. The circle of Gwynvyd is a world removed from our physical, dense plane, and yet it is woven into the fabric of this dimension; it exists side by side, only the limitations of our human eyes prevent us from seeing it. A gossamer-thin veil curtains the realm of spirit from this earthly existence. Humans fear it and yet long for it. Something within the realm of spirit feels familiar, perhaps too familiar, and to some the draw is too exquisite to ignore—they are compelled to sense it; humans have forever striven to connect to this place of spirits. We have romantic notions of its appearance, a place of eternal bliss and pleasures where skies are always blue and buttercups tickle the feet. We offer it names that evoke rest, peace, and tranquility—the Summerland, Tir Na Nog, Heaven.

Our fear arises from the forgetfulness of life, from the assumed trapping of the senses in the denseness of our craniums. But we are not trapped, and we have always been aware of this subtle realm, of our true home in spirit. This life is but a wink, a fleeting moment in the blink of existence, and yet its experience is essential to the universe that we are an inexorable part of. Your life matters; you are not a number, and your spirit in all its primordial splendor is the vehicle that sings in praise of the universe. Your spirit has existed since the beginning of time, since the initial expansion of our universe; it is only the limitations of the body that cause you to assume separation.

In Gwynvyd there is no evil, no agenda; its purpose and intent are to simply be. The mystery of Gwynvyd teaches us that evil exists only in the heart of man; in the realm of the immortals, there is no epitome of evil, no antagonist who serves to challenge a supreme being. There is no judgment here, and our desires to want fade with the brightening of the spirit as it returns home to familiarity. In Gwynvyd we are free of death; no longer subjected to the limitations of physical form, the structure of our spirit is not bound by the familiar atoms of the physical universe and thus do not degrade to the point of death. The immortals dwell here; in some cultures they are called gods, in others the Fey, the

Sidhe, the Fair Folk; they are the epitome of mystery known only to the spirit. Nothing perishes here, for this is the circle of immortality.

Doorways line its borders, cracks in the veneer of quantum flow that allow it to interact with the world of the living, for we are not entirely separated. We are woven like fine cloth, each realm touching and caressing the other; blissfully unaware, the human world may ignore it or long to know of its existence. Walkers between the worlds traverse the pathways between this world and the realm of spirit; some have awoken to the lucidity of spirit that comes from connection, a connection that further enriches this experience of being human.

We can sense the spiritual realm, and the key to its sensing is emotion. By connecting to this most subtle aspect of being human, we immediately access the world of the spirit. No proof or evidence is needed to verify the existence and power of the emotions; we feel them, therefore they exist. Their ethereal, fluid quality cannot be confined to neurology and brain process alone. They are capable of reaching beyond the density of the body to infiltrate and affect the world around us both subtly and physically. In the exploration of Gwynvyd, we begin by exploring the functionality of an extreme human emotion: grief.

Our grief connects us to a primal, instinctual aspect of ourselves; it sings of connection, it does not conform to measures or controls, it cannot be eviscerated or observed beneath the glare of a microscope, yet it is real. By understanding the process of grief, we capture a picture of the spirit; through our grief we long for it, we seek it in the darkest recesses of our being. Our emotions connect us to the subtle realms, and they act as a doorway to connect to what we cannot see.

And so through our subtle senses and emotions we journey to discover the realm of spirit.

THE PATH OF
PAIN AND FEELING

Grief is itself a medicine.

WILLIAM COWPER

I felt her body quiver as I guided her towards the morgue's public entrance. An audible, involuntary gasp left her lungs as we turned a corner to be faced with the morgue doors. Her arm was clamped around my own, her free hand clutching the handbag she held against her heart as if defending herself from the onslaught of pain she knew was imminent. I reached for the keys about my belt to open the doors as her head tilted upwards to glare at the black and white sign above the entrance way: MORGUE VISITORS' ENTRANCE, it proclaimed. Her breathing, shallow and fast, arose like the dull cry of a distant alarm. I felt a pang somewhere in my middle, around the area called the solar plexus, the center of our being. I recognized it as the stirrings of empathy, the emotional reaction one feels when confronted with the pain of another.

The doors opened, and she stood frozen to the spot. I sensed her panic filling the air around her, its effect tangible; the very atmosphere itself seemed to flee before her rising emotion. I turned to face her and held both her hands and whispered some words of reassurance. What she needed was solace; alas, I could offer none. The door to the visitors' waiting room opened, revealing my colleague, who offered only a half smile as a greeting to the bereft woman. We entered the small room, which was pleasantly decorated in pastel colors with neutral paintings hung in frames about the wall, and the smell of lilies floated from an arrangement that decorated the small table in the room's center. Leaflets bearing advice and instruction on what to do when a relative dies sat as objects of assumed consolation, and cards from funeral directors only served to affirm the nature of this place, this chapel of rest.

As we entered the inner vestibule of the chapel, my colleague stood by; her eyes closed gently as an unearthly scream arose from the woman's body. I flinched and recoiled as the sheer wave of emotion punched through the air. It dared anyone to stand in its way. Something rose within me, a sense of something familiar, something primal; I subdued its calling. I was still young in experience of such emotional magnitude. I had been instructed by my colleague to simply stand by, to assist as need be, and to act as instinct and training would permit. As the woman's knees buckled, she fell with a thud to the carpeted floor, her hands grasping at nothing in the air above her, as if reaching for something, anything that could take the pain away. My colleague simply descended to her knees beside her and softly placed her hand on the woman's shoulder.

In the center lay the dead body of her husband. A young, attractive man in his twenties, he lay as if sleeping; only his face was visible beyond the velour pall that hid his body. His eyes were closed to the world, lips slightly parted in the call of death. A volcano of pure, unadulterated raw emotion sent shock waves that reverberated around the viewing room. The decorative glass window behind me seemed to resonate with a high-pitched hum as if it too was responding to this woman's pain. I felt helpless; the plethora of questions and images that danced in my head suddenly seemed to be externalized onto some invisible screen, my thoughts appearing like images in a cinema. What could I do to ease this woman's pain? How could I dry the tears from her eyes, how could I cause her to see the wonder and magic that the world still contained? I looked across to my colleague, who had guided the bereaved lady to a seat, and there she sat, her head almost in her own lap, her body crumpling like paper.

It was at that point I realized what my colleague was actually doing—and what I should and would be doing. There was no question in her mind, no futile seeking for answers that could relieve the pain of the bereaved, which was not her duty or responsibility. I nodded to myself as I realized the purpose of our position in this place: to permit and give space in which these people were allowed to succumb to that most primal and powerful of human emotions, grief.

The British stiff upper lip always assumes a stance of strength and coping, we rarely express the way we feel, and almost never display that in public. There would have been times by influence of Queen Victoria that even in chapels of rest one would retain a certain demeanor; this is neither healthy nor conducive to the grieving process. Today we offer a space, a place in which a person can abandon themselves to the sheer forces of grief without thought of rebuke or ridicule. Words are not called for or required, and as I observed the silence of my colleague, I realized that she spoke volumes in a language that the woman's spirit understood. Grief cannot be explained by words, and at best its verbal or literal articulation transmits only a shadow of what one feels in the throes of it.

Stop for a minute amidst the pain of this memory you are reading. Consider how important is it to be afforded the space to grieve openly. Have you acknowledged this quality or have you also succumbed to awkward words in the hope of comforting another? We probably all have been in that position at one point in our lives, struggling to find words. But consider the value of a touch, of a hug, of a comforting hand that simply acknowledges and honors the power of that grief—a touch that offers the space to let go. Most people in their grief don't want words; they want the space to grieve. Consider this element when next faced with the bereaved.

I stood by silently. My colleague said nothing; only the light touch of her hand against the woman's shoulder betrayed her presence, her support. Time was not an issue at this point. The small room and the presence of two strangers served only to hold this experience, to present it to her as the reality of death. We stood by, silent sentinels to the power of the reaper to change, transform, and destroy.

Eventually she stood and, with gasping breaths that caught in her throat, moved to her husband's side. The back of her hand lightly touched his cold cheek as a single tear fell directly from her left eye to drip onto his forehead. At that point something changed. I have encountered it a thousand times since: a palpable wave descended from somewhere unknown, and the woman's entire demeanor changed. The panic slid through her body as if sinking to her feet to leach into the ground, pushed as it was by a new wave—the wave of bereft acceptance. I see it in people's eyes and sense it in their spirit; up to this point, whatever news they have received—the information that a death has occurred—exists only as data, words that fall from lips to break the heart. It is when a person is faced with the body of a loved one that it becomes all too real, and momentarily there is acceptance; to see is to believe.

Her breathing slowed and her eyes clouded over, the glaze of loss hidden temporarily by the reality that lay before her. It seemed as if the world held its breath as the information seeped into the depth of her spirit. Her entire being assimilated the scene, attempting to make sense of something that simply could not be fathomed. I knew instinctively that this calmness was truly the lull before another storm. I braced myself as I sensed the air changing yet again, heralded by a crackling of electrical charge as the searing lava of human emotion welled within her.

It was at this point that I perceived the deflector shield that I was slowly constructing, a bubble within which I stood protected from the onslaught of human emotion yet still able to respond empathically. I felt somewhat removed from the pain of this wife confronted by the tragic, untimely death of her beloved husband. I watched as her emotions bounced off my shield of defense, yet it allowed some of it to enter, to be absorbed by my own capacity to sense the pain of another and respond as a human being and a professional. I stood at the place where training can only do so much; it can never prepare one fully for the battering of human senses. I was to learn by observing and being immersed in the experience of another's grief. I listened to the advice of my colleague to her recollection of her early days dealing with the bereaved; she taught me that I should never deny my humanity, to not shun the rising of emotion within myself in response to another's grief. There is no shame in feeling.

THE AWARENESS OF ENERGY

I was changing. What was once an innocent young man was ascending into a realm of feeling and sensing; there was suddenly so much more to the world than I had initially perceived. It was death and grief that initiated this transformation within me; the subtle observation of high emotional energy was affecting me on a profound level. A nameless teacher was guiding me to sense the world in a new and fresh manner; instead of being told to believe, to have faith, to rely on another person to mediate between me and the spirit, I was seeing the subtle firsthand. I could actually observe its effects on the world as raw power explodes from the core of another individual and actually impacts their environment and the people who inhabit it. There was no denying that what I was feeling and sensing was not something of the ordinary, assumed reality that I was accustomed to; it belonged to something that at that time I could not articulate. Suffice to say, it was by proxy of the account I give above that my world began to change. I was aware of subtler realities beyond the dense existence of the physical world.

Had I known the meaning of the term clairsentience at that time, it would have adequately described what was happening inside my mind. But I was unfamiliar with such terminology and too engrossed in my new profession to strive for answers. My ability to sense new information and data, which seemed to reach me via some unknown source, was undeniable. I started to "feel" information from external sources, yet I possessed neither the skills nor the knowledge to know what to do with it or if it indeed had any meaning. However, I was sensitive enough to not dismiss what I sensed; instead, I allowed it to slowly filter through, assuming that later in life I would make sense of it. I was yet to give it voice, but I was prepared to listen.

I was changing. With hindsight I can recall the manner by which my psychic constitution was responding to the world around me, to the visible and invisible. I was becoming aware of impressions and feelings that emanated from nonhuman sources—trees, plants, even rivers and lakes. These were not conversations in any ordinary sense, though I was eventually to make sense of them as being another form of communication. This is not an unusual phenomena to those who identify themselves as Pagan; subsequent conversations have affirmed that the majority of practitioners can recall a time where the subtle and physical worlds collided.

Clairsentience is the ability to feel or sense data, information, or impressions by extrasensory means. It belongs to a sextuple group of anomalous cognitive abilities that transcend the normal, accepted, quantifiable five senses. Clairsentience—derived from the French *clair*, meaning "clear," and the Latin *sentier*, meaning "to feel"—complements the other five anomalous abilities:

- clairgustance (clear tasting)
- claircognizance (clear knowing)
- clairalience (clear smelling)
- clairaudience (clear hearing)
- clairvoyance (clear vision)

Those who are deemed psychically sensitive may embody all six abilities to a lesser or greater extent. What is apparent within my own experience is that my predisposition at birth seemingly determined which of these latent psychic senses I was likely to develop later in life.

Clairsentience is perhaps the most common of the six anomalous cognitive senses and one that permeates the experience of the remaining five. It seems that those who possess clairvoyance often report that a sense of feeling, or clairsentience, accompanies the vision; they may also hear by means of their subtle senses, incorporating clairaudience into the mix. None of the senses exist independently of the others. My dominant sense is that of clear feeling, which informs not only my spiritual life but also my professional one.

Modern occultists like Dion Fortune were convinced that we are predisposed to certain talents and attracted to pantheons, systems, and traditions of the spirit by means of an ancestrally influenced psychic constitution (Fortune 2011, 13). The abilities that we develop are in response to this constitution and define and inform our psychic abilities. It seems that we develop whichever ability is most suited to our life experience. I work in an emotionally charged atmosphere where the ability to feel and sense within that space is useful. In my spiritual life I am drawn to magic, divination, and sorcery. Clairsentience complements these facets of my life by allowing me to sense clearly and make informed decisions, whether in magic or when dealing with the bereaved. By gauging the emotional charge of any given situation, we can respond effectively; whereas the majority of the mundane world would argue that this is simply mumbo-jumbo, I beg to differ.

We all make decisions and choices based on our subtle senses, and even the most hardened muggles will admit to being able to sense the atmosphere in a space and respond accordingly; this cannot be quantified or measured, yet we all do it. The information is occult, hidden from rational view, yet the ability to sense and feel clearly is inherent within everybody. We define these situations as real by our reactions to them, which invariably arise from emotion. The issue of whether these experiences are real or not is inconsequential in light of them having real behavioral consequences in the apparent world. We are continuously affected and influenced by information that is not quantifiable. Honing these abilities into an occult talent is the task of any student of the Pagan traditions.

The exploration and expression of nonquantifiable talents must by definition be subjective, but to what extent do you understand your own? Let's take a moment to explore this.

> *Do you believe that you have an extrasensory ability? If so, how does it inform your spirituality? Of the six listed previously, which ones do you identify with, if any? Our extrasensory perceptions do not use ordinary language; even emotions do not reach us by means of language alone. Symbols, on the other hand, have an uncanny ability to access the subtle*

parts of our minds and spirits. So let's employ one that is common to Pagan practice and explore our subtle senses.

The first option is to draw a pentagram on paper and write or create a symbol for your primary talent in the middle of the star. A second option is to sit within a pentagram that you have drawn on the floor with either rope, chalk, or small votive candles to mark the points of the star. Position yourself in the center of the pentagram.

Consider your primary psychic ability. Now place the remaining five clair senses at the terminal points of the pentagram. You may wish to attempt to correspond them to the commonly attributed elemental qualities of each position, i.e.:

1: spirit

2: earth

3: water

4: air

5: fire

For example, air gives us the ability to hear, so you may place clairaudience in position 4. Clairgustance and the watery, liquid component of taste you may place in position 3.

Breathe deeply and still your senses. Be aware of the five senses surrounding you; within the center, you are a part of the entire symbol. Consider how they influence your primary talent and inform it. Recall past experiences. Did you hear something significant? Did you perceive a smell or a deep knowing, or did a vision accompany the experience?

Simply sit and consider these for the moment, with no goal other than to explore them as a whole unit, not as separate components. Later we will utilize a similar exercise to invoke memories of the dead, but for now familiarize yourself with the six clair senses and how they manifest within your life.

Permeating all six anomalous cognitive senses is emotion, as each one initiates an emotional response. In the mundane world, a term that implies extrasensory perception is discouraged; the term *empathy* has been employed to make what is beyond true articulation and measure acceptable. It is a much easier word to digest for those not of a spiritual persuasion. Empathy is inexorably linked to our emotions and our ability to respond to them and to the emotional needs and requirements of others. And yet the lines are blurred, as is often the case with matters of the heart.

In my personal practice and profession, empathy walks hand in hand with psychic abilities. I walk with the bereaved and, with my burgeoning psychic abilities, sense the passing of the dead and the spiral of grief that squeezes the hearts of the bereaved. This most extreme of human emotions, grief, and my proximity to it caused an explosion of my extrasensory talents, and slowly but surely, I started to fathom the function and necessity of grief.

THE SEASONS OF GRIEF

Ah, woe is me! Winter is come and gone,
But grief returns with the revolving year.

Percy Bysshe Shelley

Human beings are incredibly resilient. Even in the midst of immense pain and torment, the human ability to overcome is strong. In the darkest part of grief—when we feel like curling up and dying to be with the ones we love—there is a spark of the spirit that wills us to go on. It is true that to some the pain is too much and the descent into the abyss can be too overwhelming to ignore. But most prevail and rise by some unknown means to face a future without a loved one. We are naturally resilient, and even in the midst of excruciating emotional pain we may find opportunities to laugh and reminisce.

Grief has its seasons, and these express coping mechanisms that occur naturally; the brain and spirit combine to compel a person to live, to continue living. Therapists have been studying the process of grief for centuries, concluding that certain patterns inevitably affect all those in sufferance of it. The patterns of grief are remarkably consistent even if what we encounter within its throes is seemingly chaotic. I find the standard Kübler-Ross patterns of grief a little cold and unconnected to the cycles of life and have since developed my own patterns of grief that relate to the seasons of nature and my own connection to the nature-based system of the Celtic spiritual tradition. (Elisabeth Kübler-Ross was an American psychiatrist who studied death and dying. Her 1969 book *On Death and Dying* discussed the theory of the five stages of grief, identified as denial, anger, bargaining, depression, and acceptance. The system has lost favor in recent years with further studies in bereavement and psychotherapeutic methodology.)

Nature is an incredible teacher—she can inspire us and instruct us in the mystery of life and death, and the wondrous thing about it is that no religious conviction or faith is necessary. All we need is a window onto the world. Look to nature and you can see a reflection of human life and its myriad emotions; it acts as a canvas, for human nature is a part of nature, after all. Our mythologies play homage to the cyclic nature of the seasons of life, death, and rebirth. Demeter/Persephone and Mabon/Modron to name but four perpetuate the everlasting cycle of seed and grain, life and death, birth and rebirth.

Painted upon the drama of sun and moon can be seen a reflection of the human grieving process and our capacity to deal with it, for the four seasons of the year equate to the seasons of grief. But to make sense of this system, we must first examine the nature of the seasons. The seasons of the year have a tendency to oscillate; a March morning may feel particularly springlike, yet turn to hail or even snow by midafternoon. The wheel of the year oscillates in the same way as our emotions do.

AUTUMN: THE SEASON OF FALLING

Like the leaves of autumn that sigh and fall from their host, at the death of a loved one we fall into the seasons of grief. This is the time of separation, when we are confronted with the cold face of death; no parachute, no safety net, it seems, can prevent that falling from life. This phase of grief has three distinct qualities, each one a paradox, each one bringing new and varied definitions of anguish and emotion. Within this cycle we are faced with the extremes of shock, separation, and pain. But what the methods of bereavement therapy fail to inform us of is that the borders between each emotional state are not obvious. Just like the passage of a season, as autumn moves towards winter, days may be warm while frost may appear one morning and late autumn storms the next. We may fall into cycles of repetition, moving backwards and forwards between pain and numbness, shock and distress. This oscillation may confuse us further, offering us a glimpse of resilience on one hand before hammering us with debilitating emotions on the other. Grief is as personal as the individual we have lost.

Separation may come knowingly, especially when death occurs by process of chronic disease or illness. Like a leaf upon a tree, the color fades from the deep green of late summer and is replaced with ochre and umber as life wanes and death approaches. Sometimes the leaf is plucked in its glory and cast to the ground by forces beyond its control. Either way, separation causes the body to descend into shock. Like the falling leaf we descend, not knowing where we will arrive, cocooned by the air around us; the movements within it may seem blurry, numb, its edges soft and out of focus; suddenly everything else seems "out there." The reality of falling has not yet penetrated into the core of our being. We are somehow protected by the mind and spirit, physiology and brain, all coalescing to prepare us for the onslaught of emotion.

This stage of numbness is akin to a visit to the dentist, where we are injected with local anesthetic to deal with a cavity. We feel nothing at the time, only the sense of prodding, a feeling of intrusion that somehow fails to reach its destination, and yet we know that pain will follow and are accepting of that. In grief the coming pain is also inevitable, and the numbness serves to prepare us to deal with it, shifting the mind's focus to enable us to express the sheer power of human emotion in the hope that the resulting scar does not cause too much damage. I recall in the throes of my own grief my constant attempts to pinch my own skin in some vestige of wanting to feel something, anything other than that peculiar state of nothingness. Words from the lips of others seem to hang in the air before they reach the ears, and when they do they seem jumbled, incoherent. In the numbness of grief we do a lot of pointless nodding and very little interacting. The head feels dense, the world and its sounds buffeted as if the air is thick with cotton wool.

The mind may be aware that our loved one is dead—we may hear ourselves uttering the words but they don't seem real; they are distant, as if someone else is saying them. In the numbness of grief, the emotions have yet to catch up. Suddenly the intensity of separation becomes a reality, and at this point our grief transforms into oscillating waves of distress, the vocal chords are engaged, and the loss and the yearning we feel for that person shatters the numbness, sending it careening into the four corners of the world. We become a walking, breathing mass of emotion. The world feels empty, and the mind goes in search of the deceased; it is at this point that we can literally feel beside ourselves, as an integral part of our life has been torn away. The mind can see no resolution, no answer, to the pain of loss. Wave after wave of distress may engulf us as we succumb to the rawness of emotion.

In the season of falling, the very act of living can seem hard. Our appetite is lost, and simply getting out of bed is too much of a task for some to manage. The extremes of emotion may vanish for hours; we may assume a sense of ordinariness and go about our tasks, go to work, but this may be replaced with that increasingly familiar sense of numbness. We venture back and forth between despair, resilience, and emptiness, and then we may be confronted with a new torment: pain, real physical pain.

Recall, if you can, your last encounter with grief and the memory of its pain. You will find that the pain had a central location right in the core of your being; a claw, it seems, occupies that space directly beneath the sternum and above the belly button, in that section of the body called the solar plexus. This claw is merciless and crushing, and the pain is real and unfathomable. Observe a person who is in grief and you will see the unconscious attempt to soothe it; hands will move to embrace the point of pain, causing the bereaved to gasp in real physical discomfort. Yet paradoxically there is no "feeling" organ in this region; the physiology in this area serves the function of digestion, not emotion. Yet it is the very center of our person. It is our center of gravity—the place where we feel rooted to the earth. But grief tugs at those roots, and that umbilical cord that connects us to the universe is pulled as we long to go in search of our loved one.

The pain of grief should not be pacified or patronized; it must be allowed its voice. The purpose of grief is to express our loss. A stiff upper lip will serve only to bring further disjointed pain in the future. This point in the sequence of grief is not the time to be strong; it is the time to let loose the limitations of our expression, and, if we choose, to cry for the entire world to see. Regardless of whether we believe in continuation or not, we have lost; to deny our emotional processes is to deny an aspect of being human. Our loved one is dead, and even if in vision or dream we encounter them, that vessel of connection is no longer alive—it has fallen from life and turned its face from this world. We grieve for the loss of touch, of embrace, the smell of a loved one's skin, the warm holding of a hand. The unique voice and laughter of an individual alive is gone; it has been taken away from our experience of living. Grief does not mock the spirit; it honors the loss of the body.

But what should we do during this tumultuous time? In truth, the best course of action is to follow the instructions of grief; after all, it is not an enemy, it serves a distinct purpose, and to swim in its depths correctly we must assimilate its message. To be immersed in assimilation, we must feel grief without denying its ability to transform. In my experience, the worst form of grief is what is denied. Its primary purpose is to prepare for transformation, and this transformative process is the reality of living without someone. Our lives are no longer the same; they have been affected. Grief serves to prepare the soil for new seeds and patterns of living.

In the season of falling it is pertinent to succumb to the power of grief. It is a wise and tested teacher, and we can learn to trust it, but I reiterate: we must listen to its voice. Untamed grief and sheer despondency arise from the act of turning one's ear away from the song of grief. To dismiss its power and walk in the opposite direction is to dishonor its ability to initiate healing. There is no shame in grief; its purpose is vital to our ultimate well-being and the road to healing. In this season, listen to grief and ensure that there are times when you can be alone—something that those around you will instinctively attempt to prevent. But we need our thoughts, and we need that time to be at one with our grief. Find a space in your bereavement to be alone. Grief is not your enemy; it comes from you and is you. Give it the voice that it needs to form the path of healing.

To be immersed in grief does not imply wallowing in self-pity or to take to endless maudlin behavior. Turning the senses to the patterns of grief (which itself is a reaction to the loss of relationship) will inform your own personal grieving process. To smile, laugh, recall silly anecdotes, watch TV, or do the weekly shopping is not an indication that you are dismissing grief. While bereavement may seem overwhelming at the time, turn your inner ear to its voice and allow it to guide the experience; that is its function. And when the waves take you to the dark corners of tears and pain, do not fear them. They are the outward expression of love and loss.

Stop for a minute and take a deep breath. Consider the importance of the initial onset of grief; however despairing, it is essential. Within your own experience of grief, consider the following: bereavement is not an indulgence; it has a function. Within the grip of grief, take the time to stop and feel it fully. If it's happening to someone else, encourage them to be present in their grief. Dismiss the standard "try to be strong" reactions. Evaluate your understanding of grief. What does it mean to be strong as opposed to being weak? Contrary to being indicative of weakness, grief is a time to be present. How can you enable your own grief or that of another to be fully present? Consider that the first season of grief is concerned with accepting and assimilating the reality of loss.

WINTER: THE SEASON OF DARKNESS

In the hand of winter, we are in the grip of death; when we look beyond the window or walk in nature, everything is still and silent. In places the world may be blanketed in white, while others may see only stunted growth and the skeletal forms of trees. Shades of gray occupy the landscape, and it is as if color has been leached from the world. Our ancestors feared this season the most, for they had no real assurance that spring would return, that the world would come alive once more. In the seasons of grief, as the leaf that fell in autumn decomposes into the earthly tomb, we may be faced with the dark night of the soul: pain and separation, numbness and shock are replaced by more primal emotions.

The experience of grief moves from the center of the being as it is assimilated by the process to encompass the entire body. It is during this phase that our grief affects others; it leaves the confines of the body and spreads almost like a virus to affect the world around us. We are in sufferance of pain. Invoke again the memory of grief and that sense of anguish that comes from separation to recall the extremes of emotions. *The whole damn world just carries on, ignorant of the fact that my world has crashed* through a barrier and is teetering on the edge of a bottomless abyss! Why are people milling around, going about their business? Why can they not feel what I am feeling? The mind screams at them, wants the body to rush at them and shake them wildly, forcing them to stop and feel what you feel.

"I am in so much pain, stop, stop, why can you not feel my pain? Make the world stop and listen to the emptiness that my loss has created! Why are they not crying, why does the world carry on as if nothing has happened? How can the world not know that my world has collapsed? Please, anybody, anyone, stop and listen, feel my pain!"

The season of darkness is upon us with the cruel realization that the world carries on unaffected, unmoved, yet through grief your world is totally transformed. In the season of falling, the emotions were directed inwards; in their attempts to make sense of the process of loss, the bereaved may seem distant, dense, and confused. In the season of darkness, the emotions are externalized and begin to affect the world. It is during this time that family life and relationships may be strained as complex emotions are released. We may be unable to see a way out of this and become trapped in the grip of intense sadness; severe mood swings may lash out at those who seek only to help. This despair affects them too, those who love and care for us; they may feel helpless and useless or may distance themselves from us in fear of saying the wrong thing. And then there are those who grate on the nerves with the torturous, anger-initiating, pacifying statements such as "Come on now, don't be maudlin; you need to be strong. He wouldn't want to see you like this now, would he? Don't dwell on things; they will only upset you even more."

You just want to hit them, scream at them, and yet somewhere deep inside you, you know that these words only serve to demonstrate their own anguish at your pain. They simply don't know what to do or what to say. You may be easy to irritate. You have hardly any concentration, your mood swings are extreme, and pangs of guilt crash over you.

"If only I had been there a few minutes earlier, if only I had stopped her from going out, if only I forced him to stop smoking, if only I went with her—this wouldn't have happened!"

If only!

Those two simple, tiny words fall with little effort from the lips, but never have two words been as loaded with energy and emotion as they are during the seasons of grief. They have a power and an ability beyond the normal meaning of words to puncture the spirit with nails of pain and anguish. Our entire emotional connection at this stage is engrossed with the actual death and the mere chance that we could have done something, anything, to have prevented it. A deep internal battle rages through the spirit—on one hand we understand that we could not have done anything to prevent the death, but on the other we torture and torment ourselves that we did not do all that we could. And yet we cannot fathom what that action would be—what course would have prevented the death from occurring? A million situations and circumstances go into the making of a single second, and this poses questions beyond the ability of rational, logical answers.

I recall the death of an elderly lady who was struck by a passing motorcyclist, who in turn had evaded a potential accident by avoiding a child who had run out behind a parked delivery truck. The evasive maneuver caused him to steer directly into the path of the old lady, who, minding her own business, was simply making her way home. She was killed instantly. The motorcyclist survived. Her daughter was bereft with utter grief and despair; the accident had happened in the space of two seconds, two short seconds. One can sympathize with the irrationality of the daughter's reaction—the "what if" factor consumed and steered her grief. If only she had called her mobile phone. If only the grocer had dropped her change, delaying her by five seconds, she would not have been in that precise location at that exact moment. If only she had stopped to chat with that homeless man she had given her change to. If only, if only!

It was as if the timing was caused by some external means, by a force or a power beyond our ability to comprehend, inevitably summoning that most ghastly of questioning—what if, if only? We may easily succumb to despair, and this in turn leads to the torturous cycles of guilt. We feel guilty, we could have done more, and surely there must have been something we could have done, right? Nothing can remove that response, and no amount of logical explaining or attempts to pacify the bereaved can ever remove that feeling—and there is good reason for this. It is a part of the seasons of grief; we can do nothing other than embrace it. It is all too easy to punish ourselves for how we feel or respond, but by understanding why we feel like this, we give ourselves the permission to grieve. Nobody will judge us for that.

In Pagan traditions where an individual is in possession of their own conviction of spirit, another dichotomy can arise here. So often in the grip of the season of darkness I have listened as Pagans condemned themselves for descending so fully into grief. They feel inadequate or that in some way they have failed within their own spiritual path; they believe that the spirit continues, yet they cannot hide the pain of their grief.

A deeper set of contradictory questions floats from the abyss to tease and torment the spirit as the seasons of grief open doors onto the vast storehouse of human emotional responses. We may feel that we have failed. "I can't be that spiritual; I know that they have moved on, but I feel so much pain!"

Everything is brought into question as the sense of despair grips the individual in an iron claw. But we have not failed. We are grieving, and no amount of spiritual conviction should deny that basic human response. To have faith does not make us cold, unfeeling automatons; rather, our faith should also connect us to *us*. It is by emotion that we connect to our spirits, to divinity, and to our ancestors—and, by proxy, to our dead. Whatever your faith, do not be led to believe that to grieve is somehow a bad thing, for it demonstrates the connection you had to an individual. It expresses the sacred and vital nature of relationships, and to lose that connection—at least in a physical sense—causes a natural and perfectly normal emotional response: grief. Never deny yourself the unique human ability to express the severance of that connection. It hurts for good reason, for we have lost something precious. A sacred relationship with a human being has ended. Reaching out with the tendrils of your spirit, you may sense the deceased, yet that relationship has also changed; we can only embrace that change in our attempt to assimilate the seasons of grief. You may rationalize that your loved one rests in the Summerland; however comforting that notion is, it does not alter the fact that the relationship is transformed. Your grief reflects this. Embrace it with honor.

The despair of the season of darkness can be too much for some, and it is a sad fact that many who grieve may suffer further separation. Marriages and partnerships may be torn apart by deep internal processes that simply cannot be fathomed. The individual in sufferance of grief may seem to slip away from those who love them; they may become estranged and cold. Others may feel that they cannot penetrate the shields of grief that surround the bereaved. We may fall into helplessness, but there is another way.

I am convinced that so many arbitrary problems that arise from bereavement are indicative of our unawareness of the process and what its purpose is. We live in a different world to that of our ancestors, and to a great extent we have become separated from matters of the spirit. We have different pressures that weigh heavily on overburdened shoulders; the manner by which we believe in something is different, and our coping mechanisms have shifted focus. We live in a fast-flowing world where society wants everything yesterday—keep working, earn money, get that new car, buy that bigger house. When do we actually get time to sit down and listen to the voice that dwells inside us? For so many the internal voice is unfamiliar, and then suddenly we are struck by grief and it lends voice to the stranger who lives within. We are unfamiliar with it, it frightens us, and invariably, to some, our defenses are activated and we shut down completely. We can become unfeeling, unthinking, cold, and empty, all in a desperate attempt to prevent the internal voice from calling out, from being heard.

An important facet of the Pagan traditions is to teach the essentialness of giving voice to the spirit, to the "I" who dwells within. In the Celtic tradition that I follow, individuals are encouraged to seek a deeper connection with aspects of the self, not in an attempt to vanquish certain traits or attributes but simply to give them voice. This exploration of the self is not unique to the Celtic traditions alone but is an essential component of any Pagan study and training, which emulates antiquarian Pagan values captured in the words "know thyself" carved above the temple at Delphi. To honor ourselves is to honor the spirit and our connection to the universe as vital aspects of it, not as separate individuals fighting a losing battle. But so often in life we are taught that we are alone, it's all down to us, there is only us; it's no wonder when, in the grip of extreme emotion, many will crash, weeping helplessly.

To an extent, our society has lost what it means to listen, and modern medical methodology exacerbates the situation. In 2013, the American Psychiatric Association—in its latest diagnostic manual, the DSM-5—suggests a movement to pathologize grief as a mental illness that can be treated with pharmaceuticals. While the medical profession is in general disagreement with this, it is likely that we will see a continuous promulgation of grief as a treatable condition rather than as a component of the human grieving experience. This is a dangerous concept that will invariably have far-reaching repercussions, and it is symptomatic of a society at odds with its emotional well-being or, perhaps more sinisterly, manipulating it for monetary gain.

Dark nights of the soul occur when we respond blindly to an emotional situation; let's face it, we do not come equipped with a handbook at birth. There is little structure in place to explain the emotional function of the human being. Therefore, to a greater extent, we are left to our own devices; we may go in search of ourselves with no actual point of reference to guide us. But look to the systems of ancestral traditions and one will find tantalizing clues to the art of listening. The key to understanding both our emotions and the manner we react to them is to listen.

We may hear much but listen little. Listening is a different action to hearing; listening connects us deeply. We may hear the anguish of a friend or what we consider to be someone having a good old moan, but we may distance ourselves from it by not actually listening. Spiritual traditions and teachings cause us to listen to the internal voice, to the song of the "I." By listening to it, we lend it our vocal chords and give it voice; we connect with how we feel. The process may still be painful, as invariably it is when dealing with grief, but we experience it consciously and with a lucidity that only arises from the act of listening.

In the depth of winter the solstice sun dawns anew, a glimmer of hope glistens on the horizon, the worst is over, but yet we are not so naive to think the remaining winter will be a walk in the park. There is still much harshness to come, but we can breathe deeply and sigh heavily knowing that there will be light, and yet we are consciously touched by the bite of winter and will forever be marked by it. The trick during the season of darkness is not to punish ourselves for descending into the abyss, but to honor and understand its purpose as a vehicle for deep listening.

Stop for a minute, take a deep breath, and consider the following.
Understand that in the season of darkness we are in despair, but this
need not be a state of helplessness; the spring will come and the season of

new light will begin as a spark in the gloom of suffering. Experiencing the pain of loss is an essential component of the season of darkness. Give it voice. Do not avoid the grieving; simply allow it to steer the expression of grief. Replay the death in your head if that is what your mind wishes; many will shun these thoughts, finding cupboards in the back of their consciousness to lock them into. Locking our thoughts away will only allow them to fester, and they may threaten us later in life. If the circumstances of the death continuously plague you, lend them your ear but intersperse the thoughts with pleasant memories—recall laughter and good times, love and affection, silliness and joviality. We are far more resilient than we imagine. Recall the person and their entire life, not just the moment of their death. Give voice to the memories that are both painful and soothing. Your grief is yours and yours alone; the only person driving the vehicle of your grief is you. Deny yourself nothing, but instead listen deeply to the voice of your grief, for it can teach you much about yourself.

SPRING: THE SEASON OF NEW LIGHT

The cycle of moon and sun dance to a new, subtler tune as the drama of the seasons perpetually turns to the music of life, death, and rebirth. Winter loses its grip on the land, and in the seasons of grief we are given respite from the cycle of darkness as patterns of acceptance begin to stir within the spirit. Deep in their earthly tomb, in the silence and darkness of damp soil, bulbs stir in response to the growing light; they cannot see it nor reach it, not yet, but they sense it nonetheless. Cracks appear on their hard surfaces as they prepare to send shoots upwards, ever nearer the growing light.

Humans may naively consider themselves separate from the creatures that inhabit the natural world, but on a deep energetic level we are not so different. A snowdrop that senses the growing power of the sun, whose rays reach through the dank soil with whispers of hope, is invoked from the season of darkness just as we are. Our bodies respond to the turning of the seasons, to the waxing and waning of the sun and moon; we may pay it little heed, but we are affected nonetheless. In the seasons of grief we slowly ascend from the abyss of despair and helplessness as the spirit adjusts to the reality of the body and mind living without someone we love. It is the bridge to the spirit that senses the coming of a new dawn and causes our eyes to burn a little brighter as we sigh less heavily and cry less frequently. This is not to suggest that the power of the previous season has completely relinquished its grip, for we are marked by it; it forms an essential aspect of our grief. But in the season of new light, we are given hope; things are stirring.

The stirrings of a new dawn are not immediately apparent, but suddenly one finds that getting out of bed does not feel as difficult as it did on previous days. Our limbs may not ache as much, our hearts are not as heavy; in tortoise fashion we get on with our daily tasks and look to routine to remind us of the familiar. Grief is not subsiding; it is changing. It is during this phase that we get a sense of the true purpose of grief as a transformative emotion, for it prepares us for a life without someone we love. Alas, nobody can predict how long each cycle lasts, and to attempt to do so would be foolhardy and deny the very unique and deeply individual aspect of grief. No two people experience it in the same way. Grief is as unique as a snowflake or a fingerprint; it is ours and ours alone. We may share similarities and we may traverse the same course in psychological terms, but in truth we experience it alone.

To many who encounter the death of a loved one, it may come as a friend, a blessed relief from suffering. Many of us will witness the debilitating process of chronic disease, where we actually begin to grieve before the death occurs. We may find that we sink through the first two seasons of grief while our loved one is still alive, as we prepare for the inevitable separation. In these situations the bereaved may arrive at the season of new light immediately after the funeral. The seasons of grief may be short and the coming of new light may occur rapidly, allowing the bereaved to move on into the season of becoming. This does not negate the power of grief, nor does it eliminate the first two seasons; they are simply assimilated in a different manner. To those who have swum in the darkness and been immersed in the rawness of grief when death arrived with no warning, the season of new light may take several weeks or months to reach. It cannot be rushed or artificially induced; it can only happen when the spirit senses the coming of a new dawn.

The season of new light is the time of adjustment. A little color comes back into life, and if we look to nature we can see this demonstrated in the bursts of new growth. Daffodils and snowdrops bring hues of yellow and brilliant white to the frostbitten landscape; deep greens reach out from brown grasses and gray soil. The land begins to breathe again, and to the bereaved it can often feel as if we have been holding our breaths for weeks, if not months, and then something indescribable gives way, and the lungs rise and fall as if new. As the land is nourished by the rays of the spring sunshine, grief turns a corner and the body reaches out for nourishment. During the season of darkness we may have lost our appetites and lost weight in the process. As the new dawn rises we hunger again, our taste buds slowly awaken, and we sense the little pleasures in life. Color may flush to the cheeks and the body is invigorated as we take on more nourishment. But there is a dichotomy here: the season of new light is the intellectual acceptance of death; the emotions may not quite have caught up.

Experiences of grief during the period of new light can be perplexing, and suddenly feelings of inadequacy, not coping, and guilt can engulf the heart and mind again. There are times during this season when we suddenly feel guilty that we have not been actively thinking about the deceased. During the previous cycle, in the maelstrom of despair, little else occupied the mind—then all at once we find that we were thinking of something altogether ordinary: the mind veers to daily tasks, the shopping, what to cook for dinner. Then suddenly the grief erupts again as we are left reeling with feelings of guilt. *How could I have been thinking about something else?* The emotions have not quite caught up with the intellect. Head and heart may seem poles apart.

Think of the season of spring—the coming of new growth, the days are longer, the sun a little brighter, we may enjoy afternoons in the garden or walking in the countryside, feeling warmth for the first time in months. Then suddenly we can awaken to fresh snowfall, to temperatures that plummet to near freezing or beyond. The seasons of grief mimic the seasons of nature; there are dips and bumps along the road to summer and the season of becoming. We may feel okay one morning and be surprised that we have not felt despondent or sad in a while, then all of a sudden something triggers the emotional caldera that hides beneath the veneer of coping, and the volcano of our grief emerges yet again.

I recall my own experience when I lost my little sister, Rachel. Months later, in the midst of the season of new light, I was busily making tea for a friend who had come to visit. We chatted about the weather and the seasons, about life in general and the inconsequential chitchat that is comfortable amongst friends. While chatting I placed the milk carton back into the fridge and suddenly I could see nothing clearly—tears clouded my vision, my breath caught in the topmost part of my chest, and the cries of loss erupted, tearing the chains that I believed fastened them down. I could not fathom what had caused such an outpouring, and it wasn't until the next day that I realized what had occurred.

It had been five months since my sister died, and the placing of milk in a refrigerator hardly seems a likely trigger for an emotional outpouring. However, upon the fridge door—amidst the tat of fridge magnets and postcards—was a photograph of my two sisters, my brother, and me all together on a sofa, smiling, happy, four siblings together. Of course, one of those is no longer present; we are now three instead of four. It was this that caught my eye, and yet it had been there all the time. But on that fateful day, something must have drawn my attention to it, and in the middle of an ordinary action something extraordinary occurred; my grief wanted a voice. I cried again the next day, holding the photograph close to my heart, sensing the pull of my little sister's spirit as mine attempted to call it back. I could intellectualize my grief, but I could not reconcile that intellectualization with my emotions. They were not quite ready to swim together in harmony.

The season of new light contains a paradox: one feels the stirrings of hope, of adjustment, and yet one can be riddled with a new anguish. It seems to those who grieve that the world has long since moved on and forgotten your loss, and your grief can even seem a burden upon it. If the death was that of a partner or spouse, our sense of loneliness can be heightened; we may have feelings of guilt, of not wanting to burden friends and family with the fact that we are still grieving. Adjusting to being alone is something that we cannot prepare for; we may not necessarily have the appropriate tools to live as a single person. How do we cope? Adjusting to a life without our loved one is difficult, and we may feel that we are stumbling in the dark, arms flailing uselessly in the hope of grasping some guidance or the means to bring light into the void. But we are not alone; people are remarkably more accommodating and understanding than we believe them to be, especially when our rational minds are clouded by extremes of emotion.

The lessening grip of your grief as it assimilates and starts to find its home in the core of your being is no indication that you care less for your loss. It is simply transforming. After the bottom of your world fell away, now you are beginning to find firmer surfaces on which to walk; occasionally there are puddles and potholes that you may stumble into, but do so knowing that they are brief and stumble on, reaching firmer ground again. Previously only darkness lay ahead; now, as you look down the road of the seasons of grief, you see light peering at you over the rim of the horizon. The sun will rise, and a new season will begin.

Stop for a minute and consider the following. To adjust effectively, one must consciously give grief a voice; this period of new light is an opportune time to seek professional bereavement counseling or therapy or to join a support group. Turn to your family, your spiritual community, or to what brought your life meaning and purpose before your loss. There are many questions that arise during the season of adjustment, and it is important and healthy that they are addressed, however inconsequential they may seem.

Patterns of guilt are different now than they were in the season of darkness. Back then we felt guilty that we should have done something, been there, changed something, or forced anything to happen differently. Now we may face a new voice of guilt, one that chastises us for feeling that we are moving on, for not being immersed in clouds of tears for most of our waking hours. But just as before, lend it your voice and your ear, listen to what it is telling you, do not chastise yourself. You are not annoying anyone or imposing on anybody else's time or energy; those who care for you would rather you voice how you feel. The primary function of the season of new light is adjusting to a world where the deceased is missing, and this takes time.

SUMMER: THE SEASON OF BECOMING

The blooming of summer does not occur on a particular day or within a specific hour; it is a gradual process that cannot be forced, enticed, or summoned. Spring gradually and gently gives way to summer. It becomes the season of growth, and yet we know that the journey to summer has been tumultuous and at times frightfully difficult. There have been days when we have despaired and wondered if summer would come at all; a glimmer of light on the horizon heralded its coming, but there were times when clouds obscured your vision and caused you to doubt that the days would ever be brighter or warmer. The patterns of grief mimic the subtlety of the seasons, and just as spring gives way to summer, sighing as it bursts into fruition, so too does your grief. A lightness burns brightly within your spirit as the period of adjustment and new light heralds resolution and new patterns of living.

The season of becoming provides us with that most inspiring of qualities, hindsight. It is during this cycle that we become consciously, intellectually, and emotionally aware of the purpose of grief and its effect upon us. The manner by which we assimilated our grief dictates when and how we arrive at the season of becoming. Grief gives us a choice, and the primary key to its effectiveness has already been explored: listening. We alone choose how it compromises or transforms us; it is only our ability to listen or not listen that affects the outcome of grief.

With hindsight we can look back at the experience and clearly absorb its message, and we should honor it for the transformation it initiated. It is too easy to ignore the process of grief, to dismiss it as something that never happened, to fear it so much that one cannot and will not acknowledge it as a vital human emotion. But just as the sun shines brightly in the summer skies, the light of resolution shines within the spirit; we can acknowledge it and step out into the glorious sunshine of emotional acceptance.

The tools to effective assimilation of grief are not out there in some cosmic waiting room, nor do they belong to someone else; they exist within you. It is the denial of grief that removes the necessary tools to its assimilation and causes us to stumble from one season to another, and in some cases, sadly, the seasons become so jumbled up that the individual may be permanently compromised. As the sun rises and your grief soars to its zenith, rest assured that you need not feel guilty that you are moving on, for it is by your living that the deceased is honored. This is the core message of the season of becoming.

In the abyss of the season of darkness we may also want to die, to curl up into a corner and do anything to be with the person we loved, to end it, to have some solace and peace from the endless torment of emotion. In the season of becoming we arrive at the realization that we carry the light of the deceased within us—that to truly honor them we must continue living, to be immersed in life, to share their stories and be the voice that they no longer have. Arriving at this conclusion is difficult, but grief is not meant to be an easy process; it is a transformative device that challenges and claws at the boundaries of normality.

The limitation of time does not apply to the emotional state; only the intellectual mind may serve to befuddle us with nagging remarks of "I should be over this by now!" and the like. The season of becoming is initiated by the conjoining of the intellectual and emotional states. In the previous season, the intellect fathomed grief, yet the emotions were not ready to move on. As the trees burst into the rich greens of summer, the spirit also awakens to the realization that our emotions can be reconciled with the intellect. But there are still issues that confront us.

If the deceased was your spouse or partner, you will have to adjust to being alone, and there is more to this than first meets the eye. Socially you are no longer part of a couple, which can cause you to feel out of sorts or that something is missing when invited to social events, particularly where friends are present in familiar patterns of coupling. Sexually you may not have the means to express and expel the energy that can be heightened during the grieving process. During the initial season of grief, the libido is compromised greatly and can seem to vanish entirely, yet paradoxically within the season of darkness we may feel the need to express ourselves sexually. The reason for this is rather simple. The act of sex releases enormous quantities of hormones and endorphins and initiates a whole spectrum of emotions, and for a time these can distract from the pain of grief. Promiscuity among men in particular is not uncommon during this phase of grief; we may do anything to feel something other than our pain. Living without a sexual partner will cause emotional disturbances, and we may not be ready or willing to move on to a new partner. Again, listening is the key; do not suppress or deny your physical urges, talk to your closest friends about them, give your emotions the voice they require, thus preventing them from compromising you.

Practically, you have had to adjust to living without someone; you may have had to develop new skills to enable you to function normally. Ordinary relationship patterns with the deceased have been severed, and you will have slowly formed new patterns and rituals to replace those lost. Perhaps the person called at a particular time of day or you may have met for lunch or dinner, taken to walking, met in a group setting, or shared a workspace. New patterns will have emerged from the previous season like the bulbs that stirred in the earthen tomb; green shoots have risen, branches are heavy with flowers and growth, fruit forms into ripeness on vines. The change is subtle. New patterns happen almost instinctively; they are a product of your coping mechanisms and their ability to transform you.

The season of becoming does not imply the end of grief, for once we are touched by it, we are forever transformed by its power. It lives within us always; occasionally it may raise its head and ask to be voiced, and there is no need to deny it. If we listen, we learn that it is not an enemy. It is there to perform a vital function, and it causes the reconciliation of the emotions and the intellect. Grief is not an illness; it cannot or rather should not be pathologized or likened to depression. It is a natural response to loss, and we are designed to experience it. We are remarkably more resilient than we give ourselves credit for.

Understanding its power is the key to arriving at the portal to this new season, to becoming a person who is living without someone they loved. You have been touched by death, and it has changed you; that is its purpose and function. You are more able to recall memories of the deceased without them causing you pain and sadness, but this does not happen by means of time alone. The old adage that time is the greatest healer is not entirely accurate; it is a reciprocal process. Time assists the healing, but the majority of it happens internally by our ability to connect and understand the process of grief.

Ultimately the sun will shine and your loss will never be dishonored or unacknowledged; instead, the deceased will find a new home within the core of your being. Deep in your spirit the memory of the dead resides, and it is through this ethereal aspect of ourselves that we connect to them by means of our emotions. The season of becoming is not the end; it is simply one essential cog upon the never-ending wheel of birth, life, death, and rebirth. As the light of the sun reaches its zenith and the heat of summer dissipates, as our star declines in strength and power and the grip of winter threatens the earth, the cycle resumes. We learn that nature is a teacher; she teaches us that we are a part of her, human nature *is* nature, and as the wheel turns she whispers the sweet mysteries of life and death and rebirth. Nothing truly dies, she says, it simply transforms; this is the law of existence.

Stop for a minute and consider the following paragraph. How does grief find its home within you, and what does that mean? Evaluate the concepts of time as a healer, of periods of adjustments or the manner in which you have judged that someone else should be over a death by now. How long is the road to the season of becoming? If you have been personally affected by loss, can you mark in hindsight the progression of grief's seasons? How does your newly adjusted life without a loved one honor their memory without compromising your emotional well-being? Within the season of becoming we learn how to reinvest our emotions in other projects or relationships and come to an understanding that our living honors the dead.

EMOTIONAL RELOCATION AND
THE FUNCTION OF RITUAL

We have traveled through the seasons of grief and wondered at their paradox and fickle nature, and yet we have also seen how essential it is. It does not happen at a whim; it is a deep process that initiates a new form of living. But how do we move on from this—what coping mechanism can we develop to enable us to fully appreciate and comprehend the teachings of grief? To have an intellectual understanding of continuation is, alas, not enough to provide emotional comprehension. One cannot utilize the intellect alone to accept that our loved one has moved on to a different plane of existence. To effectively know that the deceased continues in another form, we must seek to emotionally relocate them. This process enables the spiritual dimension, or the subtle senses and realms, to reconcile the intellect and the emotions to know that the deceased continues to exist, albeit in another form.

For many, faith is not enough; anecdotes of the afterlife and continuation may serve only to frustrate the bereaved in that the messages may not be pertinent to them. In Pagan traditions we learn to relocate the deceased in the other worlds of existence; we learn to separate them from the ranks of the living and to designate them as ancestors. Emotional relocation is not a new concept. You are subtly familiar with it, as funeral services and ceremonies facilitate this function by designating the dead as "not living," and they are sent to another world, where we no longer see them. However the human condition may strive to tether the dead to this world of life, we know intuitively that they no longer belong here; their path has diverged. We may not see the dead, but we certainly feel them, for they exist on a subtler level. The relationship has not vanished with the disposal of the corpse; it has changed. For this to be assimilated as actual experience, we need to emotionally relocate the deceased.

In Paganism we have at our disposal an effective and familiar method for emotional relocation: ritual. Ritual causes the mind, the heart, and the intellect to experience the spiritual; faith is not a requirement to knowing. I experience, therefore I know. This is the nuts and bolts of Pagan practice. Through liturgy and ritualistic gesture, spiritual concepts are assimilated as actual experience, not simply intellectual concepts. Grief can initiate a futile grappling where the bereaved seek to find or locate the deceased. Invariably this leads to frustrations; in some cases, a debilitating helplessness may arise from having failed to locate them.

It is common during the early stages of grief for the bereaved to seek the comfort of mediums and psychics. But in Paganism, there is another way: ritual. By entering liminal space we move closer to the subtle worlds, where mind, body, and spirit can swim in harmony. Grief tends to cause a polarization of the emotions—too much head or too much heart; grief is individualistic rather than holistic—but ritual brings us back to the center, to a place where we can stop, be still, and connect to the whole. By proxy of this connection we can learn to emotionally relocate the deceased in a world that is pertinent to their experience, and yet by the tendrils of our spirits we can commune with them and know that all is as it should be.

The above statement is not to suggest that ritual has no function in secular society; one could argue that society is held together and given meaning by ritual activity: birth rituals, birthdays, coming of age, graduation, weddings, and, of course, death. The primary death ritual, the funeral, is a process of relocation. It generally follows set patterns of liturgy and symbology deeply familiar to the customs and traditions of the society in which we live. Unfortunately, the majority of funeral services bear no relation to the life experience of the deceased. Thankfully, this is changing, with more and more individuals requesting services that reflect the uniqueness of their living. For the Caucasian societies of the Western world, this has mostly consisted of a Christian liturgy read by a minister from an approved order of service compiled by the various church establishments. These rituals were effective for centuries, but of late it is evident that individuals seek funeral rituals that express the individuality of the deceased rather than a liturgy they do not necessarily follow.

Pagan rituals for the dead are not restricted to the funeral alone but can be utilized for all stages of the death and grief process. Rituals enable us to experience fully and lucidly the function of death and bereavement and the emotional relocation of the dead. Secular rituals for the dead are primarily communal, the funeral being the most obvious. But ritual can be something we engage with alone; we may utilize it to prepare for an anticipated death, to create meaningful rituals of farewell, and to recall and remember the dead. Examples of these rituals can be found in part 4 of this book.

Death rituals serve to sever the ties of the dead to the world of the living; the disposal of the corpse facilitates the return of the body back to its elemental constituents. In the human psyche the breakdown of the body frees its spirit from the denseness of physicality and enables its relocation in another realm, dimension, or plane. Burial rites return the body through decomposition back into earth; cremation serves to return the corpse through fire into air. On a subconscious level this disposal is symbolic of the fact that the body no longer has value; it has served its purpose (Leming 354). Its deposition in earth or combustion by fire marks a transition from human being to spirit, body to ether. This is vital for emotional relocation. In situations where a body is never found after death, the bereaved may take significantly longer or never fully emotionally relocate. Ritual is a gateway by which we internalize relocation in a meaningful and experiential manner.

Rituals key into the subconscious, and it is here that we must emotionally relocate the deceased; attempting to do so on a purely cerebral level will ultimately fail. For it to be effective, we must find a manner to internalize the process in a way that can be experienced by body, mind, and spirit. Let's return to the symbol of the pentagram that we encountered earlier and explore the function of emotional relocation by ritualistic means.

Create a sacred space in the manner that you are accustomed to; another option is to simply take yourself to a quiet room and light some candles, burn incense, or do anything that slightly alters the atmosphere of the room. Draw the following on a piece of paper or alternatively mark it out on the floor with cord, chalk, or other means, and place a votive candle at each point of the pentagram. You may wish to use corresponding candle colors suited to the elemental quality represented within the pentagram.

Now either stand within the center of the pentagram or focus on that area if the symbol is drawn on paper. Bring to mind an image of a deceased individual together with memories of your relationship with him or her. Hold the image fast for a few minutes, recalling past encounters and moments that are pertinent, personal.

Take a deep, audible breath and focus your attention on the point of the pentagram that represents earth. Consider the qualities of earth that the deceased possessed. Recall their practicalities—how they supported others and how others supported them. What grounded them? How did they demonstrate stability, security, and a sense of belonging? How did their earthiness complement or combine with your own? Consider these elements for as long as you wish. Conclude this section by saying:

"I honor your qualities of earth: [name them]. Know that I will always remember you."

When you are ready, take another deep, audible breath and focus on the point of water. Consider the watery, emotional aspect of the deceased; were they sensitive, aloof, easy to cry? Were they undone by their emotions or did they have a firm grasp on them? How did they express their emotions? How did their water quality complement or combine with your own? Consider these elements for as long as you wish. Conclude by saying:

"I honor your qualities of water: [name them]. Know that I will always remember you."

Take another deep, audible breath and focus on the point of air. Was the deceased flighty, dreamy, and prone to daydreams and fancy aspirations? How did they inspire you? Consider the way they interacted with the world through their creativity. What was the tone of their voice? How did they sound? Recall conversations, laughter, qualities that emulate air and their ability to express. How did their airiness complement or combine with your own? Conclude by saying:

"I honor your qualities of air: [name them]. Know that I will always remember you."

With another deep, audible breath, turn your focus to the point of fire. Bring the deceased to mind; what drove them—what were their passions? Were they quick to anger, quick to react, or did they burn quietly? How did they express their own inner fire? Recall their temper; did you argue? How did their fieriness complement or combine with your own? Consider their fiery qualities for as long as you wish. Conclude by saying:

"I honor your qualities of fire: [name them]. Know that I will always remember you."

Finally, turn to face the point of spirit. All the points of the pentagram interact with each other; none are independent. Imagine all the lines of the pentagram glowing brightly with all the qualities that you recalled; see them flooding the point of spirit. Know that the dead are not lost, they are as spirit returned to their original state, one enriched by a unique human personality. Repeat these words:

"I honor you as spirit. I honor you as a song of the universe. I remember."

Return your focus to the center of the pentagram and consider the symbol as a whole; it represents all the qualities of the deceased you have had in mind. It is also a microcosm of the entire universe. All things exist within this symbol, permanent and impermanent. Nothing is forgotten. Watch it pulsate with every quality that the deceased brought to their life and how they touched yours. See it as a symbol of your relationship. All is as one.

If the pentagram is physical, extinguish the candles and imagine the symbol dissolving into nothingness, but know that it exists nonetheless. If you worked with a paper version, burn it. As you do—as flames lick at its edges, as it vanishes into smoke—know that all things transform, but nothing is truly lost. A river loses its name and form, but its essence remains.

Return to the here and now, sure in the knowledge that the deceased continues as a song of the universe.

The above exercise can be combined with a ritual that can be found in part 4's section entitled "Saying Goodbye."

AN ATHEIST'S PERSPECTIVE

A dear friend of mine stands between the world of the spirit and the body; she cannot accept that the spirit is a carbon copy of the human that lived and breathed here on earth, but neither can she accept that death is the ultimate end. She needed to find a path that traversed the center, the middle of the road, a place that to her was indicative of realistic hope. I spoke to her about the writing of this book and asked if she would be willing to listen to my own theories and experience of death, spirit, and matters of continuation. She agreed. We spent an afternoon chatting about some of the concepts and theories in this book, and I was touched that she was deeply moved by them, but something else transpired from that conversation. Belief in the spirit, as most people would define it, is not a requirement for a belief in continuation.

Nothing in nature is wasted, the universe is the ultimate recycler, our bodies are reabsorbed into the experience of the world—they continue in that sense. And to my atheist friend this is enough; this in itself is comforting. She cannot accept that her spirit will continue with any form of human sentience, but she can accept that her molecules will continue, and that imbues within her a sense of hope and comfort. To her the grief process is essential; to feel that sense of loss is an experience that heralds the end of sentience and consciousness as she perceives it. Words attributed to Mark Twain caused her to consider the existential nature of her being, and I ask that you pause and contemplate them as she did. He is reported to have said:

"I do not fear death. I had been dead for billions and billions of years before I was born, and had not suffered the slightest inconvenience for it."

We all have coping mechanisms; what matters is how we connect to them and how we express them in a way that honors life and living. The quote above is worth pondering and meditating over, for it offers a different perspective, albeit one that may contradict or challenge your current thinking. Consider it nonetheless, if you will, for I believe it contains an element of truth that can equated to the spirit's overall experience, which we will examine next.

UNWILLING TO DIE

My father was the fittest man I ever knew. A devout mountain and cross-country runner, his lungs could propel his legs up steep hills with ease. But none of this was of any consequence; he was to die so young. My dad was diagnosed with terminal stomach cancer in January 2005; he would die eleven months later. My father's illness and the preparation for his ultimate death are heightened in my memory because of other events that took place that remarkable year. My father's condition was fickle; he would have good days and bad. One of the bad days happened in early July.

I was working in London on the morning of July 7, 2005. The morgue had been relatively quiet that week, with only a slow trickle of deaths to occupy our working hours. We were alerted by the radio that something terrible was happening in the city. Terrorists had detonated explosive devices in the city's public transport system. The country ground to a halt; people fled the city in droves amidst a cloud of panic, the nation held its breath, and the world turned its eyes towards London. I was due to return home that day to be near my father, as he was painfully ill, yet I was torn—I was also needed in London to help deal with the aftermath of the terrorist attack. I spoke briefly to my dad, and he gave me his best wishes and said I should go and help.

London was empty as the police car sped its way through the city, its blue lights flashing; other police vehicles joined the convoy as specialists were transported to the temporary morgue set up to deal with the fatalities. By the following morning the dead had been recovered and brought to the enormous morgue that we now occupied. A hushed silence fell on the vast autopsy suite as the first of the victims was brought in for examination and identification. None of us had any point of reference or internal regulator to help make sense of this act of senseless violence, the aftermath of which we attended to behind closed doors, away from the gaze of the media and the public. I recall the arrival of each body in turn, and the absolute respect and honor given to them for having met such a tragic and frightful death. There was nothing anyone could do other than ensure that their families were given closure and that their loved ones were returned to them for the purpose of farewells.

The scene in that place for days after the event of July 7 was of devastation, investigation, and respect for the victims who died at the whim of others. We cared for the dead as best we could, to ensure that their families could view their bodies one last time if at all possible. We served the dead and our country in the spirit of comradeship and resilience. In the midst of tragedy and terror, great acts of kindness and love emerged to soothe the hearts of those pained by loss. In the throes of this work I was called to return home, to leave the dead and attend to my father's bedside; he was painfully unwell again. I left behind the scene of mass death and destruction to be faced with the potentiality of personal loss and grief. As life would have it, he was to recover and survive for another five months.

My father never spoke to us about his illness. One could not address the issue with him; we all knew that he was dying and so did he, but something within him rejected its discussion. He was in his fifty-fourth year, a young man really, and yet his body was breaking down and aging before our eyes; his countenance became gaunt and shadowed as his body lost its grip on life. We could all sense the path ahead and watched as the tethers that held him to this world weakened. But his heart was strong, and he refused to let go of life; he would not succumb to the power of death and turn his face from this world.

My father kept his emotions to himself, yet within his suffering his fear of death was tangible; he did not want to let go of this life, however painful it was. I wanted him to reach out and voice his thoughts of death, to tell those he loved that he did indeed love them. But his unwillingness to let go caused him to avoid all topics of high emotion. His mind and heart were strong; he had a stubbornness born of an ox, yet his body continued to deteriorate. At 4:30 PM on December 11, he slipped into unconsciousness, his body no longer capable of alertness. I recall the very last words that he spoke before his voice was silenced forever. He was never to wake.

His death was exhausting; his heart battled, and the fronds of his mind were palpable in the room. He was fighting as hard as he could, unwilling to die. His fight was painful to watch as more and more morphine was pumped into his veins, causing the gulf between life and death to narrow further. When the remainder of the family arrived that evening, his fight had weakened and his breathing was shallow and infrequent. His body was letting go. I tried to reach out with my mind, with my own spirit, to sense his, to tell him that it was okay, that he could let go now and leave this suffering. But how does one do that— how does one actually will one's own father to die? He was afraid, and there was nothing any of us could do to alleviate that fear. All we had was love and the touch of a hand to assure him that he was not alone.

It was his brother who told him to stop fighting. He bent in close to his ear and told him to let go—that it was okay, that he could leave this place. And with that a certain stillness came over the room and the company; the wind seemed to hold its breath beyond the window and the blinds hung still against the night as the world quietened its pace in the early hours of the morning. At that point my father lost his battle against cancer and slipped quietly from this world, taking his place as an ancestor. I had lost a parent; his mum had lost her child. The pain of his illness had stopped, and the pain of our grief began. I had lost one of my mortality buffers and was encountering a different form of grief, one complicated by issues of identity. I recall breaking my heart in the knowledge that my father's name, that of the Hughes tribe, would die with my death. Being unlikely to father children, my paternal lineage dies with me.

Losing a parent is a peculiar affair. The world seems emptier some-how—one of the vessels that carried me into this world is gone, and all that remains are the tales that we tell about his life. He had a Christmas funeral: a large wreath of holly, pine, and mistletoe decorated his coffin, and his favorite Christmas songs filled the crematorium. I recall pressing the button that sent his coffin into the furnace, the flames of which returned my father's body to the elements that created him. He had feared death so much. From that point on, I was determined that I would seek to change my own relationship with death—to better understand it.

My father died an unpleasant death in a hospital bed, pumped into a medically induced twilight. He didn't actually die of cancer; he died of a morphine overdose. Such is the case with the majority of cancer patients. If asked, the majority of us would hope for a good death, to die peacefully in our sleep—no warning, no pain, and no distress—to slip away gently and quietly from the world. Alas, to the majority this will not happen. The greater percentage of deaths in the Western world occur in general hospitals and are under institutional control.

In truth, hospital deaths can be rather grim. The dichotomy of modern medicine is that in its attempts to cure, it does not afford us the choice to think about how we would like to die. That question is rarely asked or addressed unless in a hospice environment. In response to this, the manner by which we serve to make someone "comfortable" may actually prevent a conscious dying. The Hippocratic oath that modern physicians take vows to save lives, thus therapeutic methods are employed right until the very end whether this is of benefit to the patient or not. Drips pump saline and drugs into the bloodstream, the patient is encouraged to eat and drink if able, and various end-of-life pathways may be employed, from palliative sedation to intentional dehydration. The paradox of modern medical intervention is that the line between attempting to save someone's life and prolonging their suffering, particularly if the patient is going to die, can be somewhat blurred.

If the body is left to its own devices, it would withdraw naturally from what sustains it. Cats are a good example of natural withdrawing; they sense their impending deaths and will consciously remove themselves from their home and take to hiding. They stop drinking and eating, and death takes over. Human beings can experience the same death—it's a matter of choice, but alas, that choice is rarely offered to us. The dichotomy here is not necessarily how we die but rather the problem of what it is that is actually killing us. Setting aside accidents, suicide, and homicide, the majority of us will die of disease; the most common are the result of chronic metabolic syndromes such as exacerbations of diabetes, heart and respiratory disease, blood and brain disorders, and, of course, cancer. These are the top six causes of death.

However, the issue of dying consciously is a tricky subject when one considers that almost all of the above can cause excruciating pain. Pain relief is something that the majority of us will actually want, and it is something that will be offered. But does modern medicine strip death of its sacredness?

My father's death sent a clear message to my subconscious: "I don't want to die like that!"

My father feared the unknown; his impending death filled him with separation anxiety. His fear stifled his ability to discuss his death, to speak openly of it and his concerns. He had no religious convictions, yet the prospect of an unknown afterlife or annihilation into nothingness filled him with a silent dread. In her *Book of the Dead*, Dion Fortune said that we should learn to consider death as an aspect of growth and development (Fortune 39). But how do we learn this? My father had nobody to teach him how to experience the spiritual as tangible; nobody had ever offered him a space in which to talk freely about his death, and he had never sought it out.

Pagans can learn from this, and I encourage you to open effective, gentle channels of communication. The Pagan traditions are still in their infancy, deaths have been few and far between, but as time slips by, as the Pagan population increases, the demise of Pagans will become more commonplace. Are we actively talking about it? How do our traditions equip and teach us to deal with our death and the deaths of those we love? Consider hosting a death discussion evening as part of your grove, coven, or group meetings, perhaps to coincide with the Samhain season. Keep it fluid and generalized at this point; further discussion examples are given in part 2's "Myfanwy's Story." What liturgy does your tradition provide; does it have funeral guidelines and suggestions available to its members? Who are the "soul midwives" of your community—those who create and hold sacred space to assist the passing of the dying? Regardless of how well we think we know someone, do we know what their feelings and wishes are when it comes to death? Let's ask and offer a safe space to openly discuss our opinions, fears, anxieties, hopes, and wishes.

Nobody should have to die alone, isolated in their own fear. Consider the importance of training in soul midwifery or another death and dying–related program that serves your community. What can you do in service to those who will die?

SWIMMING IN SPIRIT

Humans are amphibians—half spirit and half animal.
As spirit they belong to the eternal world,
but as animals they inhabit time.

C. S. LEWIS

The emotional storm of grief is in response to loss, and at the heart of loss swims another emotion that has become intimately bound to death: fear. The actual process of grief, as we have discovered, is both healthy and essential, and we have explored its function and purpose and also the threat it poses to our well-being when ignored, slighted, or dismissed completely. But there is more to our relationship with grief than first meets the eye; to millions of people who encounter the death of a loved one, their hearts, minds, bodies, emotions, and spirits embark on a perplexing journey in search of what they have lost—an individual. In the majority of deaths the corpse lies supine in a cold room, a morgue, or funeral home, and yet somehow we sense that the "person" is no longer there; what ensues is the painful searching for what has become lost. In the aftermath of a death, the bereaved may go in search of answers, seeking out those who purport to communicate with the dead; these mediums and psychics may open channels of communication to the spirit world, anything that brings comfort and the much-needed proof that the person we loved continues.

On one hand, the searching is simply indicative of separation and loss; whenever we lose anything, regardless of what it may be, we go hunting for it. We may stress and become overanxious that the person, object, or thing cannot easily be located. In the case of a death, we struggle to articulate or make sense of the fact that a living, breathing person who was with us one second has suddenly vanished, leaving only a cold, dense corpse behind. A relationship ends, the emotional connection is severed; for so many it is unfathomable, and the mind, body, and spirit cannot be reconciled.

The searching naturally leads to seeking answers, and various agencies may be employed to attempt to provide a glimmer of hope, a chance that the person we loved is still out there somewhere, occupying a world that mimics this realm of the living. Millions seek comfort from the sensitivity of those who purport to commune with the dead, but this seemingly innocent process can also serve to further disempower the bereaved. We may seek too much and become over-reliant on the abilities of another to somehow reconnect us to a person with whom we no longer have a physical relationship. In a small number of cases, this method of communication can trap the bereaved in inappropriate coping mechanisms. It belies a deep misunderstanding of the nature of spirit, a disjointed hope that C. S. Lewis found entirely unrealistic when he said:

> Unless, of course, you can literally believe all that stuff about family reunions on the further shore, pictured in entirely earthly terms...We know it could not be like that. Reality never repeats. The exact same thing is never taken away and given back. How well the spiritualists bait their hook! "Things on this side are not so different after all."

There are cigars in Heaven. For that is what we should all like. The happy past restored (Lewis 23).

We may long for the restoration of the happy past, but there is another way—one that is honest and honors the body and spirit. We should find our own channels of communication that serve to provide answers. In order to do this, we must explore the realm of the spirit and what it means to be spirit. We must understand why we succumb to endless searching or become lost in the sadness of grief. By seeking to understand death and the meaning of the spirit, we develop an informed relationship with it, and by proxy of this we glean what it is to die and what it means to continue.

This chapter will focus on questions of the spirit and provide you with new ways of thinking, new patterns of relationship, because we can no longer carry on connecting to the deceased in the way we are used to. The relationship has changed, and if we do not respond to that change, we become lost in the search for what we have lost. To forge a new relationship with the spirit is one of the healthiest tools you can develop in life, for it will cause you to understand what it is to be human and what it means to die. Without even realizing it, you have been programmed by life, society, and our teaching systems to be separate—to believe that all that exists is here and now, and that if it cannot be seen or touched, it is mere fantasy. We have been disempowered.

To stand in your own power and to come to know what it means to die and what happens to the person beyond that point is something you must discover for yourself. Too often we stumble through life avoiding such thoughts until inevitably they come knocking intrusively at the door; we then find ourselves having to deal with it. But imagine for a minute that you are equipped to deal with it; this does not imply an easy ride—far from it—but it does provide you with the necessary tools of understanding the nature of death, the mystery of the spirit, and the meaning of relationship. But even to those who have embarked on a spiritual path and are immersed in teachings of mystery, death may still be that last bastion of fear. And it is this emotion that we must naturally explore next, for it blinds us from an authentic relationship with the spirit.

FEAR

We fear the unknown, but there is a paradox here, for to be fearful is an inbuilt protective device. It kept us safe when we lived at the mouths of caves, wary of the wild animals that lurked in the darkness. A fear of heights may keep us from venturing too close to a cliff's edge and thus prevent potential death or injury. Fear is essential to maintain the status quo, but it can also serve to harm. It is because of fear that we may develop inappropriate coping mechanisms and become disempowered by our own inability to confront or embrace any given situation that is new, challenging, or causes separation. Death strikes the match that lights a bonfire of fear, for we have been inadvertently taught to fear it.

Many adults will strive to protect children from the reality of death, and thus begins the descent into fear; a parent may unwittingly transfer their own insecurities or inability to articulate death to their offspring. But look to a child who has encountered death; they are far more accepting and resilient than we may imagine. They have an innocence that has not yet been programmed by misinformed fear, and they are also closer in time to the point where they entered this world; their minds are still open to the truth of immortality. The doubting adult mind has yet to grip them in its fist of cynicism. So why do so many adults fear death so much, and why do many transfer this fear to children hidden under the veneer of "I know what's best for them, they shouldn't be subjected to death, they are too young" and similar remarks? They do so out of fear. The fear is referred to another—in this case, a child—in the subconscious hope that it will lessen the attention of their own fear and dampen its voice, thus preventing its ability to debilitate. We may assume that the fear of death is instinctive, a built-in device, but this is not necessarily the case, and the fear of death is not the same as the fear of dying. I am not a psychologist, but having been immersed in grief and human reactions to death for over two decades, I have observed the effect of fear and have come to realize where and how it develops.

In the Western world we have been taught to fear death. Death is bad, it separates us from the status quo, and it interrupts the flow of life; it causes us to feel emotions that we can barely understand, let alone express. So the most effective way of dealing with it is to carry on regardless with a stiff upper lip and hope that it never returns to bite us on the backside. Invariably it does, and our relationship with death collapses into a heap of inappropriate coping mechanisms. Our immersion in centuries of revealed religions has done nothing to calm our fear of death; it has caused the exact opposite. We fear it even more, for we are told that the afterlife is a paradise that many feel they can never reach, for the degree of perfection is beyond their capabilities of being human. The alternative is to be tormented for an eternity in a hell dimension of perpetual terror and isolation. It taps into the heart of identity and our insecurities; it is powerful stuff. No wonder we fear death so much!

In stark contrast to the animistic pre-Christian traditions that continue to be perpetuated to this day, the revealed religions can be defined as "death religions," for they serve to prepare us for the afterlife—not necessarily the act of dying itself but what comes after. They instill a fear based on the assumed fact that we are the same person when we die. The animistic traditions are instead "life affirming," for they focus on being immersed in living, and by proxy of that living we glean an understanding of death and a knowing that comes from having a relationship with the spirit. The revealed religions serve to instill the fear of death, whereas animism encourages understanding. The

Celtic tradition is, at its heart, an animistic path that looks to nature as teacher. Nature's teachings are that of continuation—there is no judgment, no retribution implied; life, death, and rebirth are all facets of existence. Fear is eliminated when we understand, and understanding arises from relationship. It is because of fear that we have fallen out of relationship with the spirit, and therefore we find ourselves not knowing and thus on a perpetual path of seeking or avoiding the whole thing as much as possible. This may cause us to fear death so much that we forget to live fully and with lucidity. But what exactly do we fear?

THE LOSS OF IDENTITY

We have been taught that when we die we are, in fact, exactly the same as we were in our earthly life. We have two arms, two legs, a torso, and a head; we carry with us the same personality and traits, habits and opinions, quirks and peculiarities. In fact, we have been led to believe that nothing at all has changed other than the body has been buried or burned. The spirit, however, is a carbon copy of the body and is now flapping around in another world, either having a jolly good time or being stabbed by searing hot pokers in a pit of glowing embers. In Paganism there is an assumption that we exist in perpetual lands of summer, with some believing that these "Summerlands" are places of respite prior to reincarnation. And for some reason we are perfectly happy to accept this as gospel—this is what happens to us when we die; nothing changes at all. Even followers of the revealed religions perpetuate a belief that the deceased is immediately in the company of God, whereas in Christian scriptural teachings that is not true. The dead are dead until the Last Judgment. They are held in the embrace of nothingness until the end of times. Identity is suspended until the sea and death and Hades give up their dead to be judged (King James Bible, the book of Revelation 20: 5–15). For the judging to be effective, the identity must be intact. For the Summerlands to be enjoyed, the identity must be intact. This manner of thinking is part of our inherent social programming. Regardless of what tradition we may now follow, this revealed-religion sense of the spirit influences the alternative and even animistic traditions. But think on this for a minute: how much sense does that actually make? How logical is that reasoning, and does it equate to the teachings of nature?

The concept of the identity surviving death arose in response to control; if you want to control the populace, you really cannot have them going through life knowing stuff about the hereafter. That kind of information must be secret and privy to only a select few—a select few who manipulate the minds and imaginations of the people by causing them to fear something they have no control over. Suddenly everyone is a little more compliant; they do exactly as they are told. If they do not, then the outcome is obvious: you will die and you will be punished. This threat is reliant on a very powerful notion, one that still grips the heart in cold fear, that we are the same person when we die. Therefore, what we fear down here will be transferred over there; all our weaknesses and innermost desires and secrets will be laid bare for the purpose of our humiliation. We can then be given our just reward or punishment. This plays perfectly well with the general insecurities that have been instilled within us since our infancy. We fear that we will be punished, but that punishment is only effective if "we" remain unaltered after death. In stark contrast, science informs us that there is nothing beyond this life, and this existential view has given rise to a new level of fear: nothingness.

Historically, our ability to explore the facets of the spirit for ourselves has been discouraged. If we want to know the nature of the spirit, we must listen to the words of those who know about such things; we are not worthy or able to seek such answers for ourselves. We must have faith, and faith is drummed into us by a person in a position of power and influence, but faith is blind and not based on experience. To have an actual experiential relationship with the spirit is something we are all more than capable of developing, and the process is remarkably easier than you may imagine.

In general, the majority of people in the Western world who believe in some form of afterlife assume that we are the same individual on the other side. But this is an assumption, and not an informed one; as we have seen, we have been programmed to believe this. Our fears and insecurities of death and the matter of continuation boil down to the very simple concept of identity, but we can overcome this. We are products of our environments and relationships, but our apparent identity, i.e., the one we believe we are right this second, is forever changing, growing, diminishing, and evolving. We are a million different individuals to a million different people; in fact, we are products of our and other people's realities. Our personalities are forever responding to our environments and to the individuals we encounter in life.

Stop a minute and think of your life thus far; who have you been to myriad people with whom you have formed relationships? Think of family members, work colleagues, schoolmates, housemates, the lady you speak to briefly each morning in the local grocery store. Who are you to these people? You will find that you are one particular person to your mother and yet a completely different individual to your partner. To your grandmother you are the delightful grandchild she adores; the sun shines from you regardless of your actions or life choices. To your peers you may be someone who instills envy, jealousy, or dislike. How can you be so many people all at once? What does this tell you about the nature of your personality? Is this really who you are?

Your apparent identity is a constant flowing stream that moves through a landscape of other streams; every now and then, these streams become rivers that flow together for a while. They may become deep pools or lakes of intense relationship and then separate again to form new rivers on new courses, altered and affected by their environment. Each bend, each twist of the river, is unique and special; it is new and different, and yet something remains unchanged—the actual substance of the stream itself, for it carries within it the essence of its origination. But at every point along its course, it is interacting with its environment and the people and creatures that connect with it along its course. Your life is no different to this river.

Stop again for a moment, take a deep breath, and consider or meditate on the following statement:

A river loses its name and form when it enters the sea, but its essence remains.

Your apparent identity is a continuously evolving thing. The person you were ten years ago no longer exists; you may feel like the same person, but in fact you are not. Your body has changed its shape; you may no longer like certain things and yet are drawn to new things in your life. Your relationships may have changed beyond recognition. The infant that you were in your early years has certainly vanished from existence, and you probably have no memory of your formative years at all, yet you know that you existed. Your memories carry and affirm your life; they cause the development of your personality and bring to it meaning and value. We become products of our memories, but we are also so much more.

Our bodies respond to life in a different manner than our minds. Our physiology, our brains, are influenced by genetics; deep cellular mysteries form the shape and patterns of our bodies and affect aspects of our personalities. The rest is created by the mind. Our relationships with the world and those who inhabit it drive our needs and desires; we become programmed to want certain things in life that bring comfort, meaning, or fulfillment. We look for repetitive patterns that mimic or reflect those memories that made us feel good about ourselves. These can be as simple as a taste or a smell, or as intense as a sexual or loving relationship. But things are never constant. Life moves at a steady pace, and we are caught up in its drama however much we attempt to slow its drive. We may sometimes long for the "good old days" when everything was much better than it is now, yet somehow we can never replicate those times, and for good reason: they no longer exist. They were the good old days because they were new; we were experiencing something for the first time, and that creates an impression of perfection in the mind. We can become frustrated when we long for that perceived perfection and just cannot, no matter how much we try, re-create it. And yet, ten years from now, *these* will be the "good old days." We move on, we change and evolve. Our apparent identity is a constant moving stream.

THE WATCHER WITHIN

Beneath the veneer of body and mind, each one reacting to its environment and forming new relationships and new patterns of behavior, there is something else, something that has never changed. This "thing" is beyond the formation of memory and personality. Think of yourself for a minute and imagine describing yourself to a stranger on the telephone who cannot see you—how would you describe yourself? Chances are the conversation would go something like this:

"I have brown hair, I have blue eyes, I have a square jaw. I have a tendency to laugh inappropriately, and I also love to procrastinate. I am a thinker; I like silence and time to reflect on things."

Make up your own description that adequately describes you at this moment and then pause and think on this—who is the "I" that you speak of? Many of the descriptions are fleeting, your tendency to like something over another may have greatly altered within five years, you may have colored or lost your hair. You may no longer procrastinate or will have developed a tendency to be more mature and serious than flippant and frivolous, and yet the "I" remains. Something else exists within you, and this "I" has never changed, ever; since the beginning of time it has remained a constant.

Some refer to this "I" as the inner observer who watches and experiences life, tastes it and assimilates it into its own experience. It is the spirit that is observing. The spirit is the real "I" who dwells within the field of your current existence and is the conduit that sings of the relationship between your body and spirit and mystery. The bridge that forms from this relationship can be called the "mind." The spirit, however, has never been born, and it cannot die; it is permanence, a constant. It cannot be punished for the traits of your human self, for it is more than the sum of your current human existence. It is immortal. Immortality implies a continuation from before the dawn of time. Therefore, if your spirit is immortal, then why is this fleeting existence the one that dictates the appearance of the hereafter? Do the other experiences of the spirit in movement wane in contrast to the experience of being human? No, on the contrary—this life is merely an experience the spirit finds itself inhabiting for a while; it is not the be-all and end-all of all existences.

> Consider once again the words attributed to Mark Twain that we encountered earlier: "I do not fear death. I had been dead for billions and billions of years before I was born, and had not suffered the slightest inconvenience for it."
>
> This time, let's remove some of the provocative words—death, dead—from that sentence and see what happens. "I do not fear, I have existed for billions and billions of years before this life, I suffered not the slightest inconvenience for it."

Consider the implications that the inner "I" has indeed existed since the dawn of time. How does this affect, challenge, inspire, or influence your current thoughts on continuation and identity?

It is by acknowledging, perceiving, and developing a relationship with this inner observer that the body and mind reconcile with the spirit and begin to "know" it. And by "knowing," we are free from having to believe, for what we begin to perceive is based on experience and that arises from relationship. When we experience something as real, we are no longer restricted to believe in it by methods of faith alone. Our fear of death arises from the fear of losing our identity, but, as we have seen, our identities are constantly changing; they are not indicative of the original "I," and yet it is tied to it. Naturally, we are human beings who are immersed in life, and this life is incredible—to be alive on a planet as beautiful and diverse and experience it through our human senses is wondrous. This becomes the only reality, for it is the one we are fully immersed in, and yet paradoxically that immersion can cause us to fear death, for it seems such a terrible intrusion. It interrupts the flow of life.

The forgetfulness of life causes us to have temporary amnesia. We forget that we have always existed and will always exist and that this life, however wondrous and magical, is just a fraction, a split second in the experience of the spirit. However, the act of living is never dismissed as futile or something that needs transcending; we do not need to prepare for death to such extremes that we forget to live. In order to be fully alive, we need only become aware of the inner observer. The answer that soothes our fears lies in knowing the spirit. The irony is that we have always known; we simply forget, and life happens.

In essence you cannot die, for you have always existed and will continue to do so as a vital aspect of the universe; you are the universe singing in praise of itself. Your spirit selected this body, this life; it is attached to an evolutionary machine that feels, thinks, sees, tastes, touches, and interacts with the planet it lives upon. The body forms relationships, the mind interacts, and the spirit observes neutrally from the depths. It has no agenda; its only purpose is to be. Think of the hard drive of a computer. It comes equipped with certain attributes, and yet in order to be enriched by the experience of being your computer it needs input, so you come along and download new software. Software can be removed and even deleted, yet it leaves a trace on the hard drive, which has been touched by the apparent fleeting nature of the software. This analogy can be equated to the spirit; it is our hard drive, our original state, our "factory setting," if you like. Our human lives act as the software that leaves traces of living on the spirit; the spirit absorbs this experience as a vital component of the greater universe.

When we become aware of our spirits and, by relationship, realize that it has always been there and that it sings of the origination of all things, we suddenly have that "eureka" moment. We cannot die; it is only the apparent identity that dies. The constant permanent identity continues. This can be a little hard to swallow, for it implies that the personality perishes at death, ceasing to exist in the form that you are familiar with right now. It is this that initiates fear, for we believe that we are our personalities, but as we have explored, we are so much more. Energy cannot be created nor destroyed; it simply transforms. Consequently, if we are not the same person when we die, the concept of reward or punishment is invalid; it does not apply. These human concepts can only be applicable to our apparent identity. At the point of death, the spirit takes this experience into itself and carries on. There is no retribution, no recompense, no judgment; nothing has truly changed other than the relationship the mortal body had with the physical world. The interaction the body has with the world around it defines the experience and expression of relationship; death causes the cessation of this relationship in a physical sense.

We fear death so much, for we fear losing our identity, which is why we strive to search for our loved ones in the hope that they continue unchanged in another dimension. But when we realize that the people we loved were facets of our realities and products of the magic of this world, we can conclude that they have reverted back to their factory setting. They continue as they have always been—energy in motion, touching and experiencing life in a billion different forms, singing in praise of a wondrous universe. The spirit is touched by this human life; it is not negated nor dismissed but honored deeply and assimilated into the greater experience of the spirit. Nature wastes nothing. We are more than the sum total of this life, and it is this that continues at the point of death.

Death does not threaten the permanent identity; it cannot, for death only equates to a mass of cells programmed to deteriorate. The body must die—it is bound by laws of the physical universe—but its death is only one experience in the river of spirit. When you die, your spirit does not leave; it doesn't go anywhere, it is already there, it has always been there. Fear is eliminated when we grow into relationship with the spirit. We grieve, naturally, for we have lost someone; that person—the being, the physical body that we related to and its unique personality— is dead. It is gone, never to be replicated or re-created. It was a product of this place, and consequently should be honored as such. In a magical sense this is wondrous and awe-inspiring, for as aspects of nature—as integral parts of the song of this earth—we are uniquely expressive of our planet's story. The spirit is not separate from the experience of the body, and the body is not separate from the experience of the earth. Combined it creates the beautiful lyrics that sing to the music of the universe.

This life is amazing, through good times and bad. This act of living is an act of magic. But eventually it must die, as all things in the material realm must. What remains constant is the spirit, and upon it is the imprint of the human that lived and breathed here in this world.

BEING SPIRIT

There is surely a piece of divinity in us,
something that was before the elements
and owes no homage unto the sun.

Sir Thomas Browne

In the realm of necessity we experience being human—we swim in the wonder of life and the limitations of living. We exist in a world where all things must die, from a single-cell organism to a star; all things eventually consume the energy attributed to them and perish. The inner observer—the spirit now separated from the physical form it had attached to—assumes its ordinary place in the realm of Gwynvyd. Its perception of perfection comes only from the human inability to articulate something that is beyond the limitation of our intellect. We cannot conceptualize it fully, therefore we equate it with the epitome of pureness or perfection. There is no suffering here; it is a place of the cessation of want, need, and evil, and the laws of the physical universe do not apply to this place of energy in motion. This is not to be confused with the biblical heaven of the Christian tradition, which by definition is reliant upon the apparent identity surviving death in order to be rewarded in the afterlife. The Celtic Gwynvyd differs in that it is the ordinary state, not a state to which we ascend. A million things influence our perception of the hereafter or the spirit world. Call it what you will, let's take a moment to examine your impressions of it.

Stop for a minute to read and consider the following. What are your perceptions and beliefs of the spirit world or afterlife? What does it look like? What happens there? Where have these concepts and ideas come from? What point of reference do you utilize to give them substance and credence? Does the afterlife of your beliefs mirror this world—does it contain material objects and things that are important in an anthropocentric manner? If so, why? Consider the Christian concept of heaven, a city of immense wealth and treasures; what happens here—what does one "do" here for all of eternity? Consider the nature of the spirit world as you know it now.

The realm of the spirit is real. It exists beneath the fabric of our physical universe and is intertwined with it; it serves to power the universe we currently inhabit. It is what brings consciousness to a vast universe of matter. In order to adequately articulate this realm of spirit, one must utilize the imagination and an analogy.

Imagine a large, busy airport; vehicles pull up outside in the hundreds, dropping various people off at the terminal doors. Beyond these doors stretch the vast halls where check-in desks wait for eager travelers; here there is anticipation and sometimes sadness as we bid farewell to loved ones who embark on far-flung journeys. Anyone can approach this area; no permission or authority is required to enter. It is a place where travelers and those left behind mingle before the final step. This terminal building equates to life and to the living, the ordinary interaction between people. To carry on, a passport or ticket is required to cross the border into a place that exists betwixt and between. In this analogy, the ticket equates to death.

Beyond this point we are no longer a part of the ordinary world; we exist between it in a no man's land at the threshold of adventure. The ordinary world cannot infringe upon it; it is not permitted to enter. Within this "departure lounge" we cease being people and become travelers; if we were to pause within this analogy, we would notice that our relationship with the individuals in this place is fleeting. There is a lot of coming and going, and yet, were we to stop a while, we would swim in relationship as we connected to another spirit in this place. One can see this in life; delayed in an airport's departure lounge, we may befriend others around us and share in hours of connection, laughter, and the joys of companionship in a world that we create to resemble the one we left behind. Then, with a wave, the travelers move on, yet the experience has touched the spirit.

Beyond the edges of the departure lounge, gates call the travelers to venture to new places as aircraft transport them from the liminality of between-ness. In this analogy, this equates to the spirit connecting to a new form in the physical universe and becoming a part of a new experience. This concept may appear to follow the pattern of reincarnation, but in fact it does not; it differs in that no process of learning is implied. There are no lessons that the spirit must achieve to move on to another plane; it is the experience that matters. In this cosmic place between lives, we are true travelers who are not intent upon arrival. It is the journey that counts. The Celtic tradition differs greatly from the Hindu and Buddhist doctrines, which concern themselves with perpetual cycles of reincarnation until a state of enlightened perfection is attained. That theory is dependent upon continuation of the identity.

Imagine yourself in this place of spirits in perpetual motion. Look around within the analogy of the departure lounge; what do you see and hear? If you note the point of entry, you will catch glimpses of the ordinary world, fleeting images of people immersed in life. You cannot hear them, at least not clearly, but you can glean a little of their nature by observing the passing of emotions upon their countenance. Communication with the world of the living is possible here, but it is different. We may think fondly of those we have left behind and employ an emotional connection to the living, ordinary world, yet we are fully immersed in the experience of the "between" world. Cell phone signals may be jammed or poor, preventing the use of technology to commune with the living. Only vestiges of relationship remain to bridge the gap between this world and the one you left behind, yet paradoxically you are still a part of the ordinary world; you are within it and yet beyond its ordinary touch. It is the mind that is anchoring this experience to what it encountered previously.

You find a seat in a quiet corner and sit awhile to observe further; there are individuals here who are not travelers, and they occupy a different state. They reside here almost permanently; their point of entry and exit is entirely at their own will. They may serve the travelers or simply may be there for reasons unknown. In this analogy, these are the immortals—spirits who differ from the ordinary traveler, for they have assigned themselves as advisors or ambassadors of this realm and those that exist beyond it. In some traditions they are called gods; in others they are known as angels or angelic beings. To others they are the spirits of mystery that embody archetypes that those in the physical universe revere and honor. They differ in that they have consciously or by response to a deeper mystery excluded themselves from the process of attachment to the physical universe; instead, they observe it from this place of spirit.

Eventually your gate is called, and you rise to traverse to your point of exit. You pass structures that emulate life beyond this place—cafés and shops, vending machines and information booths serve to mimic the physical world, and you acknowledge them as you pass them by. At the gate, you rise into the sky and vanish from this place; it becomes a blur, a memory that quickly fades as your spirit embarks on a new adventure of connection.

THE WORLD OF SPIRIT

The spirit world does not exist in some far-flung corner of the universe; it is right here, right now; we are immersed within it. It is only the limitations of our physical eyes and their connections to our brains that prevent us from seeing it. And for good reason! We are more than willing to accept that there are things in this world that we cannot see; our physiology prevents us from seeing every spectrum that exists to preserve our sanity. We would surely become overloaded with sensory input were we able to view all that exists in this world. Imagine being able to see every spectrum of light, every microwave and radio wave, radiation waves and particles that permeate our atmosphere. Imagine being able to witness the thousands of television and radio channels being streamed through the air, a mass of information in baffling form; we would surely lose the fronds of our sanity. And yet we know that these things exist here and now; we do not need to see them in order to verify their existence. The same can be said for the power of the wind; we feel it, we do not see it, we can only see what it makes contact with. A person may claim to be in love with someone else; this cannot be proven empirically, but we would not necessarily doubt the claim. The key here is feeling. We *feel* the edges of the spirit realm.

Be assured that your loved ones have not actually gone anywhere; it is only the denseness of their bodies that has faded from memory. The memory of their personalities lives on in you and in those who tell their tales. The essence, the spirit, continues, for it cannot be destroyed, and its continuation sings the songs of memory. The world of spirit may well reflect aspects of this planet, but it does so only by means of the experience each spirit brings to it as a reflection of the universe experiencing itself. Aspects of the spirit world and the manner by which it appears to the spirits who return there are also temporary; the spirit can create a world similar to what it left, but ultimately even this begins to fade as the spirit continues on its perpetual journey of experience.

Things naturally fade with time, both here and in Gwynvyd. Human beings need to know that things will be familiar; we hate feeling insecure. The concept of a spirit world that exists as a carbon copy of this world brings some comfort. But when we consider the fleeting nature of all things in this universe, that concept loses its rationality. In 10 billion years' time, our solar system will no longer exist, having been swallowed by our bulging star as it collapses in on itself and dies. The earth and all the planets will disintegrate and vanish from existence. There will be no trace of our blue planet; nobody will remember it. In another 10 billion years from that point, our galaxy will no longer exist, and yet humans maintain that the spirit world is exactly as our current world and will remain so for all time. Why? The spirit will have experienced other forms of life in other parts of the universe, and yet no single experience of living is greater or more important than another; it all matters. Our need for familiarity and security is all tied to identity and the human struggle to rationalize that this life is as the ancient Druids claimed: the midpoint of a long existence. But this implies change, and we don't particularly like that much—and yet change is the only thing in life that we can be assured of.

As we have seen, our identities are fleeting, for they are products of this reality and this place; they are formed and molded by the relationships we forge, and they imprint themselves on the very fabric of the spirit. When the body dies, it truly dies, and the personality dies with it. It becomes one again with the makeup of this planet; whether by interment, cremation, or other means, our remains are recycled into the constituents of this planet. Even then, the tiniest components of our physical form continue, recycled, a part of this wondrous planet that we call home.

Who we are in Gwynvyd is who we have always been; as we have explored, it is fear that prevents us from knowing this, from feeling this. This life, however magical and amazing, is but a blink of an eye in the spirit's experience. This life, this body, and this experience matter, but they are just tiny cogs in the great wheel of life, death, and rebirth. Do not fear; death does not annihilate the qualities of the persona entirely, it simply assimilates it into the song of the universe, and your song matters. In realistic terms, a loved one who has died cannot exist beyond this life in exactly the manner in which you knew them here, for as we have explored, so much of them was a product of your reality; they were, to some extent, what you wanted them to be. The personality truly dies, as it is reliant entirely on its surroundings and the relationships it forges, and it is the death of the personality that terrifies us; that is too much change for most of us to handle. But nothing is truly lost, the personality has indeed perished but its signature, its echo, is carried with the spirit. However, there is still a connection, and it is the emotional bonds of relationship that we utilize to call, sense, and feel the spirit of our loved ones in Gwynvyd.

COMMUNICATION

The dead no longer have human functions; they operate on a different frequency, if you like; the spirit world does not conform to the unique environment of this planet. Communication channels are different, and in order to communicate we must first gain an understanding of these new channels. Postmortem communication points of reference are now vastly altered. We are accustomed to touch and to speech primarily, and these are then decorated with expressions, sounds, smells, and emotions. But primarily we speak to those we are in relationship with; this is the most obvious channel of communication. When a person dies, we struggle with the fact that we cannot hear them anymore and however loud we shout or call to them, they do not answer. Somehow the logic of this passes most of us by—the dead no longer have vocal chords and do not exist on a planet that is essentially a closed circuit consisting of an atmosphere that allows and regulates the passage of sound waves. We live in a physical world; they do not. In order to communicate we must adjust our perception filters, for both parties are beyond the normal methods of communication.

This may sound hopeless, but it is not; there are effective methods of communication, and they can be utilized by any one of us. Do not be put off by the claims of psychics that one must be born with the talent to communicate with the dead—you are essentially spirit, as are they; it is only your perception that must be altered. We know what it is to be spirit; it is our natural state, and that realm is not limited to the ordinary forms of communication that, as humans, we have become accustomed to. When someone dies, our instinct is to call them back; in the midst of grief we just want them back, we want to hear their voices clearly as if they were standing right next to us. But the truth is, this does not happen, it cannot happen, for the ordinary channels of communication have been severed. In order to sense the dead, we must do just that: sense.

To initiate effective channels of communication, we must first deprogram ourselves from the plethora of input we receive primarily from the world of entertainment. We are led to believe that what we see on prime-time supernatural dramas is real; in a bizarre twist of perception, many now believe that these works of fiction are reflections of reality and that we can glean comfort from them. In fact, the opposite is true: they can cause us to despair by providing a false sense of perception. Anything other than having a ghost stand before us as from an episode of *Ghost Whisperer*, looking and dressed just as they were in life, is just not good enough. We become programmed to believe that the dead are exactly the same as they were in life, with absolutely no differences, and they continuously strive to tell us that they are okay. But most of us know that this is not the case. The dead have returned to their original state as spirit in perpetual motion, but we can continue to perceive the essence that contains the memory of the living human being. But to connect to it, we must alter the way we have become programmed to perceive ourselves.

> *Stop for a minute. Think of the nature of what we are in essence. Instead of relying on someone else to provide you with snippets of information from the spirit world or longing for the connection a fictional character has in a TV drama, arrive at your own conclusions. Stop and rationally think about the nature of this life, your identity, and your loved one's identity and how we have existed since the dawn of time and we continue to exist beyond this life. Meditate on the following statements, saying each one out loud in turn:*
>
> *I am more than the sum of my physical body.*
> *I am more than the sum of my actions.*
> *I am more than the sum of my ego.*
> *I am more than the sum of my thoughts.*
> *I am. Before this life was, I am.*

In order to sense the dead swimming in the permanence of the spirit, we must adjust our perception filters. Our perception of death and dying is continuously influenced by social and religious programming. We can alter this with remarkable ease. Just as grief is the key to healing, our emotions are the key to communication. In many traditions it is held that the emotions transcend the physical plane; this is demonstrated in the Cabbalistic system where the realm of Yesod, which is above or beyond the physical realm of Malkuth, is the sphere of feeling, and our emotions can straddle the two worlds. Therefore, effective communication with the dead is by emotional means, and we do this by the magic of relationship. When we call to the dead, we do so by means of the relationships we have forged in life. Remember that the spirit is not in some far-flung dimension; it is interwoven with this realm. When we reach out through memory and emotion, we can sense the spirits of our loved ones within the realm of Gwynvyd; the spirit senses that connection, and a channel of communication opens. When spirit encounters spirit and is linked by the fronds of relationship, a symbiotic communication channel is instigated where the trace memory of human life and experience is recalled by the spirit in response to your calling. What follows is a channel of communication based on the familiarity of the relationship you had with the deceased in life. The quality of communication and the sense of familiarity we receive are as a result of our creating that person within our own realities. This does not negate the communication process—it is still one spirit calling to another—but it is sensible to acknowledge that the channels of communication are different and that the relationship we have with the dead has fundamentally changed.

Our expectations may hinder the depth of this communication by telling us that nothing other than hearing their voices clear as day, as if transmitted by radio, will do—that if they do not appear from a mist in front of our eyes, then we are just deluding ourselves. We have become alienated to the subtle; we are bombarded with color and vibrancy; streams of information and sensory data blast our brains with powerful, mind-altering effects. If it's real, then we can see it, hear it, taste it, smell it, or invariably control it. But death and the spirit are beyond the limitations of these facets of our reality. Our perception filter must be set to "subtle" to sense the continuation of the spirit.

Before we attempt to call the dead into our minds and connect with that essence that swims in eternity, it is wise to consider the following.

Why do we need to call them? In all probability it is the epitome of selfishness, which is central to grief; we are crying for what *we* have lost, not necessarily for the deceased themselves.

What do we want to hear, sense, or feel? Anything that alleviates or diminishes our own fear of death and the unknowing that comes with it, to hear them or sense them would at least provide us with a momentary reassurance that they are okay, and if they are okay, then so shall we be when we meet our own deaths. Again it is based on fear with a smattering of selfishness thrown in.

Why do we need to know that they are the same as they were in life? This alleviates the terrible intrusion or interruption that death embodies. If we know that they are just the same, with the same likes and dislikes, personality traits and quirks, it appeases our programmed belief that we survive death intact—and that the same fate awaits us. It is a distorted form of comfort that comes from a misguided belief; it is not one based on experience.

Ask yourself the same set of questions and examine your own answers; do they differ to those that I offer? If so, why? On what basis do they differ—what point of reference do you utilize to answer these questions? Examine your own programs of belief in relation to what you know. It may be difficult for you to accept that the spirit, in essence, has continuously existed, and that this life is only a fraction of its experience, and for good reason. You have been led to believe otherwise.

Silence is key to effective communication. Take yourself to a space where you will not be disturbed for a while. Create atmosphere by lighting a few candles and placing a photograph or memoir of the deceased on a shelf, altar, or table. Still the internal noise of your chattering mind; an effective way of achieving this is to shift your awareness so that you watch your thoughts as if they are on a movie screen. Take a few deep breaths and recall how the person made you feel; play back the memories you have of them. Allow these thoughts and emotions to flow from you and into the world of spirit; do not force it, just feel it.

Tastes and smells in particular are powerful tools for connecting to the subtle. For example, when I move to sense the spirit that occupied the body of my great-grandmother, I use a hard-boiled candy called Everton Mints as a tool within the ritual. This may, on the surface, sound rather silly, but she loved them and they are something I intimately associate with her. I place some in her honor on my ancestor table and pop one into the corner of my mouth when reaching out to the spirit. The effect is almost instantaneous. The sight, smell, and taste of the mints are enough to fill my mind with memories. For several minutes I am consumed by thoughts of my great-grandmother. The spirit reciprocates and moves towards that emotional connection.

This feels different to physical relationship but can be equally as profound. Sense them in this transformed state; swim in memory and recollection. The individual, physical personality has died, but the spirit remains a constant, and imprinted upon it is every single second of the human life it experienced in this world. This is what you are connecting to. Think or speak questions out loud if you wish, but do not force or expect a response. Allow any impressions or emotional responses to filter through; now is not the time to analyze them. Just relish in memory and connection.

Finish this simple exercise by thanking the spirit.

Messages that you receive from the spirit are not restricted to ritual activity alone; images and impressions may arrive later during sleep, when we are closer to the spirit world than at any other time. In dreams you may see them as they were in life; at other times it may feel like a new file of information has been slotted into your mind, complete with an emotional attachment. Do not dismiss these subtle channels of communication, for they are unique to you and the relationship you had with the deceased.

Memories of the dead are remembered by the earth. They are a part of its story. When we meditate on our ancestors, this is one stream of communication that can be opened: the memory of earth. Our closed planetary circuit does not forget anything; we are a component of earth as an organism. The wisdom of our ancestors—the connection between their minds and the land—continues to echo from cloud and stone and sand. We may sense ancestral wisdom in this manner, but rather than connecting to the spirit of a dead human being, we are connecting to the memory of them held in earth's embrace.

THE PROBLEM OF GHOSTS

We may all love a good old-fashioned ghost story, even if we find the concept of ghosts difficult to believe. The majority of people are accustomed to the idea, and many more are quite willing to accept their existence even if they have never experienced one. Ghosts are appealing, for they embody a certain romanticism about death and the possibility of continuation. Not only do they appear as they did in life, but they may also seem to go about their ordinary business as if nothing much at all has happened. The paradox of ghosts is that they frighten us, but why?

This may not be true of a certain minority of folk who are quite comfortable dealing with the supernatural, but to the majority the thought of seeing a ghost is terrifying. Popular fiction and the movies have served to program us to believe certain things when it comes to ghosts; quite frequently they are lamenting, wailing, crying in drafty corridors, baying for blood, or suffering. We may be told that terrible things happened within a certain building or piece of land in which the poor tortured soul was tormented in life and has not yet fathomed its death. How utterly ghastly; why would an otherwise sensible and rational person die and then be subjected to an eternity of wallowing along corridors? It makes very little sense.

Ghosts are identified with spooky places, old buildings, castles, and mansions; there are several old structures surrounding my own home that are renowned for headless ghosts and "gray ladies" that float about during the witching hour. In all honesty, the majority are simply products of an overactive imagination or are associated with legends and myth. More people die in terrible suffering in hospitals than have ever died in old castles, and yet our hospitals are not generally renowned for being haunted. Frankly, when it comes to ghosts, a good smattering of common sense is needed as well as an understanding of the spirit and the world which it inhabits.

There is a very real aspect to ghosts, and if one were to look at them closely, one would find recurring patterns that can be true of a great proportion of accounts or stories. A quick glance at any Internet-based ghost-hunting website will demonstrate these recurring patterns evident in many hauntings; numerous accounts tell of ghostly activity that follows a particular routine. The ghost may be seen to walk the same path and appear at certain times or during particular ambient conditions. Few ghosts seem to acknowledge or interact with those who witness them; they seem to be driven by some automatic pilot beyond the comprehension of the most adept ghost hunter. One theory for this is the "cinema of time" concept, which claims that energies released by organic life forms can be trapped in the earth's atmosphere and played back, almost like a recorder, and it may do this when the conditions at play emulate those during recording. The result is a noninteractive apparition that seems to go about its business in a repetitive fashion, paying no attention to its actual surroundings. It is possible that these ghosts are simply echoes of past events; they may well be supernatural in that we do not understand them fully, but the question of whether they contain any actual consciousness is doubtful.

This cinema of time does not negate the concept of ghosts; in fact, it gives credence to it as a possible, viable phenomenon. The earth is a closed circuit; it can be argued that by means of natural processes those elements of the past can be recorded by the organism we live upon and played back. In mediumistic circles we may hear of this phenomenon as "residual energy"; in my Pagan traditions we glean a sense of the ancestors by means of this phenomena. We may sense their presence within rituals and rites that serve to transport us through liminality to a heightened sense of awareness, and within this state we are more easily able to perceive the past and its echoes. In the realm of spirit there is no such thing as yesterday and tomorrow; there is only now. As energetic beings we leave a trace of our existence, and this trace can be replayed and consequently observed. To many, these encounters will appear ghostly, otherworldly—apparitions that serve to terrify us from the edge of beyond—whereas in actuality they are nothing of the sort. Even ghosts can embody and transmit mystery.

But what of those that interact with humanity—how can we define them? Seemingly the violent spirits that cause chaos have often been attributed as energetic projections from living human beings. Poltergeists in particular have been pinpointed to the maelstrom of energetic release from the bodies of pubescent children. These so-called noisy spirits can be explained as disturbances caused by the living, not by the dead. But there is more to heaven and earth, as the saying goes, and it would be foolhardy of me to offer this portrayal of ghosts without giving credence to something beyond understanding.

We are not the only species on this planet to be in possession of spirit; in an animistic sense, everything on this planet is a receptacle of the spirit. For centuries, if not millennia, humans have long encountered the spirits of plants and trees, all of which appear oddly humanoid in shape. This begs a question: why do they seem to appear human?

The answer, I believe, lies in relationship. The human spirit is more than capable of sensing another spirit that may inhabit a different species. Let's take a tree, for instance; its spirit is traditionally referred to as a dryad, and in some folklore it is recorded as being a "hooded one"— it appears humanoid in shape. Through my own experience of these things, I offer this explanation. The human spirit senses another spirit and reaches out towards it in communication; when the matrix of the other spirit is sensed and responds, the human mind gives it shape and form that is acceptable and comprehensible to the parameters of belief and acceptability of the individual. The spirit of the tree has no actual shape or form other than that of the tree it inhabits, yet we will more often than not perceive this spirit as humanoid—for a simple reason: it makes sense to us. In order to engage with it, the human mind needs it to look familiar, otherwise it may not fully engage with what it senses and or sees.

We are surrounded by the spirit world, and in various altered states of being we are more than capable of transferring thoughts and projections onto the matrix of spirit, causing fragments of it to appear in accordance with our expectations. These can appear as ghosts. In the throes of grief we may call on the spirit of a loved one and it may well appear, but I believe it does so by the fragments of relationship that we cast and project onto its energy matrix. This does not imply that the spirit is devoid of the memory of the deceased; it retains it still, it's simply no longer governed by it. What remains is a residual trace of the human being without the personality that drove its human experience. In this manner the apparition or ghost may feel ethereal, serene, or peaceful. In essence, it only looks like the person you have lost because of your expectations and needs.

In the same manner, aspects of the personality can be trapped in the earth's charged atmosphere and then sensed by those who are sensitive to such emanations. These too can appear as ghosts. Heightened emotional states send out immense energy, the impact of which most humans can sense; the old adage of being able to "cut the atmosphere with a knife" refers to extreme human emotions somehow caught in the very air itself and transmitted to an observer. We may never fully understand this principle, but nonetheless we are able to sense it, and the majority of folk are familiar with this phenomenon. But where does that energy release go?

In my experience, it remains within the closed circuit of our planet, trapped in the atmosphere, in stone and clay and crystal, in minerals and rock. This gives rise to the phenomenon of psychometry, the ability to sense a memory from an object. To those who are gifted with the sight, the clairvoyants, they may sense this energy and by means of reciprocal awareness see its shape and form. However, projections of emotional energy that contain residue of personality can be confused with the spirit when, in fact, they are something altogether different. The manner by which we sense the difference is that residual energy does not alter or change—it is merely a playback—whereas interactions with the realm of spirit can change and develop. Budding psychics would do well to develop an awareness of the different forms of energy lest they confuse one for the other.

The knee-jerk reaction to a ghost or ghostly happenings is to fight or flee, and so often people of the New Age may rush to banish such things without first attempting to understand it. Memories are complex things, the matrix of which can be trapped in our atmosphere and replayed over and over and over. We may encounter these as troublesome or frightful and may seek ways to eliminate them, but pause and stop a while in their presence. Push away your fears—they are generally illogical and arise only from misunderstanding—so when in the presence of a ghost, reach out to it with your own spirit, with emotion and empathy. The results may surprise you.

THE ACCEPTANCE OF DEATH

Myfanwy lived a life of permanent pain; her features would contort under the strain of immense physical agony and discomfort, yet she held an extraordinary strength. Years before I met her, she had been involved in a terrible motor accident that had practically pulverized her hips and smashed the joints of her legs and arms. Weeks of hospitalization and treatment brought back some movement, but she would remain practically crippled.

She was as round as the earth, with long blond locks that framed her jovial, kind, and infinitely wise face. Her spectacles were as thick as toughened glass, causing her eyes to seem magnified behind them; we would jest that she could no doubt still see Halley's Comet through those things. I adored Myfanwy and would pounce at any opportunity to spend hours and hours in her company. Her sagaciousness imparted much wisdom and knowledge to me, and I will forever be grateful to have had such a wonderful yet unassuming teacher of mystery.

We would spend whole nights lost in chatter and exploration, and would scowl as the sun awoke a new day and other commitments that would take us away from the sanctuary of her living room. She used a wheeled walker to get about, and cripple or not, she certainly got about. As Druids we have always been the outdoorsy type, continuously finding beautiful places to spend days and nights in nature, and Myfanwy, despite her disability, would always be present. She would look beyond the pain and relish instead in the company of those she loved. And we loved her back, so much. When times were difficult or petty arguments would rise at home, I would escape to Myfanwy's. The absence of my toothbrush alerted my partner that I had indeed gone to Mivvy's (our term of endearment for her) and would return at some point in the next twenty-four hours. She was a sanctuary, a shelter from the storm of life, a place where magic felt so near and mystery not so out of reach.

She would listen deeply and think much, surrounded by a haze of her favorite cigarettes; with her spectacles covered in greasy fingerprints, she would let out streams of words that could adorn a conversation with pearls of wisdom. She was so ordinary in many ways, and yet she was an extraordinary priestess. She would often describe herself as a "Sourceress"—a play on words: a priestess who sought to sense and feel emanations from the Source. It was this connection to spirit and soul that propelled her through her pain and allowed her to be in the world fully, to enjoy the gift of life despite her constant agony. She was an advocate of magic and the arts of spellcrafting and conjuration, and indeed much of her strength and fight came from intense acts of magic. Her mind would frequently leave the confines of her crippled body to find solace in the painless domain of the spirit; here she would rest awhile and find respite from her pain. She would return to her battered body refreshed and able to battle with the constant agony that life had dealt her, but she did so with valor and immense courage.

I recall a Summer Solstice celebration; typically in the United Kingdom it was raining, and we were camped in the forest. Having feasted, we settled for the night and anxiously awaited the coming of the solstice dawn. Alas, Myfanwy was unable to lie on the cold, hard floor of the tents and chose instead to sit in a large camping chair next to the fireside. It was raining hard and she sat quietly under a long piece of tarpaulin that at least served to keep her dry, even if the sight of it was somewhat comical in hindsight. I lay in my makeshift bed watching her from the open doorway; only the occasional glow from her cigarette belied that she was moving. She sat as still as the night, lost in the rapture of being here in this place. I felt at that point that something was changing—that Myfanwy was changing, that somehow she was on borrowed time.

As it turned out, a new pain had risen to plague her, to torment her further, but this was different. It was pancreatic cancer that caused this newfound agony. It was terminal; she was given a maximum of six months to live. She had been admitted to hospital, and the days were once again nearing the rise of the Summer Solstice. I held her hand; she was keen to see the cover of my first book, which I had printed for her; she would not, alas, see the actual book itself, and we both somehow knew this. Her hair hung about her face as usual, and her glasses still magnified her eyes beyond what was normal. She smiled brightly and squeezed my hand, proud to the point of bursting. I held her small hand with both my own and said, "Why do you have to die, Mivvy?" I choked at the thought of her leaving.

"I fear I must," she replied. "I can't take this pain anymore, Kris; I no longer have the energy to carry my body and live in the world fully. If I can't be of this world, I don't want to be in it at all."

"I don't know what we are going to do without you; I shall miss you so much," I cried.

"Just live—relish it and live! Laugh, remember to laugh. We have memories; they never die, you know." She squeezed my hand reassuringly.

"But we still have the solstice, Mivvy; we could all come over and take you to the hospital rooftop to watch the sunrise!" I exclaimed brightly.

"We'll see, yeah. Let's see how I feel."

I leaned over and kissed her soft cheek and stroked her hair; something tore inside of me, something indescribable. I knew somehow that this would be the last time I would see her alive. She nodded her head and smiled and gave me a jovial little wink, which looked rather bizarre from behind her glasses, which resembled reentry shields more than spectacles! I turned at the door to look at her one more time; her little body sat upright in the bed. She seemed so small, so insignificant, and yet the impact she had on my life was quite the opposite. I felt the invisible claw of emotion grip the center of my body and allowed the tears to well up as I walked away from her room.

On the evening of the Summer Solstice, just as the sun went down, Myfanwy turned her face from this world and died.

I felt cheated initially, to have lost my teacher and friend, to be abandoned to find my own way through matters of the spirit. It took a while for the message of her death to filter through the grief. Death is not an enemy; it is just one step along a glorious adventure through existence. She once said to me, "I want to be there when I die, I mean to actually be there, fully present and aware, to know it's happening, to sense its coming and feel the tethers of this life break away. I don't want to be pumped full of morphine and left to die in a stupor. It's only going to happen the once, and it will be the biggest adventure of my life."

She had no fear. She accepted the coming of death and held out her arms to greet it. She slipped gently from this world, conscious until the last two hours. Her ailing body had caused her mind to wander to the realms of the spirit, and it was here that she found herself immersed in mystery and magic. It was through her pain that she found her spirit, the silent witness within. She was a true walker between the worlds. She once told me that those who fear death are those who suffer terribly at its threshold. Unwilling to let go, the body fights against the inevitable, causing the individual to suffer a tormented death; I had seen this at my father's deathbed. Those who have no fear slip from this life as if walking through a door. I was unsure what to make of this until it happened to her. She had been diagnosed with cancer only three weeks previously, and no active treatment had begun as yet. But Myfanwy had had enough. She had suffered the indignities of pain, and she would suffer them no more; she certainly would not be held ransom to the often undignified death that cancer brings.

What can we do to ensure a good death, or even one that is good enough? Planning ahead, especially when one is in good health, seems a little odd, but a little forethought can alleviate an enormous amount of uncertainty and doubt when the inevitable does happen.

Consider compiling an advance statement or a living will that specifies what kind of treatment or care you would like to be given were you to become mentally incapacitated and unable to make decisions due to illness. Whilst these statements are not legally binding, they do provide guidelines for the medical profession and families to understand your wishes. A general Internet search using the keywords "living will" will provide useful results.

Previously you were encouraged to open general discussion channels within a group setting. Now consider devoting an evening with your grove, coven, or group to discuss particular aspects regarding your own deaths in a practical manner. This exercise would be ideally suited for the Samhain period. Within the supportive structure of a group setting, you could consider the following:

- If given the choice, where would you want to die?
- If given the choice, who would you want present at your death?
- What advance statements would you prepare to ensure you died with dignity?
- Support each other in exploring the intricacies of creating a living will.
- What forms of care and or treatments would you like?
- What medical interventions would you not like?
- Have you considered a "do not resuscitate" order?
- How would the manner of your death and passing reflect your Paganism?
- Are there any rituals you would like performed at your deathbed?
- Consider compiling a death plan that specifies your wishes and offers guidelines to your family on how to prepare for your death and disposal.
- Consider your funeral service; whom would you want to officiate?

This is not a maudlin, gloomy exercise but one that will initiate fascinating discussion and implement a real change in your life.

the Realm of Infinity

PART 3

THE CIRCLE OF CEUGANT

IN WHICH THERE IS ONLY
GOD/THE GREAT SPIRIT

I was a multitude of forms
Before this consistency.
I was a droplet in the air,
I was the radiance of stars,
I was a word in writing,
I was a raindrop in the shower,
I was a spark in a fire.

TALIESIN IN "THE BATTLE OF THE TREES"

A triad states: "The three things that none but God/the Great Spirit can do: to endure the eternities of Ceugant, to participate in every state without changing, and to ameliorate and renew everything without causing the loss of it."

To be immersed in mystery is to seek to understand it and be transformed by its power. We exist in human form; trapped in the density of matter in this realm of necessity, we are limited. The limitations of our intellect and our ability to conceptualize what is beyond the comprehension of human intelligence can only realistically be expressed by means of our creativity. The human creative force has forever striven to make sense of mystery, and through poetry and writing, painting and song we serve to make sense of the infinite, but one cannot conceptualize what one has no concept of. This is the paradox of the circle of Ceugant.

This is the place of high mystery; prophets and priests have perpetually struggled in their attempt to articulate this realm, this place where they believe only their God or Great Spirit resides. Its fronds reach into the realm of spirit, into the circle of Gwynvyd, surrounding it; it is the mystery that breathes motion into the spirit and animation into the body. It is the vastness, the nothingness, and yet, paradoxically, the "all things" on the edge of reason.

All things exist as an expression of Ceugant, and yet it is beyond the limitations of human constructs, which strive to personify it as a single humanoid being. It is from Ceugant that existence originates, and it is to Ceugant that the universe sings—not in worship but in praise of being. The universe sings in praise of itself, and it does so consciously; its threads of being connect it through the veils of Gwynvyd and to the infinite mystery that lies beyond it. All of existence and the quality of that existence abide forever within high mystery, be they animate or inanimate in nature. All things exist as beautiful and good varieties of the soul that brings the quality of existence to the great mystery of origination.

Ceugant cannot be measured nor its size defined; it is beyond our concepts of duration, and no extremes exist within it; it has no beginning and no end, and there is no middle to it. It is at the edge of our universe and it is the mystery that permeates all things; it is beyond our articulations of God/Gods/Great Spirit. We have long attempted to personify it, and yet truly we cannot; it is outside our limited abilities.

We humanize the great mystery in an attempt to understand it, to alleviate that terrible human condition that is fear of the unknown. I also am limited in the exploration that follows, but I have striven by means of living and tradition to bring a fraction of sense to what is beyond measure.

And so we ascend through spirit and the place of the gods, all gods, and onwards still to what sings the universe into being.

TOWARDS INFINITY

To see a world in a grain of sand,
And a heaven in a wild flower,
Hold infinity in the palm of your hand,
And eternity in an hour.

WILLIAM BLAKE

We have explored the realm of the spirit by means of imagination, experience, and tradition, but what is next? Does everything end at the edges of the world of spirit or is there a further continuance—another form of permanence that whispers from the edge of beyond? According to several traditions, there is something else that exists beyond our limitations of understanding the spirit. In New Age circles one may often hear the phrase "they have moved to a higher level of existence" uttered as a remark to describe some sense of the spirit's progression from spirit to something altogether different. Upon further pressing, one quickly realizes the answers are rarely forthcoming, and we descend into obscure concepts and the grabbling for anything that may make any sense, however vague or unconvincing. So what do I know?

In the expression of these thoughts, I raise my head above the parapet and perceive the guns of disagreement that may well be aimed at my head, but this is unavoidable, I fear, for in a universe of infinite possibilities and potential, there can be no absolute truth. We can only strive to serve our truth by our unique connection and perception of it. The previous chapters have ascended in profundity, beginning with the body, which was my initial point of reference, then floating through the ether into the world of the spirit by proxy of the physical experience and my exploration and practice of spirituality. However, we now ascend to a greater mystery, and it is only by means of my visions and meditations that I present this information to you. I go beyond my own tradition's teachings in exploring this realm; indeed, not many traditions offer answers that traverse the circle of infinity. Only snippets of wisdom reach down from that lofty place to tease the spirit. In a manner it is almost too vast, too obscure for our little minds to grasp, and we may shake our heads at any thoughts of it.

It's too complicated, too much for me to deal with, I can't go there!

I would, however, claim that we *do* know something of this place, even if our ability to articulate that knowing may be limited, but in the depths of our spirit swims the knowingness of Ceugant. It is the realm of origination; it is not a state that we achieve, and there are no long and arduous tasks of learning that we must traverse to reach it. We came from here and we return here, regardless of the diversions along the way. Our memory of Ceugant is confounded by the fact that we are twice removed from it; the realm of Gwynvyd lies between the here and now and the edge of infinity. When one considers that even memories of the spiritual state may at best be vague, they are even vaguer when we attempt to align the mind with the circle of Ceugant.

This book's progression through profundity is at its penultimate stage, and the information in this and the following chapter may baffle and confuse, so I suggest that you read it a few times, think and meditate on the information presented here, and explore these constructs and concepts by means of your spirit. My aim throughout this book has been to offer a window, a unique insight into the world beyond death from a new perspective. You may never have contemplated what exists beyond the spirit; all I ask is that you suspend any doubt you may have and read the following with an open mind. Know that I do not offer this information as dogma but rather as personal insight that complements my life and my spiritual path; by means of this, I hope to inspire you to seek the edges of knowing and reach for infinity.

This chapter acts as a bridge that spans the gorge between the spirit and the soul. The final chapter will focus on that most mysterious of concepts, the soul; however, for now we will explore the transition point from spirit into soul—but why the differentiation between the two? In my tradition, the spirit equates to a fragment of the soul that experiences the universe as an individual entity; it is the experience of individuality, yet it is simultaneously connected to the source, to the soul. Spirit, derived from the Latin *espíritus,* is taken to mean "breath" or "to breathe"; it implies movement and animation. It is fluid, forever flowing, moving in and out of experience. The soul is the constant that houses it; another way of explaining this is that the soul is the house of the spirit, and this concept will be examined fully in the next chapter.

The circle of Gwynvyd has a border. If we were to visualize the spirit world, we would see its edge as a place of mists, the vapors of which reach into the realm of spirit. Gwynvyd's endless activity is of the comings and goings of spirits, who move knowing that eventually what lies at its edge will call them back into itself—back to the source of all things. This is the point where the spirit surrenders the process of experience and returns to the singularity of the soul or to a higher plane of existence. This does not imply that the spirit is governed or is in service to a higher being; it is only in service to itself as a facet of the source. This may sound, on the surface, to be a description of monotheism, the concept of a singular, intelligent, humanoid God, but I must stress that this concept differs vastly. It is not monotheism that I describe here; the energy that resides in Ceugant is beyond the mystery of deity—it is what, in fact, breathes life and essence into the gods. The concept of gods and deities will be discussed a little later, but for now it is sufficient for me to say that no god or gods exist in this realm. They belong in the realm of Gwynvyd, where spirit is in the process of interaction on a conscious level.

The realm of infinity is beyond our understanding of consciousness and can only realistically be portrayed in a hypothetical sense. Regardless of what tradition or religion we adhere to or follow, each interpretation of infinity is hypothetical. Nobody has monopoly over its truth, for there are no absolutes here. To explore the hypotheses of Ceugant is to transcend concepts, and this is no easy task, especially for a writer in the throes of describing it. Writers deal in concepts—we conceptualize and bring forth words from the realms of possibility—but in essence writing is a form of art, and the manner by which we connect to infinity can only realistically be expressed by artistic means. However, even this method is flawed, but by means of artistic expression we bring forth elements of the spirit and soul and share that inspiration with the world. We make manifest what was previously unmanifest; we take from the nothing and bring forth something. But there is a dilemma here, a paradox, for as soon as we attempt to rationalize or conceptualize infinity, we make it "something," and this immediately limits it; it ceases to be a permanence by its very defining. We sense infinity, and this sensing is a tricky thing to articulate, but for centuries we have striven to do so, to make the concept of eternity bearable. Ceugant is that place of "no-things," yet "all-things" swim in its sea of eternity; as humans we cannot help ourselves—we long to make sense of it, to bring meaning into mystery.

MAKING SENSE OF ETERNITY

What does that fickle little word embody? Look at it: eternity. Quite a pleasant word, really; it's pretty and yet has the ability to relay so much mystery. But what, in fact, is it, and are we really capable of grasping any sense of the eternal, of the infinite or immortal? A component of us is indeed eternal, and we are capable of getting a sense of that—of reaching through the density of matter and to the spirit, where we feel the meaning of eternity. However, the general teachings of many spiritual traditions and religions are that you have a spirit that will live for eternity, that it belongs or is in service to some über being that is vaguely human, and that we resemble it in form. You just have to believe this, and that's it; if you can't sense it, then you are immediately made to feel inferior to those who are obviously of greater spiritual aptitude. But you do not need anyone else to tell you that you are a part of eternity; you can discover this for yourself. Before any ascent into the lofty realms of the spirit can begin, one must descend into the material realm. By going in and back, we begin to grasp what it means to be eternal, to be an inexorable part of everything.

Herein lies the beauty and the magic of the Pagan traditions. There is no sense of denial, and no process of transcending is required or necessary; the keys to the spirit lie in living and in life. This world, in all its splendor, is an essential part of spiritual lucidity; it is never denunciated or besmirched as an experience that impedes or prevents some form of enlightenment. To be enlightened or to transcend implies denigration—that this living, this life, serves only to remove us from the lucidity of the spiritual, that the human persona must be overcome in order to ascend by means of lessons learned to a greater spiritual experience. In truth, this is once again a reflection of the fallacy that the personality survives death, which, as we have discovered, it does not; it perishes. The concept that lessons are essential to traverse the path of eternity and be rewarded with ascension to a higher plane, to escape the perpetual cycles of reincarnation until we have learned our lessons, perpetuates the belief that we are essentially a single personality capable of being rewarded or punished. It serves to control, to make those of less lofty spiritual experience feel that they are being controlled by some higher power that they have no relationship with. Not everybody has the time to invest in continuous exploration of the spiritual and ascend to the ranks of priests, who are then raised on pedestals of spiritual superiority. We are all capable of developing a relationship with the spiritual and through it glean an understanding of life, living, and eternity. By proxy of this connection, we remember the spirit and its purpose: not to learn—this is too human a concept to be universally applicable—but to be. Just to be.

Life itself holds the keys to eternity.

These keys hide in the message of sum totality, and I offer two examples of this that serve to demonstrate our eternal nature. One is based firmly in the physical and takes us on a journey through blood and ancestry, through the rivers of immortality, the spirit, and ultimately to the soul. The other takes us inward, deep into the core of our being and further still into the reaches of inner space, wherein we shall discover the ever-present, omnipotent soul.

The problem with eternity is that it is so damn difficult to comprehend. We may have highly developed brains, yet our ability to conceptualize time is oddly limited. Most people are only capable of conceptually grasping around three generations; after that, time simply becomes a series of numbers. Take my own personal spiritual path, Druidry; it invokes the memory of a caste of priests from around two thousand years ago and more. I struggle to remember last Tuesday—two thousand years is beyond my human ability to grasp! It is too much time, and yet in the grand scheme of things it is hardly a blink. So if we struggle to make sense of time itself, how can we ever hope to make sense of eternity? For this we must utilize the imagination.

SUM TOTALITY MEDITATION 1

Read the following meditation a few times to get a grasp of its structure, then close the book and settle yourself down somewhere comfortable—there's no need to sit cross-legged until your muscles groan. Just be comfortable and in a position where pins and needles won't serve to cause mischief. Focus on the rise and fall of your chest and the inhalation and exhalation of your breath. Allow your eyes to fall gently closed and listen to the sounds around you—hear them all and become aware of everything around you using all your senses except for your sight.

Now imagine the following (don't force this, don't assume this must be in 3D Technicolor brilliance; use your imagination, not your eyes):

- Imagine your parents standing behind you, Mum on the left, Dad on the right.
- Now imagine their parents behind them.
- Imagine the thousands of people that stand behind them.
- Imagine these people forming a country, and that country forming a continent.
- Imagine the creatures we were before we evolved into human beings.
- Go back further; imagine the primate ancestors and the trees and birds of our early earth.
- Imagine the planet, blue and green, a billion creatures and plants, now just a mass of connected organisms on one organism: the earth.
- Imagine the earth as a ball of glowing fire, arising from the searing heat of a shrinking star.
- See the light of the star shining brightly among a billion others.

- See the searing light of our own galaxy's core as it bursts into being.
- See the darkness beyond, and sense any movement within it.
- Imagine all this energy streaming out from a single point.
- Imagine the inconceivable explosion at the beginning of our universe's time.
- Imagine—keep going back and back through time to when there was nothing.

As you imagine this reversal, keep going to the point where you simply cannot fathom anymore, then speed back through the springing of light and galaxies, stars, and planets and the first stirrings of organic life, and forward through time to the coming of humanity and eventually to you. You are all of this; you are the sum total of everything that has ever existed before you. You stand at the pinnacle of being, immersed in eternity. Nothing is lost—unremembered perhaps, but never truly lost; you have at the tips of your fingers and the murky edges between mind and spirit the ability to tap into and know the mystery of the universe, for one simple reason: you are it.

SUM TOTALITY MEDITATION 2

Now, instead of going back through time, we shall go inward. Sit comfortably and look at the palm of your left hand. Focus on one of the lines that decorate the skin there; look closely and pick one crease. Really look at it. Now close your eyes and imagine the surface of that tiny fragment of skin. Move closer towards it in your mind, further and further until the cells that make up your skin can be perceived by your imagination. Imagine yourself passing these cells; they are enormous, full of structures that appear alien to you, their outer shells covered in a forest of cilia. Imagine that the cells you see are the size of a large car; you can see the workings within and you zoom in on a single cell and enter it.

- Imagine you pass through the cell walls; cilia appear like trees around you.
- See other structures passing you within the cell's body.
- Imagine what it must feel like to glide through the thick cytoplasmic fluid within the cell.
- Mitochondrion and ribosomes swim around you, and in the distance the nucleus of the cell pulsates like the center of a galaxy. Move towards it.
- Enter the cell's nucleus and imagine even more structures within, such as chromosomes and chromatin.
- Imagine the particles that make up these cell structures.
- Imagine the smallest things in our universe: atoms.
- Now imagine these atoms as circles of energy attracted to one another.
- See them move through space, drawn to one another; protons and electrons spinning in an alien universe.
- Now see the space they move within.
- It is empty.
- Imagine that emptiness, that space, nothing.
- Imagine yourself within this nothingness.

We may see the physical universe as solid, whereas in truth it is not; it only appears as a solid by the forces that act upon it. In essence it is countless atoms and particles that coalesce to appear solid. And the force that drives this solidity is energy, and we may call that energy "soul." As each facet of the physical universe condenses and appears solid, it begins to experience the universe within the density of a physical form. The fragment of the soul now caught in this experience can be defined as the spirit; it swims for a while in the rapture of existence until the physical form loses its shape and is no longer able to sustain life. The spirit is released, and yet between the spaces, within the emptiness, there is something we all share: nothing. And it is nothing for good reason, and this hypothesis is worthy of reiteration here, for if it was something, we could define it, and were we able to define it, it would not be a permanence. Permanence is beyond definition. As soon as we attempt to define it, it is limited by our own limitations.

Within the two meditation examples above, it becomes clear rather quickly that the mind is unable to grasp certain aspects of the journey. It becomes too big, too vast for us to comprehend and define, even if only internally by our own inbuilt program of language. As you journey, what you will note is that there comes a point where you must and can only rely on your senses to journey deeper and closer to the edge of intellect. Articulation loses its grip, and we realize that we can only sense the mystery. And from this sense a profound message will filter through your spirit and into the mind: eternity is not out there waiting for you; it is right here, right now, for you are eternity.

The awareness of our place in eternity and of our individuality and the permanence of the spirit focuses the mind on the wonder and magic of life. Agendas and power struggles fall by the wayside as we perceive the web of magic that connects all things, and it is because of this connection, this deep relationship, that we learn to live with a positive morality. To know that all things swim in the sea of eternity is to acknowledge the interconnection of all things; with this awareness rises natural positive morality. We don't need anyone else to tell us how to live; if we are guided towards a "knowing," the rest simply follows suit. No commandments are required or necessary; look at that word *commandment*, to command—hardly something that harbors or encourages inspiration and seeking. Finding your own place in eternity and seeing all things reflected in the "all" nurtures positive morality; those who have awoken to the lucidity of spirit and soul cannot help but be intrinsically good.

The physical universe is the soul in expression, and its sparks are the breath that brings life to the material realm; the soul imbues the physical dimension with spirit, and the spirit causes matter to sing in praise of it. Death is an essential part of the process of living and expression; without it, the universe could not sustain itself and would lose momentum, and its own permanent death would follow.

BEYOND BLACK HOLES

A dear friend of mine is a particle physicist and a practicing Pagan. She combines the wonders of magic and science, reconciling one with the other in her incredibly intelligent mind. I often spend hours chatting with her about the wonders of the universe, and most of it serves only to baffle me and leave me in awe. I do not claim to understand a fraction of what she can grasp with her intellect, but I can certainly feel the magic within it. Recently we got to chatting about death and the ultimate demise of the universe. Like most people, I have been led to believe that our universe is constantly expanding and will continue to do so until it runs out of steam, when it will then experience what scientists call a "cold death." All at once the universe becomes inert and unable to retain its form, so it collapses in on itself and blinks out of existence.

The question of what exactly the universe is expanding into or what is the space it will leave behind when all its lights go out is beyond the capabilities of the human brain to comprehend. The majority of people will quite happily accept that this is the nature of our universe—it expands into forever, and it must expand within something, right? Even the most skeptical of folk can accept this concept of eternity and yet will dismiss the concept of spirit or soul. Perhaps ultimately it is fear that prevents the majority from exploring the universe in both a

physical and spiritual sense. But what of the death of the universe—
what then? Doesn't its death negate the whole sequence of existence?
On the contrary, it seems that even the scientific community believes
there is more than initially meets the mathematical eye.

When our universe experiences its "cold death" and shrinks back on
itself, it collapses to a point, and within this a black hole appears. Every
ounce of material in the universe will vanish into a nothingness that
will consume it in its entirety. But further magic may be afoot; where
can all that matter go? The belief is that beyond the black hole is a
white hole, which is the expulsion of the material into the creation of
another universe; in other words, our black hole will create a big bang
and the birthing of another universe. The same may well be true of
the deaths of stars that collapse and form black holes that suck everything into itself; this vanishing act potentially creates a white hole in
another universe, causing material to spring into existence and taking
the essence of one experience with it to begin another.

The soul remains a constant; it is beyond the dance and drama of
universal births and deaths, and yet it permeates it all. It creates an
interconnected web of magic that defies logic and reason and breathes
mystery into everything that exists. If you look deeply with a telescope
through the boundary of our planet's gossamer-thin atmosphere and
into the vastness of space, you may perceive the gaps between stars and
galaxies to be empty, but they are not: they are filled with energy and
vitality, with potential, and each section of darkness is an extension of
you—nothing and nobody is truly separate.

THE WEB OF MAGIC

Imagine if you could see the strands of connectivity throughout the
physical universe—if your eyes could be adjusted to perceive the tendrils of energy and potential that connect all things, you would see a
web. This universe-wide web has been referred to and used by human-

kind since the dawning of our civilization. We have called it many things: Akasha, the Web of Wyrd, the Holy Spirit, Ein Sof, Awen, Chi, Imbas, the Zero Point Field, God, Nwyfre, and the Vacuum State. The plethora of words that we have utilized as a species serves to demonstrate the complex, conflicting, and paradoxical nature of interconnection, but they articulate our attempts to make sense of the universe and our place within it. And yet we seem to always return to the concept of a web, and even our common language uses the metaphor of a web to express connection—World Wide Web, for instance.

A web is a simple image to visualize; we are familiar with its shape and form. We encounter spiders' webs frequently, making them everyday symbols that we can easily connect with. The invisible forces that act on our universe can be effectively imagined as a vast spider's web that connects every single molecule and atom in the universe to each other. We have explored aspects of this web previously by descending through matter and into the space between all things; this river of energy and being can be seen as a web. When we wish to affect this web of being, we will resort to the subtle, to the power of prayer, spellcasting, conjuration, and sorcery. We have been doing this for millennia in one form or another, only the words that describe this course of action differ. It is almost as if, when we realize the limitations of the human being, we instinctively appeal to the universe by magical means. It seems programmed into us that there is more, that we have abilities beyond the limited capabilities of our human forms.

Magic is the conscious attempt to create change and to influence a situation, circumstance, or individual to do our bidding. It works in accordance to the will, where we impress the power of our wishes onto the subtle realm in an attempt to cause change in the physical. Many may scorn the use of magic, yet its presence has been a constant throughout our human history, and we find acts of magic in surprising and sometimes everyday places. Followers of religions, spiritual traditions, and even those of no religion or spirituality may utilize the powers of magic without even realizing they are doing so. Prayer is the plea or the beseeching of a supernatural being to cause change in accordance to your will; the casting of a spell is the attempt to cause ripples of change that sound through the web of connection, and the same can be said for sorcery and conjuration. The lighting of candles on a birthday cake is the utilization of the elements—in this case, fire to carry the desire or wishes of an individual to a subtle realm where it will be activated and then manifested on the physical plane; it is an act of magic. The casting of a coin into a wishing well uses the mystical qualities of water to cause change, another act of magic. Humans have forever solicited the power of the elements as bridges that carry our wishes to a dimension or realm where they are activated. Magic is not new or unusual; as humans we are programmed to invoke the subtle in times of need or desire.

In essence, magic is the ability to identify the individual strands upon the universal web and observe their pathways, to identify how each strand is connected to the other. The mind is then able by means of the spirit to arrive at that strand and pluck it; the subsequent vibrations then carry the will of the magician along the web of being until it arrives at its desired destination. This plucking transmits the will from one point of the web to another, thus causing change in accordance to the will. This may be seen as some form of exclusive power, but it is not; every human being has the ability to enact and alter the web of existence. It is the understanding of the nature of the web that decides the outcome and effectiveness of the act of magic.

The subtle is forever affecting our lives; powers and forces invisible to the naked eye can be sensed and may defy logic and reason. Take the emotions of another individual: not a word needs to be spoken, and yet we may sense and identify a problem or issue by means of senses that science would have us believe do not exist. The ability of magic to cause change cannot be disputed by those who have had it proved to themselves, though it cannot be observed in a laboratory or subjected to control testing, and yet it is something that we instinctively utilize. When all else fails, humans will naturally turn to magic.

Our ability to identify and tap into the web of being to utilize the power that inherently lies within it causes us to sense the connection between the body, mind, spirit, and soul. It is the awareness of the nature of each facet that makes effective magic; it is only the limitations of our language and expression that complicate it.

Memories are stored in the web of being, and accessing these memories is an act of magic. Every single second of our lives, every emotion and thought is recorded in the web of being and retained there as essential experience of the universe. When we call to the dead we can sense their memories stored within the web, and our emotional connection to that brings them back into focus for a while so we can share memories and reminiscence; we do this by means of magic. You can glean a sense of this by recalling your own memories and then dissecting their origination; did they exist as fragments of data within your brain or are they stored elsewhere? My belief is that our memories exist in the field of the web and that our brains simply select that data and cause it to coalesce into a set of symbols and language that the human body can then express. The brain acts as the receiver of the mind, which lives in the web of being, which in turn is activated by the spark of the spirit.

We exist in the unfathomable web of body, mind, spirit, and soul, each one connected to the other and blissfully swimming in the rapture of being. Whatever words we choose to describe the influencing or movement of this web will naturally be limited, but in my case I am happy to go with "magic." I like the awe that it evokes, the mystery that it holds, and the potential that hides within it.

THE MYSTERY OF DIVINITY

Death stands above me, whispering low
I know not what into my ear;
Of his strange language all I know
Is, there is not a word of fear.

WALTER SAVAGE LANDOR

The bridge between the spirit and the soul has been blurred by the attempts of humanity, religion, and tradition to define it. To find the house of God and be secure in the knowing that God lives somewhere out there is ultimately beyond our ability to conceptualize, but this has never prevented us from trying. God, this concept of a single superior being that exists beyond the realms of physicality and the spiritual, is inevitably a part of our understanding of mystery. If it's too much for our brains to cope with, if it defies all logic and reason, then just call it God and be done with it. Even within the rise of the Celtic romanticists, the word *god* has been utilized to describe high mystery. One cannot judge its use too harshly or condemn those who used the term for doing so; they were products of their time and the society they lived within. The usage of the word *god* was inevitable. It served to identify high mystery, but it did so in a rather limited manner for it created God in the image of man. Suddenly the whole universe is anthropocentric—in other words, it all revolves around human beings and our form. And the greatest one of them all—the most powerful, all-seeing, ever-present God—was created and housed in the realm of infinity; it was beyond the limitations of body, mind, and spirit. It was firmly placed in the realm of Ceugant.

We assume God, or gods, to exist in the realm of infinity—that they are beyond rationalization or definition, that they exist as the epitome of mystery. I, however, beg to differ, and in my experience of the spiritual I have concluded that the nature of the gods is not quite as convoluted and complex as we have been led to believe. This theory is certainly not new and can be seen within other traditions and philosophies, but generally it is a little too radical for many to accept, so bear with me and allow me to explore the nature of God and the gods.

I make mention of the singular term "God" in a monotheistic sense simply because the majority are familiar with the concept, and also because the great inspirers of the Celtic tradition used this term as a matter of course, even if the philosophies they explored were somewhat anathema to the Christian society they lived within. But from this point onwards I shall bunch that singular God in with all the other deities that make up religions and traditions, for they all share something in common: conceptualization. They are indicative of the human limitation to perceive anything beyond anthropocentricity. So what are the gods, and where exactly are they? As I mentioned earlier, in a universe of infinite possibilities there are no absolutes, and this simple truth is also applicable to the gods; therefore, in accordance to my own experience, I offer the following answers, but bear in mind that each one is as true as the others.

ARCHETYPES

It is human nature to create personifications that appear very much like we do. We may take the concept of a spirit or spirits, adorn them with humanoid features and traits, then clothe them with personalities and attributes. Human beings have done this throughout time to personify the powers of nature, where natural forces have been given human names and qualities, be they powers of thunder and lightning, storms, hurricanes, heat, and cold. In order to make sense of these and enable connection, our ancestors constructed them as archetypes with very human identities. Rationally we instinctively know that thunder is just a sound, a natural phenomenon that has no actual shape or form but exists as the rapid expansion of air as the result of pressure and temperature changes caused by lightning. Our attempts to connect to thunder and understand it gave rise to the gods of thunder; in the Celtic tradition he is called Taranis, from the proto-Celtic *toronos,* and can be seen in the Welsh word *taran,* meaning thunder. Human qualities and attributions can be seen emulated in archetypal forces, from love and hunting to birth and death.

When we think of the gods, we naturally believe them to resemble human shape and form: that they have bodies and organs, two arms and two legs, hair and clothing; we believe them to be actual people. But in essence what we have done is invented a person to make sense of a natural phenomenon or attribution, to give it a human aspect that we can identify with.

To these constructs we attribute powerful words that provide them with further identifying features, and these words are entirely dependent on society and language. To some they are gods, to others they may be angels or demons—spirits that archetypically embody a force, power, or attribute, to make sense of it and allow humans the ability to appease it or plead with it for favors or mercy. But something happens to these archetypes: they seem to take on a life of their own; fed by the imagination of humanity, they appear independent of their creators.

What are your thoughts on archetypes? Do you attribute anthropocentric names and images onto natural phenomena? What role do archetypes play in your own spiritual expression? Perhaps you are a devotee of a particular archetype; how did this relationship come about? How does a relationship that you may have with an archetype differ from any other form of deity or spirit?

APOTHEOSIS

This is the elevation of an individual, archetype, or construct to the ranks of a deity; it is the process of deification. It is believed that the gods of tradition started their lives as spirits of a place or object, a nature spirit, or that of a long-forgotten ancestor; they may arise from myths or legends. Over time this spirit is nurtured and fed and elevated to a position above and beyond humanity; it becomes a deity. These are beings that have been created by the relationships and connection human beings have to a particular location, mythology, or spiritual construct. The power of feeding it creates a thoughtform that has the ability to survive in the human imagination and also beyond it in the collective consciousness of a tribe or people. A deity is born.

This divine roller coaster takes the deity on a journey of perpetual transformation as each generation of worshipers or devotees connect to it in individual manners. The deity will continuously evolve until it is no longer revered or honored. Even then it does not cease to exist, for it may be captured in myth and legend and reawakened centuries later. But the illusion that they are very much human and exist without the power of human imagination is simply that: an illusion. Gods and goddesses created by means of apotheosis need humanity in order to sustain their form. Without reverence and devotion, they descend back into constructs and back further to their original power.

The birthing of deity by apotheosis does not negate or denigrate their existence. They are very real and powerful entities, albeit created ones, for they bring with them the power of what they represent. Apotheosis is our attempt to make sense of mystery. By giving it a human face, we strive to understand it better and perhaps fear it less.

What is your understanding of apotheosis? Take, for example, the Celtic goddess Cerridwen. There is no evidence to suggest that she was a goddess in antiquity, and yet she has since been deified. Does this affect the manner by which we connect to her as a goddess? Is her identity as a goddess warranted? Is it valid? Can one be a witch in one century and a goddess in another? What defines a spirit from a deity, a mythological figure from a god? Are there any deities in your tradition that you can identify as products of apotheosis? Consider the implications of apotheosis and the origin of the deities you have relationship with.

PARALLEL BEINGS

Within the Celtic tradition in particular there are several gods and goddesses that appear as humanoid, supernatural creatures with powers and abilities beyond the capabilities of humankind. Some are offered no description other than what may be discernible within the meaning of their names. Interestingly, those that have become known as deities are not referred to as such within the various chronicles of the Celts. They have subsequently become divine; apotheosis plays a part in this category too. What can be fathomed from the presence of these entities, of which dozens exist in the Celtic tradition alone, is that many of them do not reside in our world but inhabit another world that may appear similar to ours, yet is quite different in nature. Perhaps the most significant of the Celtic "otherworlds" is a mysterious realm known as

Annwn (pronounced ANN-oon); the word is derived from the Old Welsh meaning "deep" or "abyss." It implies that this world somehow exists beneath the fabric of our world and yet is accessible. Legends and tales abound of human encounters with this otherworld. For centuries it was assumed erroneously to be the land of the dead; however, Annwn is defined as somewhere other due to the actual absence of the dead. It is another world, separate to ours yet linked to it. It can be described as a parallel world that exists in another universe. The creatures that inhabit it, although seemingly human in form, have abilities and powers beyond our own, and consequently they are identified as deities.

> Do otherworldly realities play a role in your Pagan practice? If so, do you perceive these otherworlds as being in a separate universe to the one we currently inhabit? Consider some of the common Indo-European otherworlds—Annwn, Hades, Mount Olympus, Asgard. They all seem to have corridors that link them to our world; what does this mean? Barrows, rivers, groves, and hills are all common access points. Do you live by any? How do these places make you feel? How do we create a cosmology from this—do we need one? Consider the deities of these otherworlds; how do they differ from their counterparts that are an aspect of our universe? How do you experience them? Do you frequently interact with deities who inhabit an "other" or parallel world? If so, what defines them as "other"?

BEYOND INCARNATION

If you journey by means of the mind and spirit to the realms of Gwyn-vyd, you will encounter beings that are beyond immediate explanation. Within the dimension of spirit it seems that there exist entities that no longer return to the cycles of life; they exist within the realm of spirit without material attachment to the physical. These observers are synonymous with deific beings that may once have experienced human life and subsequently are interested in watching it. These beings may have no actual mortal shape or countenance; their legends may be vague, with no location specified. They speak to us from the realm of spirit and are beyond our understanding, but they may well have an interest in the business of humankind and have long since become accustomed to devotional acts. In this manner they may assist humanity or imbue the meaning of mystery to their adherents. These beings may be the collective thoughtforms of cultures and beliefs; they may be the accumulation of imagination and connection that is filled with the memories of dead human beings. These deities represent high mystery.

Consider the value of not knowing and deep mystery to the Pagan traditions. We don't have all the answers, but were they available to us, would we want them? There are certain concepts that we cannot conceptualize; they become too vague and lose their form when we consider them. Take, for instance, the Cabbalistic sephiroth of Kether at the very top of the Tree of Life. It is beyond human articulation; to attempt to define it would limit it. Do you consider there to be deities or spirits that emulate this quality, those that are above and beyond mere human consideration? Meditate on this vast unknowingness and record your impressions.

In essence, the concept of divinity is inexorably connected to the human imagination; many developed from myths and legends, and some of these became religions. We may never truly understand the nature of deity, but we can be certain that they exist and that they do so by the magic of relationship; without this, they will fade into obscurity and memory. The gods and goddesses are not stationary, and if they become so—just like our universe will—they will lose the confines of that experience and transform into something else. In order to survive, they must be in constant motion, moving to the beat of devotion and reverence.

THE MYSTERY OF DIVINITY

The soul cannot be truly limited to being a god or goddess; its magic lies in something far more profound, something beyond our ability to articulate fully. What is your relationship with divinity? How do you define deity, and what, if any, influence does it have on your life and spiritual expression? Questions of divinity can only realistically be addressed by means of your relationship with it. These intriguing beings—however we perceive them—offer us something of value, as we have been revering them for millennia.

THE GRIM REAPER AND DEITIES OF THE DEAD

Surrounded by mists that stretch back countless millennia, engulfed in mythology and tradition, the image of Death personified is as familiar to today's society as it was centuries past. Artists pondered over it, poets wrote to it, composers etched out music of melancholy and gloom to it. The Gothic era lavished in its symbology to an extent that balanced on the border of worship. Continuously, through the etheric mists of time, this enigmatic figure has entrenched itself into the popular imagination and into the nightmares of society. The Grim Reaper is a symbol of Death personified and represents the collective psychopomps of antiquity—the gods of the dead.

With wisps of shadow, the cold breath of Death personified is etched into the Western mind as a creature of some stature, adorned in billowing black fabric from which a bony, skeletal hand extends. Brandishing a scythe as sharp as the crescent moon, it holds it aloft, threatening to strike those for whom the hourglass has ceased its limited dance of sand. The personification of Death embodies the belief that death truly is beyond our control, and that some force in an invisible realm fastidiously observes the passage of human life and heralds its end. When the reaper comes, there is very little one can do to prevent the scythe from falling. Death personified does not necessarily bring about the action of death but rather the gathering of the soul after death has occurred. In some cultures the image of Death personified is one laced with violence and destruction, perhaps exemplifying the paradoxical, contradictory nature of death, an event that brings about confusion, anxiety, and sadness.

Death personified has the ability to change its outward expression in accordance with socio-cultural evolution and development. Inherently it is dependent on the human imagination, yet it would be foolhardy to state that this alone is its only source of power. Death within the Christian tradition is a fearful entity, for it is associated with sin, and sin is regarded as something in opposition to the true will of God. The book of Romans 6:23 states, "For the wages of sin is death." Death is portrayed as terrible, as punishment for the weakness and sinful nature of humankind, requiring the repentance of God's forgiveness to ensure the passing into everlasting life. In the book of Revelation, Death is named as the fourth horseman of the apocalypse; it rides upon a pale horse. It is sentient and able to respond to the commands of God, it is the destroying angel, it does God's bidding, yet paradoxically God and its servants within the church scorn Death as being evil and violent.

The New Testament perpetuates the fear that humanity feels towards death, yet in the Old Testament the story is somewhat different. The book of Job describes "angels of death" called the Memitim, not an individual but rather an army of angels who mediate over the lives of those at death's door. Collectively they are known as the Mal'ake Hamavet, to whose ranks Azriel, referred to as an Angel of Death, may be assigned. In Judaic texts it states that the Angel of Death was created by God on the first day to facilitate the departure of the human soul to its origination in the realm of God.

Throughout the majority of cultures, Death personified is perceived as a psychopompic figure, not necessarily as a destroyer. Psychopomps, from the Greek *psychopompos*, can be translated as the "guide of souls"; their role is not to take life but to facilitate the journey between the conscious and the subconscious worlds. They part the veil and allow passage between the worlds of the living and the dead. In many cultures they may be perceived as various animals, most commonly those belonging to birds of the corvid family; in other cultures they assume an anthropomorphic identity. Interestingly, throughout most ancient cultures, in particular Slavic, Scandinavian, and Celtic, the image is feminine. It is only within the last four to five hundred years that Death has erroneously evolved into a masculine figure, probably as a direct result of Christian influence in that the Christian angelic forces are mostly perceived as masculine and rarely feminine.

Polytheistic traditions have nearly always assigned a god figure to act as psychopomp; these so-called gods of the dead developed through time to become what the popular imagination calls the Grim Reaper. The presence of Death personified can be found within the mythologies and sacred texts of all traditions and spiritualities. To the ancient Egyptians it was Anubis and Osiris, to the Celts it was the Morrigan and Gwyn ap Nudd, leader of the Wild Hunt. The Germanic and Nordic tribes identified it as Odin, whose earlier title was Grimnir, from where the prefix *grim* of Grim Reaper originates. In Hindu mythology it is known as Yama, the lord of death, and the list goes on and on, reaching back into time through cultures and peoples, each one expressing the need of humanity to understand death.

The symbology surrounding the imagery of Death personified has also become entrenched in the popular imagination. The skeleton is a common symbol of human death, as it embodies the stripping away of flesh and identity; beneath the skin we are all the same, we are as one, and in death we become united. The scythe, commonly held aloft by the Grim Reaper, is a significantly ancient symbol with obvious associations with the harvest and the cutting of wheat; it is synonymous with sacrifice, and its ultimate adoption by the figure of Death is a natural succession of ancient symbology. Black has long been associated with death and grief, although not exclusively so; some cultures may well adorn in white during funerary rituals. However, black is generally seen as something sinister or gloomy, perhaps as a result of the fact that black is in actuality the absence of all color; it is the visual impression experienced when no visible light reaches the human eye. It is both nothing and all things simultaneously. It is mystery, as is death.

The Grim Reaper is firmly entrenched in the popular imagination and is quite valid to the Pagan traditions. It acts as a skeleton that one can clothe with the characteristics of other deities of the dead. In the absence of relationship with a particular psychopompic deity, the Grim Reaper is an ideal substitute. The primary psychopomp that I work with is the Celtic deity Gwyn ap Nudd, who is associated with the Wild Hunt; his chariot appears from the sacred mounds at the festival of Samhain, and he goes in search of the spirits of the dead. The Black Book of Carmarthen, an ancient Celtic manuscript, records a dialogue between Gwyn ap Nudd and a dead man called Gwyddno Garanhir. The poem also associates ravens with death and dying; these birds of the corvid family are typical psychopomps of the Celtic peoples. During the waxing half of the year I perceive him as an antlered god of nature; during the dark half I see him as the Grim Reaper, clothed in a black gown, scythe in hand, although I do not envision him as skeletal. I combine two images with which I am familiar.

What is your understanding of a death deity? Vision journeys to meet the personification of Death can enrich your spiritual understanding of its function and help develop relationships with your psychopomps. Let's take a moment to meet one.

Read the following and memorize its details as best as you can. Take yourself to a space where you will not be disturbed for twenty minutes or so. Be comfortable; set the scene with candlelight and incense. Close your eyes, breathe deeply and slowly, and bring to mind the following images.

Imagine that you are standing about thirty feet from the edge of a cliff, beyond which there is a vast ocean of nothingness. Visualize this as a darkness or outer space. Ahead of you, merely inches from the edge of the cliff, stands a portal made of two standing stones, each one thirteen feet in height. They demarcate the liminal space between life and death; the cliff upon which you stand is the world of the living, and the vastness beyond is the realm of the dead.

Focus on the space between the standing stones and say or think these words or similar:

"I address thee, O Death; from thee there is no concealing. Permit me audience with your form."

Imagine that a form takes shape between the stones. A black cloak billows in the ethereal breeze, blacker than the darkest night. A movement heralds the extension of arms wrapped in delicious darkness, a hand extends from beneath the fabric, and a golden, sharp scythe appears from nowhere. You cannot see the figure's face, as billowing black fabric occludes its head. Say or think these words or similar:

"I address thee, O Death; from thee there is no concealing. Permit me to gaze upon your countenance."

Imagine yourself slowly walking towards the figure, and as you do a breeze catches the hood that obscures its head, and suddenly a face comes into view. It is androgynous and benign, its eyes are pools of darkness, and its mouth is curved in a gentle smile. If you are in relationship with a psychopomp, project the image that you are familiar with onto this form. Approach the figure so that you can sense its presence and energy.

Gaze at the figure's eyes and say or think these words or similar:

"You have been where soldiers were slain, from east to west; I am alive, they in their graves. You have been where the dying lay, from north to south; I am alive, they in death. O Death divine, bid me counsel, teach to me your mystery."

Now, stay within this space and allow what questions you have to project from your mind to the figure of Death. Know that it will do you no harm; you are quite safe to take its counsel and be in its presence. Do not force or expect any answers; simply experience the vision. Speak to the figure and converse with it as you would with a teacher. When you feel the vision is near its end, take a few steps back from the figure and say or think these words or similar:

"O Death divine, from thee there is no concealing; permit me to leave from your presence."

Sense the figure's energy dissipate and watch as it dissolves into the fabric of nothingness.

Take a deep breath, slowly return to the here and now, have a drink, take a snack, and forget about the vision. Sleep, and on the morrow recall any impressions in a notepad or journal.

Now let's move ever deeper towards the source, towards the place of high mystery; the bridge from Gwynvyd beckons us to step over the gorge that separates something from nothing.

SEEING THROUGH TRAGEDY

I vividly remember the night that my little baby sister was born. My mother never quite made it into the maternity hospital, and little Rachel arrived in the parking lot! A ray of light that beamed through the dark October night, her radiance shone brightly if only for a while. Over two decades have since passed; Rachel is no longer with us. She lived boldly and with a passion and determination that belied her young years. She was the little treasure of the family, the youngest of four children that my mother begot. She was a beautiful child, sweet natured, funny, and gentle; she had a countenance that made the heart smile. I loved her so much.

In her pubescent years Rachel developed idiopathic epilepsy. Her first seizure was terrifying, yet she and the family learned to live with the infrequent episodes, which thankfully were rare. She lived with her epilepsy, taking her medication as instructed, and she got on with life unimpeded by her affliction. She was a popular girl; she made friends easily and laughed wildly. She shared my tendency to procrastinate and would lounge in her bed until midmorning at any given opportunity. She grew quickly as the years sped by and as we all got lost in the drama of living.

Rachel longed to be a mother, and on January 25, 2009, that wish came true. She gave birth to her son, Harvey, who entered this world on the feast day of the Welsh patron saint of love, Saint Dwynwen. She launched herself into motherhood and the joys of connection that it brought; her little son—the candle of her eye—beamed a new radiance into the world. She took to motherhood like a duck to water; a new kind of purpose came to her as she took to her role as matriarch. Alas, her body was to deal a cruel blow in the peak of her life, at the time when she was most complete.

It was an epileptic seizure that was to summon her death; she took to her morning shower, with her little son entertained on his play mat on the bathroom floor. With his mother in plain view, his world was secure and as it should be—until Rachel's brain fired every neuron within it. She lost her consciousness immediately and fell to the shower floor, striking her forehead on the faucet. In an instant, Rachel was dead. She had shared only eight short months with her baby son. Her body had other plans, it seemed; it could no longer sustain its status quo. Harvey would grow never knowing his mummy or having a vivid memory of her as a living being. It was my other sister who discovered Rachel's body and the terror of finding little Harvey bereft atop the staircase, not knowing where his universe had gone.

The youngest sibling of four, our mother's youngest child was dead. The heart of the family imploded in sheer utter grief. Rachel lay cold and silent at the morgue, and my brain struggled to deal with the image—a thing so familiar to me, yet beyond terrible. I felt like I was choking standing there, not knowing what to do, what to say, what to feel. Her partner entered the room with little Harvey in his arms and collapsed onto Rachel's body, at which point the baby, upon smelling the scent of his mother, reached out for the comfort of her breast. This was too much for everyone in that room to bear; screams of grief rose into the stuffy atmosphere, my knees buckled and I recall placing a hand out to prevent my falling too hard. A cry that had been voiceless emerged from within my being and pierced the air before me as a new pain cracked the beating of my heart.

My mother had lost her child; how does a woman recover from that? A piece of her lay dead in the morgue, and the primal, terrible scream that crashed from her chest to punch everyone who stood in its way was beyond belief. It was a scream I believe that only a mother can produce in response to the loss of her child. The family broke down into bitter tears and the beginning of grief. How could such an unjust thing happen? How could such tragedy befall such a beautiful and innocent young girl, to sever her from being the mother she longed to be? How could a power out there have allowed such a thing to occur? The cruel nature of her passing was beyond belief, and our emotions dealt with it in the only way we knew how, by grieving.

A few weeks later, I lay in bed not knowing if I was awake or asleep, but somewhere between. A strange heaviness came upon the bed, and my eyes opened to be met with Rachel sitting on the edge of the bed. I stared at her incredulously and opened my mouth to speak, when she said, "Do you know that you can die without actually knowing that you have died? It happens that quickly."

I sat bolt upright. Rachel was not there, but her words hung in the air like dew. I grasped the pillow next to me and wept into its softness; how could my little sister have died like that? This was so unfair. I awoke the next morning and called to the power of death, to the reaper itself; I demanded to know how it could have betrayed me by taking my sister.

"I gave my life to you! I have done nothing but serve you, you bastard, how can you do this to me!"

The reaper did not answer; nothing answered. I was lost in the pain of grief, and it would last for as long as its course was necessary and unobstructed. A tragic death tears away at belief, as people cannot fathom that a benign superior being could allow such things to happen. How can there be a God if it allows this to happen? I hear those words so often, falling from the lips of the bereaved. We are programmed to accept that something controls our lives, that our living and our dying are predestined by a superior being who governs all these things and meddles in the affairs of humans. And when things do not go according to plan, we focus our resentment on an external force, even if we have previously paid it little attention.

It was not the reaper or God or the gods that called to Rachel's spirit that day; nothing beyond this world caused her death. Her body is what died, and it did so because it was flawed, like all our bodies are—a little something was out of place, and on that day it failed. Her body fell from this experience. The tragedy, however, remains, for we are confronted with the glorious face of her little son who lives without his mother. He will learn of her through us, through the relationship that we had with her, and we continue to call her memories from the web of being. She exists within us now, Rachel, the little girl who became a mother, a sister, a daughter. The friend and companion that we knew has gone, but the spirit that chose Rachel's life continues, and I can sense it beyond the veil of living. I reach out to it with the memory of our relationship, and I sense it tingle at the touching of spirits in collision.

I miss my sister; I cry still for her loss. She was important to us, and she is important to the soul to which the experience of her life now brings to it another ray of brightness.

Rachel's death taught me the function of sadness; never before had the seasons of grief been so tangible, so powerfully apparent and real. When a sudden death strikes, we are stunned by our unpreparedness; it cripples us. Preparing for an expected death is one thing, but coming to terms with an unexpected and tragic death is quite another. Sadness has a function; we may deplore it and resent the pain it causes, but it forces us to take time out. The expression of sadness, a sagging lip line, and narrowed eyelids all serve a function, for they elicit empathy and compassion from our fellow human beings (Bonanno 31–32). Sadness has a defined function and is vital to the healing process.

We are remarkably more resilient than we may give ourselves credit for. Tragedy may temporarily stun us into inaction, but beneath the veneer of sadness we can still function, and we invariably do. The majority of bereaved individuals do not suffer long-term damage as a consequence, but they are undeniably transformed by it. There are always exceptions to the rule; to some, grief strikes too hard a blow, one from which the individual does not recover.

Consider the function of sadness and how it initiates, perpetuates, and assimilates the seasons of grief.

REACHING FOR THE
SOUL'S MEANING

I backward step into the abyss,
where the form ends and nothing is,
Where nothing ends and all begins.

Ross Nichols

O ne cannot help but arrive at this chapter with a degree of trepidation, for the vast unknowingness of the realm of infinity questions everything; it is a place of contradiction and paradox. This is the
place of high mystery, the place where all things are and no-thing is. I
have my own take on the realm of Ceugant, my own deep understanding of it, yet I am daunted by the attempt to articulate it. In truth, this
is *my* truth; it can only be mine and mine alone. This lofty place, the
source of all things, is too vast for the human mind to fully express, but
in our attempts to do so we move the mind closer to mystery, where we
attempt to make sense of our place in eternity. It is in its exploration
that we glean a little of the immense potential that swims within our
universe; it is by sensing our origination in soul that we learn to know
our place as vital facets of universal mystery. In this spirit, this chapter

will focus on the essence of soul, but forgive my limited abilities to fully articulate something that is truly beyond the power of words.

Within the introduction to the realm of infinity you will have noted the inclusion of a triad. These snippets of triadic wisdom are prevalent throughout the literature of the British Celts, and they transmit a storehouse of knowledge, information, and wisdom in bite-size pieces, allowing the keepers and transmitters of tradition to memorize them with ease. There are hundreds if not thousands of these triads recorded, one of which appears in the introduction and states thus:

> The three things that none but God/the Great Spirit can do: to endure the eternities of Ceugant, to participate in every state without changing, and to ameliorate and renew everything without causing the loss of it.

If we look at this a little closer, we can discern some of the mysteries of Ceugant and its nature; however, all is not as it seems. Triads are fickle little things, and they need careful examination if we are to discover and absorb their wisdom. If we take the first sentence, we are introduced to the concept of Ceugant as the three things that none but God/the Great Spirit can do—to endure the eternities of Ceugant.

In the previous chapter we explored the concept of God, gods and goddesses, and I concluded that those who penned the triads—in this case, the Celtic revivalist Iolo Morganwg—had no other point of reference for a realm or power as singular in appearance as Ceugant. Frankly, the majority of folk would perceive this great oneness as a god or superior being, for we have been programmed to accept such concepts for something so incredibly obscure. This is simply demonstrative of the limitations of language, yet some folk may consciously choose to refer to this place as God, and there is no harm in that whatsoever—we can only connect to it by means of our own parameters of understanding and knowing.

As I previously explored, the realm of Ceugant is beyond the limitations of an anthropomorphic God; it is, in essence, a singularity, a collective consciousness that is beyond comprehension. And yet we are informed by the triad that only a god or great spirit can endure the eternities of Ceugant—so what is meant by this? To begin with, we must strip the terms *god* or *great spirit* of their anthropomorphic associations and find another word that adequately explains singularity without the limiting factors of personality, agenda, and motive. Bear in mind that the two terms in both their revealed religion and Pagan sense are anthropocentric; they refer to a humanoid being. Therefore, in this exploration I shall use the term *soul* to replace the preprogrammed understanding of a god or great spirit.

> *Stop for a moment. Read and consider the following paragraph. Close your eyes and invoke what you have been programmed to believe represents a god or great spirit. Hold the image for a few seconds and then cause it to dissolve into nothing, but know that its omnipresence remains. It is not and does not resemble a human being. With its dissolution it becomes simultaneously No-thing and All-things, including you. This expansion that encompasses the entire universe is not separate from you; you are it, and it is this understanding that enables the endurance of eternity.*
>
> *If we become trapped in the belief that all things revolve around a single entity that is human and more or less acts as a human being, then we are forever locked into patterns of apparent identity. This cannot endure eternity. It is the elimination of fear and the true understanding of the nature of self and being that causes us to awaken to the lucidity that arises from the interconnectivity of spirit and soul. As a consequence, we are able to endure the eternities of Ceugant, for we ascend to the realization that we are Ceugant—it is our original state.*

The spirit in the realm of Gwynvyd is closer to this truth, for it has returned to its original state beyond the density of matter. It is the denseness of our physical world, familiarity, and personality that cause us to fear the return to the source. But when we capture a glimpse of this in life, the world shines brighter for we can sense the movement of spirit and soul singing within the conglomeration of matter. We see and therefore know the magic that lies in existence. For many, the concept of eternity and its enduring is too much to bear—it is too vast a thing to contemplate, and there is great fear here. Within its singularity we sense a dissolution of "us," and this can grip the human heart in terror. But as we have seen throughout the course of this book, the "us" that we have been programmed to believe is fleeting. We are taught to fear that death can bring about other forms of death, repetition in a hell dimension where we are caused to die over and over again, or, as some traditions claim, complete annihilation. And what do these things teach us? Fear. And if we fear, what chance do we have to know the spirit and soul and the knowing that we can endure eternity? For we are eternal.

The passage between Gwynvyd and Ceugant is not, as some would describe, a form of spiritual suicide; it is simply a return to the source of all being, to the vast cauldron of potential whose waters continuously stream throughout all things. It is the conscious movement from the realm of experience to the place of potentiality. We are able to endure it for we are, in essence, what the Celtic revivalists called God or Great Spirit; we are a spark of the source swimming in experience. Hypothetically this singularity may be giving birth to a multitude of other universes where the sparks of the soul, the spirit, return again to the playground of experience.

As we move on to the next section of the triad, we learn another facet of high mystery: to participate in every state without changing.

The soul is the house of the spirit and permeates all things; it is the heart of all knowing. It is what whispers mystery to the spirit, which in turn sings it to the minds of those who inhabit the physical universe. It is within all things; it is the constant that imbues the visible and invisible worlds. The soul is able to participate in every form of life and living, and experiences every state of being by proxy of the spirits that bring those encounters to it. The spirit is in constant motion, falling in and out of experience, attaching itself to life and the living material universe, yet the soul is the constant that houses it; it never changes. The soul remains the original driving force that causes something to come from nothing by becoming aware of itself.

Within the Celtic tradition we capture a glimpse of this mystery through the words of the prophet Taliesin, who was born of the goddess Cerridwen. His words appear in the introduction to the realm of infinity and are repeated here:

> *I was a multitude of forms*
> *Before this consistency,*
> *I was a droplet in the air,*
> *I was the radiance of stars,*
> *I was a word in writing,*
> *I was a raindrop in the shower,*
> *I was a spark in a fire.*

Taliesin speaks of several states of being or existence, of which only a fraction is shared here; you will note none of the states refer to a human being. This reiterates the Celtic belief that not only do we survive death but we go on to experience other forms of existence in other states; the human experience is only one aspect of being. He speaks of his human form by referring to his current consistency; this is the voice of the human that speaks of high mystery, and within these words we can observe the constancy of the universe—the soul.

What is essentially being transmitted here is the mystery of continuation and permanence. Taliesin has existed in numerous forms, yet his essential spirit—the "I," the inner observer—is ever present. Each line of the poem begins with the word "I"; he is speaking of an inherent aspect of himself that is above and beyond his apparent human personality and identity. The "I" is indicative of the soul and its ability to participate in every state without changing. It may experience myriad changes by means of the spirit's attachment to the physical, but in essence it remains a constant. You captured a fragment of this in the sum totality exercise in the previous chapter, and the above verse from the wisdom of Taliesin is worthy of further meditation. An Internet search using the key words "Taliesin Battle of the Trees" will provide you with the full text.

The third and final section of the triad states "to ameliorate and renew everything without causing the loss of it."

Here we are introduced to the concept that nothing is lost to the soul; all things are retained despite their constant state of renewal and flux. The memories of the universe are stored upon the warp and weft of the soul's fabric and stored there as an essential aspect of the universe's song. All things exist and are renewed and made better by the perpetual spinning of the physical universe bringing new life into being. New experiences arise, and the spirit attaches itself to them as messengers of the soul. It is the soul that drives the energy of the universe; it is that invisible force that can be perceived in the vast unknown nothingness between all things. We may die and our personalities as we know them perish, but our memories are energetic and cannot be destroyed; they are transformed and stored in the warp and weft, and there they sing the song of existence for eternity. Within the continuous transformation of all things, we may assume that things are lost, for they no longer appear as they were, but the soul teaches us that this is not so. It retains the memory of the universe. We are, in fact, the universe experiencing itself.

When the physical body dies, other than the disintegration of the corpse and the death of the apparent identity, nothing, in fact, is truly lost; it is simply transformed. It no longer serves or is bound to the experience of the human being, but the soul retains that experience as the spirit carries it towards the depths of infinity.

WHAT'S IN A WORD?

Are we able to glean a sense of the soul, of the inexorable interconnectivity of the universe? Yes, we are, and the manner by which we do this is by exploring the meaning of the word *soul*, which may surprise you. We previously explored the etymology of the word *spirit* and its qualities of breath, or essential breath, and expression. Here you will discover that the etymology of *soul* is strikingly different and refers to something that we are all more than capable of identifying with, and by proxy will cause us to deepen our understanding of the nature of soul.

Soul is derived from the Proto-Germanic word *saiwalo*, meaning "to come from the sea" or "belonging to the sea" or "to be of the nature of the sea." The usage of the word to describe the disembodied aspect of a dead human being was only first used within the English language in the year 971 of the Common Era (according to the *Chambers Dictionary of Etymology*), but it seemingly was utilized to describe something of greater mystery prior to its familiar meaning today. The connection with the sea bears a striking similarity to the Celtic belief that the soul emanates from the sea and upon death the spirit of an individual returns to the soul by way of the sea. With this in mind, it seems probable that the word *soul* has long since been synonymous with the power and nature of the sea, and perhaps for good reason, for it tells us something of the nature of soul.

The oceans and seas of our planet exist as a single mass of briny water. We may identify it with locality-specific names, but they are, in fact, a single entity. Wherever we may be on the planet, the sea connects each part to the other. To be immersed in the sea off the southern coast of Britain is to be standing in the same body of water that washes onto the islands of the Philippines. It is the same mass of water that lies frozen and silent at the poles. By being immersed in the sea, we gain an understanding of the true nature of the soul—it is omnipresent, it is the constant, and this can be seen metaphorically in our oceans.

By meditating on the quality of the sea, one can deepen the understanding and perhaps more essentially the relationship we have to the great mystery. Celtic mythology exudes oceanic mysteries, none so apparent than in the Four Branches of the Mabinogi from Wales. These tales abound with the sagas of gods, goddesses, and their offspring, but the Fourth Branch itself is worthy of mention here. If you are unfamiliar with the myths of the Mabinogi, read the Fourth Branch to get a sense of the story (see mabinogi.net/math.htm). An early episode of the tale sees Aranrod's virginity being tested by the great Druid/magician Math, the son of Mathonwy; as she steps over his wand, she gives birth to a large, strong, yellow-haired boy. In her shame she makes for the door and drops a small "thing" from her loins. Pertinent to this book is the significance of the first child, for Math has a name already prepared for him: Dylan eil Ton, meaning "sea heir of wave." The almost insignificant statement that Math has prepared a name for a child that surely he had no idea would be born hides a deeper mystery and is perhaps indicative of the magician's inherent power. He commands that the child be baptized, which, according to scholarship, is significant of assumption into human society. However, Dylan rejects this process and immediately takes to the sea; at the shoreline he takes on the nature of the sea and, as the medievalist Will Parker eloquently puts it, "regresses into undifferentiated unconsciousness" (Parker 550).

The implication here is the total dissolution of Dylan's human self. He becomes sea.

In a mystical sense this is significant, for the Celtic mysteries elaborate that the student/initiate must be "touched by the spray of Dylan's Kingdom" to achieve transformation (Ford 136). This can be taken to suggest that in order for the mysteries of the universe to be assimilated into the experience of being human, one must first understand the nature of singularity—of soul. The sea offers this key.

Read the following brief meditation, and memorize its details as best as you can. Then settle yourself, breathe slowly and deeply, and bring to mind the following:

Imagine a small male child, his hair bright yellow, like sunlight. He stands on a sandy beach, his back to the sea. His small body is covered in drapes of seaweed, and his eyes are as black as night. He smiles at you, and these words fall from his lips:

"All things know me. All things have shared my citadel beneath the waves."

The tide rushes suddenly and his form collapses into the water, dissolving into the very fabric of the sea. Imagine the waves now rushing towards you at incredible speed. In an instant the cold sea is waist deep. Take a deep breath and imagine yourself falling backwards into the water. Recall the words "all things know me; all things have shared my citadel beneath the waves."

Imagine yourself dissolving to become the sea in its entirety. Sense the Mediterranean, the Caribbean Sea, and the Pacific and Atlantic Oceans all singing to you. Sense the different lands they interact with, but also sense the constant that remains unchanged. You are an aspect of that constant.

Add a practical element to this exercise when you are next at the ocean by lying flat on your back in the sea with your ears submerged. Listen to the song of the sea, recall the meditation, and dissolve into undifferentiated unconsciousness.

The qualities stated in the triad we discussed earlier can be seen emulated in the sea; it is a constant transformative power. It serves to change and mold landscape and seascape; it corrodes and it creates. The land it interacts with is continuously being transformed and renewed by its power, and yet it, the sea, remains. Its essential nature is not detrimentally affected or altered, yet it absorbs the quality of land into itself. The creatures that inhabit its body are affected and transformed by it, they swim within its substance, they are a part of it, and yet their experience of life is different in its locality. The same metaphor can be applied to us.

Within the ocean of our bodies exist a trillion organisms, each one with its task, with its own experience of living, and yet they exist as a part of the whole, the one. We in turn exist as 6.6 billion human beings that share a world with countless other forms of life, and yet we are a part of a single being, the earth. The earth, in turn, sings the song of the solar system, which is an aspect of a greater whole, and on and on ad infinitum, and all of this can be seen in the nature of the sea. To stand and gaze at the shores of our oceans is to look upon the face of mystery and magic; the sea acts as a teacher, a transmitter of truth, that enables the body and mind, spirit and soul to flow as one. It teaches us the connection between the body, mind, spirit, and soul, and within it we can see clearly the message of continuation and permanence. In the throes of grief our emotions heighten, and the power of those emotions reaches out into the world as we go in search of our dead. In the midst of this pain and anguish, take yourself to the sea and sit there in quiet solitude and listen to its ability to transform and yet remain a constant.

BEING NOTHING

During the process of formulating this book and deciding what each chapter would contain, I struggled with this one in particular, for ideally the only true representation of the realm of Ceugant in this context would have been a blank page. How does one describe nothing? What, in fact, is nothing? Perhaps a blank page would have served the mystery more effectively. "I backward step to the abyss where the form ends and no-thing is," said the Druid Ross Nichols, who penned the words that open this chapter. Within it he captured an echo of high mystery; some of the words, however, instill a foreboding in most— none of us truly like that word *nothing*, as it feels too close to the concept of annihilation.

But things are not quite as clear-cut as we would initially believe. You will have learned by this point that the fear we have for this "nothing" has its basis in the illusion that we are what we are now and must remain so; anything other would be suicide. But by the teachings of our ancestors, through experience and a discourse with the sea, we learn that there is so much more to the concepts of living, death, and the afterlife than we have been led to believe. But there is still the problem of the "nothing." Had you been faced with a blank page, I imagine you might be a little befuddled by my actions, yet many may have sat and pondered the fullness of that empty page and perceived the mystery that lay beyond it. Ultimately (as is clearly evident) I decided to continue writing, and I pray that you forgive my limitations of expression within this section; this concept of nothing is tricky business.

This idea of nothing is not new, and it can be seen as teachings within other traditions. One of the most obvious is the quality of Ein Sof in the Cabbalistic tradition. The words combined mean "no end" or "unending"; it is the epitome of something that cannot have an end. In the usual usage of language it is said that Ein Sof, also known as the negative veils of existence, is the essence of God prior to manifestation and the production of spiritual and physical dimensions. These are complex subjects, but what can be deduced from them is the fact that what exists prior to manifestation lacks substance and form; it has no density to give it pattern and being. It exists as pure nothingness that is, in turn, pure potential. And yet within this description I am aware of the limitation of language and wonder—had I been bold enough to have gone with the blank page idea, I may have served the soul better. For within these words that flash before me are concepts such as *exist* and *existence*, which of course are words that define, yet in attempting to define the nothing, we limit it. Paradox.

The Celtic Pagan tradition seeks to invoke the meaning of deep, profound questions by questioning the enquirer. In this manner the questioner must look within to discover answers, for that is inherently where they lie. The teachers of the tradition act as guides that take the enquirer by the hand to a point where they must then venture alone to discover the heart of mystery. The old teachings of the Celts are crammed with snippets of questions that invoke the seeker to go deeper into the realm of the spirit by means of their minds. Within the mysterious Celtic manuscript known as the Book of Taliesin, there is a particular question that is indicative of the nothingness at hand. It refers to a state that we partake of each day. We may give it little thought, but within it there lies a profound mystery: "Do you know what you are when you are sleeping, are you a body or soul, or a pale and mysterious thing?"

At no other point in life are we closer to the essence of what we are than during sleep. This little death takes us on a daily sojourn of several hours into the blissful rapture of nothingness. Time ceases to exist as the brain disengages its strongest tethers from the mind. Our bodies slow down and the heartbeat and rhythm of blood and hormones decrease as the body rests and the mind takes its place in the infinity of the field of being. When asked to describe the state of sleep upon waking, the majority recall only a sense of bliss; no other human emotion or sense seems an adequate description. It is simultaneously nothing and yet there is something there, but it's beyond our grasp, beyond the ability of our words to describe. We have no sense of our bodies while asleep other than the vague references to it in dreams. Our lives are governed by time—seconds, minutes, and hours that dictate our movements and actions. And yet in the depth of sleep, time becomes meaningless; it is of no consequence. It is here in the wonder and naturalness of sleep that we perceive what it is to be of the soul; it is in this state that we sense our origin and our final destination. Perhaps this is why sleep provides such comfort and solace; it is the manner in which we recharge by returning each night to the edges of mind, spirit, and soul.

It would be unusual for an individual to fear the state of sleep; most welcome it as a respite from the tumultuous drama of life, a time to recharge our batteries and take stock of the day as the brain sorts memories into long- and short-term packages. These flit before the mind's eye as dreams that rise from the density of the brain to become imprinted on the field of mind in unison with spirit. It is here within this nothingness of sleep that the soul can be sensed—but this sensing is unlike our normal patterns of perception.

We are programmed to accept or believe that the spiritual is out there somewhere, in some far-flung corner of the universe, and we seek to find it by looking outward. This perception is quite incorrect, for the state of sleep tells us that the no-thing and all-things of the universe exists within us; it is imminent. We do not sense the soul as we would sense another being or person; we sense it as an intrinsic and inherent aspect of ourselves. Generally our data comes from external sources; methods of communication reach our bodies through the medium of air or waves or electricity, and we feel, hear, and see them. They exist beyond our bodies, and these are the normal patterns of sensing that we have become accustomed to. In this manner we imagine that to be aware of the spiritual, it must somehow touch us from on high or from somewhere beyond ourselves. This is not so. We explored earlier the necessity for engaging our perception filters, tweaking our understanding of how we sense. The soul exists within you; it is as present as your mind. You do not feel your mind as such, but you know it to be there by sense, and it is part of the ordinary state, as is the soul. We sense its flow by shifting the consciousness into its stream of movement, and we do this at least once a day in sleep.

Are you a body or a soul, or a pale and mysterious thing? Perhaps the latter is the most intriguing aspect of the verse at hand, for it describes something that has no form; it is amorphous, without substance, and evokes mystery. We are pale and mysterious things, and we become this whenever our consciousness is altered, be this by means of meditation, sleep, pathworking, or ecstatic ritual. These and other similar states that cause brain frequency to be altered release the mind from the restrictive denseness of the body and allow it to cross the rainbow bridge between body and spirit with ease, without obstruction. The brain is a wondrous machine, but it can also serve to impede, for it will do anything in its power to maintain the status quo; its primary task is to maintain the functions of the body and ensure homeostasis. It is also the receiver of the spirit, and it is this bridge between the spiritual and the physical that is expressed as mind, the perfect balance of spirit and body, the mind being the relationship between the two.

The spirit is unaffected by the restrictions of the brain; it simply observes, whereas the mind is affected by the density of our gray matter and the manner by which our bodies react to it and to the outside world. This facet of the mind can cause traits that may denounce or reject any concept of the spiritual, for the mind is deeply affected in life by the personality that is woven into it. Upon sleep or death, the body and personality—the active aspects of our lives—dissolve in the same manner as Dylan's dissolution into the sea: the mind is released from the confines of the body, and the spirit absorbs it into the warp and weft of the soul. The pale and mysterious thing speaks of the mind during its temporary release from the restrictions of the body.

The functions of sleep are understood by modern science, yet there exist aspects of it that continue to baffle the most genius of scientific minds. If we consider the matters of the spirit in relation to the body, we can see the soul at work in the makeup of the physical universe. As light levels alter and twilight descends, our brains release a hormone called melatonin that prepares the body for sleep. If we succumb to this hormone release, we enter the first stage of sleep, called the hypnogogic state. This peculiar state of consciousness is familiar to us all, but I suggest next time that you take note of its effect upon you. You will note that as you enter it, the mind is greatly altered—it becomes more neutral in behavior, and the personality is temporarily suspended. It is that state where one wouldn't really care what happened in the world; it is the onset of bliss. The body seems to fall away from the mind, and if we are to suddenly become aware of our density, we may jerk violently and involuntarily. "I was just drifting off," we may say if disturbed during this period. An interesting phrase, although I would claim that what is actually happening is that the body is drifting as it releases its grip on the mind and spirit. The body maintains a status quo in response to physical forces, but seemingly the brain itself is programmed by something beyond scientific understanding to initiate a temporary release from the normal physical state. As we descend further into deep sleep, the mind is released, and we experience this as the memory of blissfulness.

As we move towards waking, we enter a phase known as the hypnopompic state, which is characterized as the point where the mind is reunited with the brain and we become conscious again. But there is a peculiar aspect to this state, for if we were forced to awaken during this state, we would struggle in our attempt to make sense of the real world and will appear confused and sluggish; our speech and other senses are impeded, and we may speak in gibberish. The mind has not fully coalesced with the body's functions, and it seemingly cannot fully engage with physical reality; for this to occur, the brain must come into play. As the hypnopompic state progresses, the brain initiates the release of a hormone called cortisol, a stress messenger that arises from the adrenal glands by the instruction of the pituitary gland that sits deep in the brain. The effects of cortisol enable the waking individual to orientate the self in time and space; in other words, the body must initiate a process that "docks" the mind to the experience of the body it is attached to. So what is going on here?

Our plane of experience is that of the body; this, in turn, imprints the personality onto the mind, which acts as the bridge between the physical and the spiritual. The forces that act upon the body cause it to select the spirit that experiences this life and absorbs it as part of the story of the universe. However, we encounter states in life, daily and ultimately as death, that cause the separation of the body, mind, and spirit. Powerful hormones are necessary to ensure that the body reengages with the energy that drives and sustains it; without these forces that act on the body, it would be unable to maintain life and would fall from that experience. The human state upon waking without the initiation of messengers that "dock" the mind to it is almost a zombie state; there is nothing present, only basic functions that enable the body to perform as a machine. The human body is constantly striving to maintain the link, or the docking mechanism, that ensures the attachment of the body, mind, and spirit. The soul is the constant that underlies it all. It is the force, the mystery that we sense when we disengage from the limitations of our bodies when we sleep. Understanding this as the daily equivalent of death initiates the realization that death is not a state to fear; we actually experience it every single day of our lives. We return to the familiarity of the source, and in that place we impart the experience of this living as lyrics in the song of the universe.

PERPETUAL BEAUTY

You cannot truly die; you have existed forever and will continue to exist forever, for you are forever. You share the same soul as all the gods that have ever existed; they are aspects of the soul just as much as you are. You are the soul of the universe, and you exist here and now as a spark of that mystery, and each night as your head touches the pillow and you snuggle deeply beneath your duvet, you become the spirit that you have always been. And in that state you know of the origination of all things and the magic that you are the universe experiencing itself, swimming in the rapture of being—with no purpose other than to be. You are the beauty of the universe in perpetual motion.

Your body will die and your personality will dissolve, its memories imparted onto eternity. Your spirit will encounter other forms of existence, and it will impart those memories onto the fabric of the soul. You are a body, a soul, and a pale and mysterious thing; you are all of these and more; you have been more and will be more. Nothing is lost, it simply transforms.

Rest, close your eyes, sleep, and reach for the soul's meaning.

LOSING AN ANIMAL COMPANION

Millie found us. Winter Solstice dawned in hues of pink and crimson; yawning, I ventured into the garden to greet the sleeping trees with blessings of Midwinter. To my surprise a small gray cat sat curiously in the middle of the lawn. She looked at me as if she had seen me a hundred times before as her tail swished gracefully from side to side. I was somewhat perplexed; we live in the middle of nowhere, hardly a metropolis for cats. But this was not the first time a cat had arrived mysteriously at our door with an imaginary suitcase and a look about its face that proclaimed "I shall live here!" Fidget the black and white tomcat did the same, coincidentally (or not!) five Winter Solstices past.

I greeted the little gray cat, who immediately came to me. To her, human legs were objects for rubbing, and her tail curled about my calves. Being a rather sentimental old fool, or perhaps having succumbed to the spell that cats can expertly cast, I fell in love in an instant with the little gray cat. And with that our little family extended by one furry feline. A few inquiries with the farmer down the road over the holiday period enlightened us to the cat's story, who by now had been named Millie.

Millie had had a rather unpleasant life. She had been neglected and abused by her previous owners, and when they left the house that had been her only home, they did not take her with them. Instead she was locked in the empty house and left to die. A few weeks later, a potential buyer found what appeared to be a dead cat lying in a dusty corner of the empty kitchen. It was Millie, but by some miracle she was still alive, barely. It transpired that a diet of insects and water from the toilet bowl had, in fact, saved her little life. She was rescued and nursed back to health. Eventually she was taken in by the farmer next door and given space in the barn with the rest of the farm cats. Now don't get me wrong, a farm cat's life is not a bad life, albeit they are not pets, but a warm mezzanine, food, and straw keep the majority in good health and spirits. Alas, not Millie. She had sensed that the Pagans next door were a much better option. And so she arrived on that pink Solstice morning and became a part of our family.

I find myself pausing as I write these words, filled with emotion for my little gray cat, and I am aware of the words that are yet to come. Fingers tremble slightly on the keyboard; I watch the words dance before me and become blurred black dots as my eyes wet with tears. The emotional arc that captures the heart when one loses a pet is heartwrenching, yet I have not quite relayed the tale. Memories arise even though I believed them to be fastened down. I am in two minds: remove this tangent or keep it in; "Keep it in!" my heart says, for grief must be given its voice when it arises.

A deep breath.

An animal companion is not just an animal but a complex individual with a distinct personality. Millie was no exception, other than her persona was distinctly queer and rather eccentric. She liked to walk beside me in the same manner as a dog; a tap to my thigh and a click of my lips and she would take to my side. Our evening constitutionals were divine affairs, a human and a cat lost in the delights of companionship beside hedgerows and trees. We would take in sunsets and crimson horizons, moonlight and starlight, and although no human words were exchanged, I will remain forever convinced that we engaged in meaningful discourse.

At home she became my writing companion; a crocheted blanket on her own chair beside the desk was her daytime position. She performed the same ritual daily where she would sit on her bottom and gaze at me as I fired up the computer and took to writing. For minutes she would assume that same position, watching my fingers tap at the keyboard; a little purr would sing to the silence, and then she would settle and sleep. If I stopped typing, she would rouse from her slumber to offer a curious look that seemed to say, "What are you stopping for? Keep at it—my food isn't gonna buy itself!" At night we would snuggle beneath duvets and blankets, her purring lulling me to sleep. She was my friend, and I adored her.

Three wonderful years went by. She was spoiled to within an inch of her life, and she relished the love and attention she received. But her life was nearing its end. With little warning, she developed nasal cancer. There was little that could be done. It was too near her brain for surgery, and it impeded her breathing. We were devastated. We took solace that Millie's last years had been wonderful and that she had been loved so much. The vet prescribed her some effective pain relief, which helped immensely, but her life was slowly slipping away.

Her favorite place in the summer months was beneath the fragrant lilac tree. She would watch the garden pass by and occasionally rise to make sure that the house and her domain was in order. It was a Friday when she came to me. Gingerly she climbed onto my knees and sat, most unusually, facing me, lifting herself so she was as near to my eyes as possible. Her nose touched mine, and I knew in that instant that the time had come. We decided that day to take her the following week to be put to sleep.

Millie, however, had other plans. She took to her lilac tree; its flowers had just since passed their best, and as purple petals floated to the ground on a gentle summer breeze, Millie turned her face from this world and died. She died on her terms, in her home, surrounded by the things and people she loved. Free from pain, she fell into eternal sleep.

Society has inadvertently created a hierarchical tier that defines the quality and meaning of a death. I don't think this is necessarily a conscious decision but a natural process that expresses our coping mechanisms. Society would cease to function effectively were we all emotionally debilitated by the empathic outpouring to someone's death that does not directly affect us, so we naturally tier our responses to other people's grief. We can read an account of three hundred people killed in an aircraft accident and empathize, but we are not debilitated by grief. The death of a child registers high on our empathic radar, and we may find our hearts bleeding for a parent whose loss has torn their world apart. We can adequately project a torrent of sympathy towards someone who has lost a spouse or a parent, a sibling or close relative. But when it comes to pets, our reactions can be different. Try telling your boss that you can't come to work today because the cat has died. The death of a pet that is not our own generally registers low on our empathic radar, and our ability to sympathize in the same manner as the death of a human being is greatly reduced. Why?

The quality of relationships cannot be quantified, and to be in sufferance of grief is, as I have previously explored, indicative of an irreversible change to that relationship. The relationships we develop with pets are unique in that rarely are they expressed beyond the home unit.

We can gauge the quality of people's relationships with human beings because it is a language that we inherently understand. We talk about our human friends and families in work, in groups, and at play, and there are similarities that every other individual can appreciate and see emulated in their own lives. But the language that we employ with our pets is different and one not fully articulated by language. Yes, of course we speak to them, but the true method of communication between a pet and its human is voiceless. It is an emotional connection, and that is something that is difficult to express beyond the confines of that relationship.

Our pet companions are always there, at home generally; they become a part of the fabric of the home and an expression of its personality. Close friends and family may have an appreciation of that, but it is perhaps one that colleagues and distant friends cannot fully comprehend. Consequently people who lose a pet often find that they can be ridiculed for grieving for an animal, which can leave them feeling even more bereft. Grief is not limited as a response to the death of a human being alone; animal companion deaths can be equally traumatic. To many people, the relationship they have with a pet is their primary relationship. To the elderly, the isolated, the introverted, and those who have no family, a pet may be their only expression of meaningful relationship, where the love that the companions share is unconditional. To cause someone who has lost a pet and is grieving to feel ridiculed is an errant fault, and one that can and should be avoided simply by extending a hand of sympathy and compassion.

In response to the death of an animal companion, we ourselves may feel foolish and may even attempt to disguise the fact that we are in sufferance of grief. A whole storehouse of emotions can come into play, particularly if the animal has had to be put to sleep. To make that decision is perhaps the most difficult one for any animal lover. It may seem like the kindest option, but the heart can rarely rationalize such a notion. To the majority it still feels like murder. It is perhaps the most difficult decision a pet owner will make. In the immediate aftermath of an animal being put to sleep, guilt is normal and something that must be experienced in order to assimilate the grieving process. Finding yourself in this horrid position is never easy; it hurts.

The relationship you have with your animal companion is unique and special; with this in mind, if you find yourself in the position where the decision to euthanize is imminent, reach out to the animal with your emotions and let them know what is happening. They are not automatons—on some level they understand what is happening. They are more than capable of sensing your emotions, therefore cocoon them in that love during the whole process. Flood the ether with your compassion and reflections of your lives together. If you can, be there for them as they die—now this is tricky, and for many a task that they cannot bear to undertake. But consider it; however difficult it will be for your emotions, it will be far more difficult for that animal to die without you being there. Your love and your connection and that out-pouring will make easier their passing.

Honoring our animal companions should be incorporated into our Samhain traditions and rituals, with photos of them placed on the ancestor altar. Sharing stories of our pets' lives is equally as valid as those of our human companions, and should never be ridiculed or belittled as not being "true grief." When our pets die, they leave a void that can rarely be filled; do not denigrate or downplay the loss of an animal companion. They are as much a part of your life as any other member of your family or circle of friends.

Ritual and Practice

PART 4

PREPARATION, PRACTICE, AND RITUAL

Death is the end of life; ah, why
Should life all labor be?

ALFRED TENNYSON

Rituals and ceremonies that honor the dead can bring solace, comfort, and a sense of continuation to those who are left behind. Paganism in general embraces connective rituals that serve to honor the dead and can be incorporated easily into everyday life. Honoring the dead is remarkably different than pining for them and constantly attempting to call them back.

Look to nature—look to a mighty oak who may allow a tired bird to perch and rest its wings; they swim together for a while, two beings blissfully enraptured in relationship, but the bird will eventually spread its wings and take to flight, and the oak will never attempt to call it back. We can be like that tree, allowing the freedom that the spirit of our loved one deserves to fly free while honoring it for the life it experienced in this world. Death is never easy, but there are little things we can do to honor our loved ones and celebrate the impact and influence they had on our lives while simultaneously acknowledging their continuation as spirit.

The industrialization of the funeral industry has served to disempower us by taking the emphasis of care for the deceased away from the family or community unit. Thankfully one can see changes in this trend as more and more people move towards taking control of funeral services and other aspects of dying and death rituals. These small steps are immensely empowering, and slowly but surely the modern face of death rituals is being transformed. In a Pagan sense it is important that we develop new liturgy and rituals that reflect the individual's spirituality. In a book of this length it would be impossible for me to offer rituals and ceremonies that would accommodate all traditions. What I offer instead are rituals that I have some experience of in the hope that these will inspire you to create your own.

Examine the rituals that your tradition has in relation to dying and death. How do they reflect the requirements of the dying and the needs of the bereaved? Have they actually been implemented or put into practice? Perhaps your group, coven, or grove is not yet in possession of death rituals; if so, it may be time to address the issue. Consider the function and effectiveness of death liturgy within the dynamics and tradition of your group.

A VIGIL FOR THE DYING

For death and life, in ceaseless strife,
Beat wild on this world's shore,
And all our calm is in that balm—
Not lost but gone before.

CAROLINE NORTON

I f a loved one or fellow Pagan is dying, it is important that they receive as much spiritual comfort and support as possible before and during the time of passing. To be present at someone's death is a special and privileged occasion; the majority of us, if given the choice, would wish for those we love to be there for us as we transition.

There are several circumstances where the following ceremony could not be undertaken, particularly if the dying individual is in an intensive care unit or is dying of a contagious disease; access to these in particular will be limited. However, it can be adapted or performed remotely; take from it what inspiration you can. If the death takes place at home or in a hospice or general medical unit, there is no reason why this ceremony cannot take place. Always be considerate of others who may be present, particularly if they do not understand the Pagan element. It would be the responsibility of the priests present to explain its function. The ceremony calls for the lighting of three candles; if this is inappropriate, consider using artificial light. It's the symbology and sympathetic connection that matter.

Bear in mind that in the process of natural disease, death may not be quick; the patient may lose consciousness and remain in that state for several hours before death occurs. The dying person may withdraw from eating and drinking completely, which is quite normal and is indicative of the body withdrawing itself from life. With this in mind, this ceremony has no time limit as such and will be dictated by the dying process itself.

THE DEATHBED VIGIL

The primary function of this ceremony is to instill a sense of calm and offer the dying individual a sacred space in which to pass over. Sounds, smells, and touch are important in helping the individual to have a sense of the familiar. In most cases, the hearing is the last sense to cease operation; therefore, ensure that those present continue to speak to the dying person. Sing songs or chants to them, use drums or other instruments familiar to them, but avoid loud noises that may shock them. Hold their hands and massage their feet if you can. Call to the gods and goddesses that they were devoted to in life to assist and be present. Call to the spirits of place to attend and ease their passing. Cast a circle or sacred space according to your tradition.

When the patient loses consciousness completely and the breathing becomes labored or shallow, it is a sign that death is imminent. If possible, have three small candles ready; small tealights in glass jars would be ideal. Place one as close as possible to the left-hand side of the patient and light it. Encourage all present to recall memories of the patient's life, and say words of this nature:

We honor your body and your earthly life; we honor this vessel that we have touched and held and embraced. Long shall the memories of your physical form remain with us. Know that you

will not be forgotten. Blessed be your human body that held the
experience of this life that now ends. Let it end in peace. O gods
and goddesses of the land (if appropriate, name those of meaning
to the patient), of this place, arise, hearken to this call. Comfort
(name) and ensure him/her swift passage from this world.

Remain in thoughts of the patient's physical life for some minutes.

Light the second candle and place it as close as possible to the right-hand side of the body. Encourage all present to recall the patient's creativity, emotional expression, and the uniqueness of their communication. Say words that describe this, such as:

We honor your expression and your creativity; we will remember
the tone of your voice and the uniqueness of your laughter.
We honor the way in which you inspired others. Long shall we
remember you as an expression of your living. Blessed be your
personality; know that we will carry its memory with us. As
this life ends, let it end in peace. Gods and goddesses of the sky, of
expression, vitality, and emotion, hearken to this place! Comfort
(name) and ensure him/her swift passage from this world.

Remain lost in thoughts for several minutes.

Light the third candle and place it as close as possible to the patient's head. Encourage all those present to visualize the patient's spiritual being. Say these words or similar:

We honor you as a spark of the universe, as immortal spirit;
we honor you within the oneness of soul. As you return home,
know that we will honor the life you experienced here in this
world, and long may we remember it. Gods and goddesses

of death and high mystery, hear this call. Hearken to this
place and make swift (name's) passage from this world.

Sense all three aspects of the patient in this space, and if appropriate chant or sing as they descend closer to death. Maintain touch throughout the remaining time.

If possible, form a circle around the patient, with all participants holding hands. Recite this prayer:

Soul, since I was made in essence pure,
Without end nor with beginning.
With seven faculties that I was thus blessed,
With seven created beings I was placed for purification;
I was gleaming fire when I was caused to exist;
I was dust of the earth,
I was a high wind,
I was blossoms of trees on the face of the earth.
Soul, since I was made.

Death may not be immediately apparent, but a time will come when all chest movements stop. One can discreetly place two fingers on the wrist to check for the absence of a pulse. Pupils that become dilated and fixed are a sure sign that death has occurred.

When death is ascertained, encourage all present to imagine a pair of stout wooden doors, flanked on either side by pillars of carved stones. With arms outstretched and palms facing, move the arms out in an opening gesture while saying:

Guardians at the veil, permit him/her entry,
Ancient wisdom, open the doors!
The wisdom of sages fashioned you
Before this world was made,

You had being when the earth was young.
(Name), now go forth; take your place with the mighty dead.
Blessed be the life you lived and blessed be your death.
We will remember you.

Imagine the deceased spirit walking through the doors and dissolving into the beyond. Now bring your arms back together until the palms touch, watching with your mind's eye the stout doors closing shut. It is done.

Remain in this place for as long as required.

If the individual died in a hospice or hospital, their body will no doubt be transported to the facility's morgue. If a funeral director is being employed, the body may be removed from the place of death and held at their facility until the funeral. However, if the death occurred at home, it is vital that the body be kept as cool as possible prior to the funeral. Decomposition can occur rapidly, so it is important that if you are taking care of the body yourself, you are equipped to deal with this.

Ensure that all heat sources in the room the body occupies are turned off. Windows should be left open, curtains closed, but ensure that gauze or muslin is taped or pinned over the window opening to prevent insect entry. Putrefaction will begin within the abdomen of the corpse; keep this area cool with ice, dry ice, or cool packs. Additional ice packs wrapped in fabric can be liberally placed around the body.

The body can be washed with a solution of undiluted tea tree and lavender oils, which will help prevent microbial growth on the surface of the skin, but ensure that gloves are worn during application. Burn frankincense and pine resins or needles at frequent intervals to help create and instill a sense of the sacred and mask any odors. Portable air conditioning units are perfect for ensuring the room is kept cold. Remember, the colder the better. The more you prepare ahead of time, the better the experience will be for everyone.

PREPARATION OF THE BODY

Under the wide and starry sky,
Dig the grave and let me lie.
Glad did I live and gladly die,
And I laid me down with a will.

ROBERT LOUIS STEVENSON

In the summer of 2013 I was privileged to conduct the funeral service of a local Druid; a select number of priests from the Druid order that I head were chosen to officiate at the service. Prior to the service, we prepared his body for the earth. No words can quite describe the feeling of performing this intimate ritual. It was performed at the deceased's house, and his spirit felt tangible; we felt cocooned in his memories and the connection his spirit had to the building and his possessions. The intention of the rite was threefold:

- to honor his physical body
- to prepare and clothe him for his coffin
- to acknowledge and honor his spirituality

The ritual served also to bond those present one to the other and to the spirit of the departed. It was the last thing that any human being could do for the body. If you are offered the opportunity to do a similar ritual for a member of your community, I would heartily recommend that you do so. However, I would recommend that this ritual only be performed if the body is in good condition and not in a state of decomposition. To prevent the purging of the corpse's stomach contents, a small amount of cotton wool can be placed in the mouth and into the nostrils.

This ritual is best performed before the body is placed in its coffin.

On a massage table or other suitable surface position a length of natural cotton, linen, or muslin lengthwise, approximately 3.5 meters in length or less, depending on the height of the deceased. Place another length of the same fabric widthwise across the center of the surface being used, approximately 4 meters or so. The fabric should form the approximate shape of an equal-armed cross.

If available, have a photograph of the deceased in life, and create a sacred space according to your particular tradition or in the manner you are accustomed to. Burn the following incense recipe during the ritual; in my recipe, "1 part" is designated as a heaped dessert spoon.

> 1 part frankincense
> ½ part myrrh
> ½ part pine needles or resin
> ¼ part wormwood
> ¼ part vervain
> Few drops patchouli oil

In addition, mix together 75 milliliters, 3 ounces, or ⅓ cup each of lavender and tea tree essential oils to make a mass volume of approximately 150 milliliters and place in a wide, shallow ceramic bowl. Have small pieces of gauze or cotton in readiness next to it that are approximately 8 inches square.

Light some candles and place some of the incense onto a hot charcoal disc.

Acknowledge the spirit of the deceased:

Spirit of (name), hear us; you who occupied this physical form, hear this call. Know that we come to this place to honor (name) living. (Insert names of the gods and goddesses that the deceased worked with), hear us, attend this rite, be with us as we honor your devotee's passing from this world. Be here now.

For the invocation to a chosen psychopomp, repeat three times using your own words or the following as inspiration (from my *Book of Celtic Magic*):

Edge of darkness ravens cry
Part the veil for he/she who dies
Spirit passed beyond death's reach
Come ye forth to (name) now teach
Truths of life and truths of death
Here at edge of life's last breath
Guardians, spirits who tend the veil
Let him/her board, his/her ship to sail
Beyond the sea and to the west
O spirit, we ask you permit him/her rest.

Using the premixed essential oils, dip the gauze or fabric squares into the oil and wring out. In the ritual we performed we did not use gloves; however, if you are sensitive to essential oils, it would be wise to wear suitable surgical gloves. If you choose not to, your skin will dry and the area between your fingers will temporarily bleach. Wash your hands at the conclusion of the ritual and moisturize frequently.

Recite the following prayer (inspired by Starhawk's blessing for washing the dead from *The Pagan Book of Living and Dying*) while simultaneously anointing the stated body part with the oil-soaked gauze; note that the intention here is not to wash the body in oils but to moisten by anointing it lightly. The quantity stated is more than enough to cover the body of a six-foot-tall adult male of average build.

We honor your head, the place that gave rise to your thoughts.
We honor your eyes that bore witness to this world.
We honor your ears that heard the wonders of this world.
We honor your nose that brought breath to your lungs.
We honor your lips that expressed your uniqueness.
We honor your shoulders that carried your burdens and those of others.
We honor your arms that reached to embrace this world.
We honor your hands and the magic of touch.
We honor your heart, your seat of feeling and compassion.
We honor your center that held you to this place.
We honor your belly button that anchored you to blood and heritage.
We honor your belly, the center of passion.
We honor your genitals, the portals of pleasure.
We honor your knees that bent in service to others.
We honor your legs, strong and stable.
We honor your feet that trod the face of this earth.
We honor your body, the vessel of living.

Use the remaining oil to completely anoint the body front and back. A tip here: anoint half of the back at a time by having people opposite you reach over and log-roll the body only a few inches off the surface of the table. This will enable you to reach under the body.

Place a small stone or pebble to represent the land the deceased lived upon on the belly of the corpse and say these words or similar:

May the powers of this land return your body to the mysteries of earth.

Place a small feather on the belly of the corpse and say these words or similar:

May the powers of air and sky hold the memory of your life.

Place a small amount of natural sea salt on the belly and say these words or similar:

May the powers of our sacred seas call your spirit home unto itself.

The body should now be smudged with the prepared incense while the following is recited three times:

Back to the earth, back to the sea,
back to the spirit, one with thee.

If the deceased wished to be clothed in a particular garment, now is the time to do this. Otherwise, fold the cotton/linen/muslin that is hanging from behind the body's head and bring it forward, towards the belly, laying it flat against the corpse. Do the same with the fabric that hangs loosely at the feet end. Now take the fabric that is hanging to one side, fold it up and over the body, diagonally towards the chest; fold this around the top half of the body as many times as it will go. Fold the remaining length of fabric over the body and diagonally towards the thighs, wrapping it around the lower half of the body. The result should be a body that is completely covered in natural fabric.

Chant the following or similar as you wrap:

Back to the earth, back to the sea,
back to the spirit, one with thee.

The body should now be gently lifted and placed within its coffin. Secure the lid in place before saying the following:

We honor your seven consistencies
Of fire and earth
Of water and air
Of mist and flowers
And the southerly winds.
The first for instinct,
The second by which you touched
The third that gave you voice
The fourth with which you tasted
The fifth by which you saw
And the sixth by which you heard
The seventh to follow scent.
Blessed be the dead.

Conclude the ritual in whatever way you are accustomed to. Alternatively, sit by the coffin in contemplative silence for a while.

FUNERAL FOR A DRUID

Bury my heart on Mona
By the old bull's bay
And have a piper play for me
At the closing of the day.

ANONYMOUS

Peter planned for his funeral twenty-two years before the event. Within the grounds of his home he planted a grove of six apple trees, in the center of which was raised a seven-foot-high tumulus of earth and stone. This was to be his final resting place. Peter thought about his death; he wanted it and the decisions he made to reflect the colorful nature of his living. His focus was primarily a return to nature, to the realms of land, sea, and sky; his wish was that any sorrow was approached with celebration. In 2013 he developed terminal brain cancer, and true to his word, he approached his impending death with a sense of celebration.

He ensured that we, the local Druids, understood exactly what he wanted and how we were to conduct his funeral. I spent several hours in his company talking about his coming death. It was both a humbling and moving experience. His health deteriorated, and he was admitted to the local cancer hospice. There he retreated from life; his body pulled away from sustenance and liquids, and slowly but surely he turned away from the world. Late on a glorious moonlit August evening in the company of a dear friend, Peter's life ended.

A few days later, his body was transported to his home, where the Druids gathered to prepare his body for its final resting place. The previous ceremony for the preparation of the body was conducted, Peter was placed in his wicker coffin, and we carried him the hundred yards from his home to his grave.

A funeral rite should reflect the individuality of the deceased; the role of the celebrant is to listen to the needs of the dying and respond accordingly to create a ritual that is meaningful and deeply personal. Peter loved the mythologies of his land and the dance of the three traditional Celtic realms of land, sea, and sky, and his funeral reflected that love. The following is an account of his funeral service.

SETTLING AND GROUNDING

Priests take their position, forming a circle around the coffin. Priest 1 is positioned at the head of the coffin. Mourners are invited to form an outer circle surrounding the priests and the grave.

All participants are asked to visualize Peter, to invoke a memory of him and consider his spirit present.

PRIEST 1

> *We gather within this sacred space, upon this hour, to honor the life of Peter and to return his mortal remains into the keeping of this blessed earth. In the ways of our ancestors, it was understood that the spirit does not perish but animates a new form in another realm, and that death is merely the midpoint of a long existence. Who understands the mysteries best but those who have passed through death's door?*

What form the spirit that animated Peter's form will thus take
is not known, but Peter remains within the song of that spirit.

Travel with the setting sun, Peter, and rise again with a
new dawn in a new and different place. But know this,
that here, within this space, you will be remembered.

Hail to thee, spirit of Peter: know that we come to this place in honor
of the life you occupied in this world. Know that all these things are
in your honor, and long may your memory continue. Hail to you,
spirit of Peter: be here in this space and know that you are honored.

Leaf of tree, bark and stone, arise and come unto this place in
mourning and celebration of a life that breathed amongst you. Tribes
of the seen and unseen worlds, you of the hollow hills, you of land and
sea and sky, hear this call. Arise and join us as we return Peter's body
to this earth that he loved so much. In this wisdom we behold Peter's
memory and essence; nature does not waste anything, and we see him
as the sun glistens and shines on the earth, we feel him as the warm
summer winds cascade through the land to caress our skin, we hear
him in the songs of the birds at dusk and dawn, and we touch him in
the cool waters of our lakes; he is now all of these things and more.

Long may you be remembered!

A fire bowl with a small pyramid of wood, positioned between priest
1 and the head of the coffin, is lit.

PRIEST 2

This fire is lit to honor the flames, heat, passions, and the spark of Peter's life. It burns as a reminder that all things are transformed and changed by the powers that govern our universe. Within this sacred bowl, earth transforms into air by the powers of fire. And within this rite, we commit Peter's body to be transformed into earth by the flames of our compassion and love.

As a reminder of the omnipresent nature of Peter's spirit, the following adapted verses of "The Battle of the Trees" held in the Book of Taliesin are recited by priest 3. At the end of each line, all priests repeat the phrase "I have been."

PRIEST 3

I have been in a multitude of shapes (I have been)
Before I assumed a consistent form,
I have been a sword, narrow, variegated,
I have been a tear in the air,
I have been the dullest of stars.
I have been a word among letters,
I have been a book in the origin.
I have been the light of lanterns,
A year and a half.
I have been a course, I have been an eagle.
I have been a coracle in the seas:
I have been compliant in the banquet.

I have been a drop in a shower;
I have been a sword in the grasp of the hand,
I have been a shield in battle.
I have been a string in a harp,
Disguised for nine years.
I have been all these things and also the shape I have since departed.

PRIEST 1

All is not lost; a river will lose its name, its course, and
its form as it enters the sea, but is its essence dissolved?
No. Within the midst of change and transformation,
memory is held. We die only when we are forgotten.

We believe in a continuation, but we still miss the body, the touch, and
the sense of being in another person's company. We miss the sense of
wonder beheld in simple things and the pleasures gleaned from living.
We are permitted to miss and reminisce about a character who brought
color and panache to the world. But with that, we must let him go...

Consider, if you will, a tree, a mighty oak who will allow a
bird to perch and rest awhile, and then let it fly free without
ever attempting to call it back. Your hearts need to be like
that tree, allowing the spirit that occupied Peter's form the
freedom it requires to fly free of this place. Beyond suffering,
beyond the sunset, and into the laps of the gods.

PRIEST 4

Approaches the coffin and, with arms outstretched, palms towards the ground, says the following:

> *I call to the powers of this land, arise and hear this call. Kin of*
> *the earthly realms and spirits of this land, attend and witness this*
> *rite. Mother Goddess, Mon, nurturer and bread basket of Britain,*
> *mother of Wales, grandmother of the world, ancient goddess, hear*
> *this call! Arise and come unto us, attend and witness this rite.*
> *Accept this, the body of Peter, as we return his remains to the flesh*
> *of your body. Powers of this land, bear witness. Be here now!*

Priest places a stone on the lid of the coffin.

PRIEST 5

Approaches the coffin and, with arms forming a wide Y shape gestured towards the sky, says:

> *I call to the powers of the sky, to those of the high places, spirits*
> *of expression and breath, of inspiration, hear this call. Come,*
> *winged creatures and spirits of the unseen realms. Come, bee*
> *and wasp; come, dragonfly and fairy, attend this rite, bear*
> *witness as we return Peter's body to the earth. Gods of the high*
> *places, Beli Mawr, father of sky whose radiance gives life to*
> *earth, attend and bear witness to this rite and to Peter's passing*
> *from this world. Powers of the realm of sky, be here now!*

Priest places a swan feather on the lid of the coffin.

PRIEST 6

Approaches the coffin and, with arms stretched out to the sides, says:

> *I call to the powers of the sea, to the magic of singularity and the*
> *mysteries of the deep. Come by powers of the ninth wave. Sacred*
> *seas that surround this island, hear this call, bear witness to one of*
> *your tribe who has left this life. Gilled creatures, water breathers,*
> *winged ones of the sea—arise, hear this call. Llyr, mighty god of*
> *the sea, arise and attend this rite; hear the call of your servants.*
> *Branwen, gentle lady of the sea, come on starling wings and witness*
> *this rite. Spirits and gods of the realm of sea, be here now!*

Priest places a sea shell on the lid of the coffin.

PRIEST 1

Invites friends and family to approach the coffin and share a eulogy in Peter's memory. Priest 2 places a small cauldron of hot charcoal on the lid of the coffin. Upon completion, the eulogist sprinkles some incense onto the coals and returns to the circle of mourners, then all present say the phrase "long may you be remembered."

All priests move to the coffin and place their hands, outstretched, above it. One priest begins a steady but determined drum beat.

All priests recite the following mystery from the Book of Taliesin:

> *Soul, since I was made in essence pure,*
> *Neither for my own sake, nor for death,*
> *nor for end, nor for beginning.*
> *It was with seven faculties that I was thus blessed,*
> *With seven created beings I was placed for purification;*
> *I was gleaming fire when I was caused to exist;*

I was dust of the earth, and grief could not reach me;
I was a high wind, being less evil than good;
I was a mist on a mountain seeking supplies of stags;
I was blossoms of trees on the face of the earth.
Soul, since I was made.

Preselected bearers are summoned forward and take their position on both sides of the coffin and prepare for lowering.

PRIEST 1

Ancestors, guardians at the veil, open the doors of the dead!
Gods of death and crossing, hear this call!
Wisdom of ages, part the veils!
Spirits of this place, accept Peter's body into your domain!
Peter, take your place as ancestor!
Peter, know that we will always remember you!

Lower coffin, increasing the drum beat as it is sent into the earth.

PRIEST 1

Gods of the deep, spirits of earth, accept the
remains of Peter into your realms!

PRIEST 2

Approaches the fire bowl with a cauldron of water and pours the contents onto the flames.

As the flames of life are extinguished, so we accept that Peter
has passed from this world. Know that the flames of his
memory you now carry within you. Bear witness to them.

All priests recite:

Grant, O gods, thy protection
And in protection, strength
And in strength, understanding
And in understanding, knowledge
And in knowledge, the knowledge of justice
And in the knowledge of justice, the love of it
And in that love, the love of all existences
And in the love of all existences, the love of the gods and all goodness.

Invite mourners to approach the grave and cast a handful of soil onto the coffin.

It is done.

SAYING GOODBYE

Don't cry because it's over.
Smile because it happened.

Dr. Seuss

Situations may occur that prevent us being present at the death, funeral, or memorial, depriving us of a moment to say farewell, but all is not lost. The spirit occupies all time and all places; one can reach out and bid a fond goodbye without the need to be present. This simple little ceremony requires only three flowers, some string, and a pen and paper, and it can be conducted anywhere you wish.

You will need:

- bramble flowers or leaves
- red rose petals
- rosemary leaves or flowers
- pen and paper
- natural string

Take to sitting and have the paper and the flowers in a small bowl or pouch and place nearby. Take time to recall the deceased. Sit in quiet contemplation for a good duration of time, lost in thoughts and memories. If it helps, play their favorite music or wear their favorite scent; have photographs nearby to remind you of them. After some time in contemplation, take the paper and write the deceased a letter. Tell them what they meant to you, what they brought to your life, how they enriched your experience of living. Don't hold back; be frank and honest, perhaps telling them things that you may not have had the courage to do in person.

Place the letter on a flat surface and take the flowers in your left hand. Take the rosemary in your right hand; holding it fast, also hold the image of the deceased firmly in mind. As you place the plant on the paper, say these words or similar:

> By the virtues of rosemary, I remember you; by the power of this
> plant, I vow that your memory will not fade. Know that I will
> miss you, know that I will remember you. I bid you farewell.

Now take the rose petals in your right hand and hold the image of the deceased in mind. Say these words or similar as you position the petals on the letter:

> These petals of the rose represent my love for you. Know that I will
> cherish our friendship for as long as I shall live. By the powers of the
> rose, know that my love for you will never fade. I bid you farewell.

Repeat the same process with the bramble and say words to this effect:

By the virtue of bramble, I ask that your spirit forgive any
wrongdoing I caused you in life. Forgive my actions if they
brought you tears, pain, or anguish. If I have spoken harshly
to you or unkindly, forgive me. I bid you farewell.

Wrap the flowers tightly in the paper and secure with natural string. If you are able, or at your earliest convenience, the bundle should be burned and your messages sent to the spirit world by way of transformation into smoke. As the bundle burns, repeat these words three times:

Bramble, rose, and Mary wise, burn by flame and into sky,
(Name), your life I honor here, farewell and fond goodbye.

It is done.

DAYS OF THE DEAD

Three nights that bring the ancestors near
Through veils so thin they gather here
No rules nor neither slight nor sin
Shall spoil our somber Samhain din.

KRISTOFFER HUGHES

In 1897, in the region of Ain, France, seventy-three fragments of a bronze tablet were discovered that transpired to be a lunar-solar calendar dating to the second century of the Common Era. Referred to as the Coligny calendar after the township in which it was found, it is believed to be one of the only true accounts in existence of the division of the Celtic year. While the numerals are in the Roman style, the names of the months are given in Gaulish, one of the early Celtic languages. Pertinent to this discourse is the occurrence of the name *samonios,* derived from the Gaulish word *samon,* meaning "summer." In all probability, the later Irish-Celtic term *Samhain* is cognate with *samonios,* meaning "summer's end." This suggests that the term *samonios* may very well be the earliest written record of what we would recognize in modern Paganism as the festival of Samhain. Of particular note, the Coligny calendar makes reference to *Trinoxtion Samonii,* translated as "the three nights of Samonios," which suggests that the festival was observed over three consecutive nights.

The spirit of Samhain endures through the expression of final harvest festivals that contain elements of ancestor veneration and a preparation for the coming winter. This is particularly relevant in the Northern Hemisphere at the end of October. While little can be deduced from the Coligny calendar as to the nature of the celebrations themselves, it is apparent a festival that marked the fall into winter was observed by the European, British, and Irish Celts. Tales and legends that refer to Samhain are abundant, particularly in Ireland and Wales, and have a distinct liminal or supernatural quality. While there is some skepticism as to the amount of influence the old festival of Samhain had on modern celebrations, the similarities are compelling.

Coinciding with the period of Samhain in Central and South America is the influential festival of Dias de los Muertos, the "Days of the Dead." The primary focus of this colorful festival is to honor the dead; its symbols and iconography are rapidly being absorbed into modern Halloween celebrations. Festivals of this nature do not exist in a vacuum, and while separated by the vastness of the Atlantic Ocean, it is likely that the Dias de los Muertos festival shares a common origin with European final harvest celebrations. Professor Nicholas Rogers, in his exploration of the origins of Halloween, states that

> Halloween and the [Mexican] Days of the Dead share a
> common origin in the Christian commemoration of the
> dead on All Saints' and All Souls' Day. Both are thought
> to embody strong pre-Christian beliefs (Rogers 142).

Whilst there is scant evidence to suggest that the Celts revered the dead during the period of Samhain, its supernatural qualities have since led to a development of ancestor veneration particularly relevant to the new Pagan traditions. Today the sublime Samhain and the secular Halloween contain the spark of an ancient festival that was old when our societies were new. It has developed into the perfect blend of Pagan and Christian symbology; it is a tradition that transcends cultures, languages, and religions.

A comprehensive historical account of the rise and development of the Samhain/Halloween festival would, I fear, take an entire book. It is sufficient to note here that the evolution of Samhain/Halloween indicates a continuous interest in and fascination with the macabre latent in the popular imagination, which in turn feeds the festival, thus ensuring its continuity. Samhain "feels" like something supernatural is driving it—it almost has a life of its own, and its sheer ability to evolve and address the needs of different times and peoples is tantamount to "spooky."

It is apparent that the term *Samhain* now applies to the sublime quality of the secular Halloween, and since the rise of the modern Pagan traditions it is quickly becoming the Western world's new "day of the dead." It offers a period of reflection, contemplation, veneration, and celebration of our dead, recent and ancient. In my own tradition we have taken the Coligny calendar's Trinoxtion Samonii rather literally, and we use it as justification to spread the festival over three delicious days. This allows us to be fully immersed in the old and new traditions of Samhain in a manner that truly brings the dead to mind, while simultaneously celebrating the jovial and frivolous aspects of Halloween. When we are forgotten, we cease to exist; Samhain facilitates remembrance.

So how do we celebrate and venerate the dead? Following are examples of rituals and practices pertinent to the Samhain period. They can be added to your traditional ritual structure or used independently.

TRINOXTION SAMONII DAY 1

(CIRCA OCTOBER 30)

The Feast for the Assembly of the Dead

This modern group ritual is inspired by an old Welsh custom called *hel bwyd cennad y meirw*, which translates as "gathering food for the embassy of the dead." This tradition was still prevalent in North Wales as late as 1900 and coincided with the Welsh-Celtic festival of *Calan Gaeaf* (Samhain). The poor would journey from house to house singing a ditty in return for food. Some of the food would be offered to the dead along with prayers, while the remaining would form the *Calan Gaeaf* feast (Evans 176). The function of the ritual today is to offer a space of communal silent contemplation where the focus is entirely on the dead. After the primary invocation, speaking is forbidden, giving rise to its other modern title, "the Dumb Supper." It can be performed and adapted for group or solitary use.

This ritual is peculiarly powerful in that it breaks down social norms. Eating is a communal affair and one that engages social conversation and interaction, but the Feast for the Assembly of the Dead contradicts this. The result is oddly magical.

You will need:

- a large pillar candle
- additional candles for windowsills
- photographs of the dead or items to represent them
- a small bell
- homemade cakes, biscuits, or cookies
- a prepared meal

Place the large pillar candle on a pedestal in the center of the dining table and surround it with photographs of the dead. Ideally, when your guests are seated at the table, the candle will be above eye level.

Position additional candles on every windowsill in the dining area; one candle per sill is sufficient. If the room is windowless, position a candle against the northern wall. Prepare a meal for your guests to your own liking. In some modern traditions, the meal is served in reverse order (Day 198–199). Ensure that the room is lit as much as possible by candlelight only.

Position the homemade cakes on a stand or plate at one end of the table. Create a sacred space in the manner to which you are accustomed. Encourage all those present to close their eyes and recall their dead. Attend to your windowsills or to the northern quarter if no windows are present and, as you light the candles positioned there, say:

Hear my words, now hear this cry,
Shadows from the other side.
To this circle gather nigh,
Cross now the great divide!

Return to your position at the table and reach forward to light the central candle. Say words similar to these:

Shades of the dead, arise and be here now,
From depth of memory arise, be here now.
Ancestors of blood and heritage, arise and come unto us, be here now!
Assembly and messengers of the dead,
Accept our offerings of food and memory; be here now!

Throughout the meal, the central candle will act as a reminder of the presence of the dead at the feast. As you take to sitting, pass the cakes to your left. Each guest should take two cakes, and, holding them both, should say:

Spirits passed, here to tread,
Come by raven's cry,

Upon this night, O blessed dead,
Memory will not die.

One cake should be placed amidst the photographs as an offering, and the other should be placed on the guest's plate. Continue until all guests have placed their offering; the host should place lastly. When all the cakes have been positioned, the host should ring the bell three times. From this point onwards, the ritual meal should be served and consumed in total silence.

To herald the end of the ceremony, each guest should consume the remaining cake left on their plate. Be immersed in thoughts and memories of the dead.

Conclude the ritual by reaching forward and snuffing the central candle with words to this effect:

Spirits and shades of the dead, know that you will
not be forgotten. Blessed be the dead.

It is done. Afterwards encourage all present to share their thoughts and stories of the dead.

TRINOXTION SAMONII DAY 2
(CIRCA OCTOBER 31)
GRAVE MINDING

Grave minding and grave decorating traditions run hand in hand with the season of Samhain, and perhaps nowhere is this as apparent as in Central and South America during Dias de los Muertos. However, elements of this practice are easily incorporated into modern Pagan traditions and offer a subtle yet powerful method of honoring the dead. It is a practice that I have been personally undertaking for the past twelve years, and it has become a valued addition to my Samhain rituals.

Grave minding is an immersive ceremony where the graves of the dead are tended to and cleaned. Food, flowers, and lights are given as offerings, and a small meal is taken as a form of communion in memory of the dead. While incorporating a Pagan element, I have often taken non-Pagan friends and relatives on my grave minding tour of the region. It is a practice that can easily be adopted by anyone regardless of spirituality or religion.

A primary function of this practice is that it feels almost like a pilgrimage and a vigil combined. I rarely visit the graves of my loved ones at any other time of year, so as a consequence my "grave minding" tour is something I anticipate with some delight. I relish spending a whole day visiting my ancestors and swimming in their memory.

For this ceremony you will need:

- floral tributes of your choosing
- cakes or cookies
- a seven-day or grave candle
- old cloths, a water mister/sprayer, and gentle detergent

As you approach the cemetery or memorial park, bring the dead to mind. Recall whatever memories you have of them. Spend time cleaning and generally tidying the grave, and leave your offerings of food and floral tributes. Light the candle and imagine that the flickering flame represents the connection you have to the deceased; their memory burns in you, for you are intimately connected by blood and heritage.

Remain here for some time in meditation and quiet reflection. Partake of food and drink, and if you are in company, share stories of the deceased. If permitted by the cemetery authorities, leave the lit candle in place. Say these words:

As the veils of Samhain fall,
Sense this light, hear my call.
Blessed dead in earthly tomb,
Your memory in me abloom.

SAMHAIN RITUAL
(EVENING OF OCTOBER 31)

Create an ancestor table or altar specifically for the ritual to be performed this evening. This could be as grand, elegant, or simple as you wish. However, it should form the focal point for the coming ritual. Adorn it with photographs and candles, items, and objects that either represent the dead or belonged to them. Encourage your guests to add their own tokens of their dead to the table. In addition, place a good home-baked loaf of finest bread on the altar/table and cut it directly in half.

Position in the center of the table a large cauldron or shallow dish; have a small container of tealights next to it. Use your imagination here; in my own group, we use a full-size real coffin for this ritual, which sits before the ancestor table and takes center stage. Whatever you use, be sure that it is large enough to safely take as many candles as guests present.

Create and demarcate a sacred space in whichever manner you are accustomed to. Alternatively or additionally, place four candles at the four cardinal directions. Extinguish all lights except for one candle on the ancestor altar/table. Encourage all present to breathe deeply with the ground beneath their feet, sensing the countless ancestral feet that have walked the land and subsequently been interred within it. After three deep breaths, begin the ritual.

Move to the candle that represents the north and light it while saying these words or similar:

> *Ancestors and dead of the north, shades and spirits past,*
> *arise and come unto us. Come by strength of earth and soil,*
> *rock and bone. Arise and come unto us! Be here now!*

Encourage all present to raise their arms, elbows hinged and palms facing outwards (hereafter referred to as the gesture), and say:

Ancestors, come on this Samhain night,
Pass through the mists from shadow to light!

Swiftly move to the east, light the candle, and say:

Ancestors of the east, shades and spirits past, arise and come
unto us. Come by breath of air and expression, come by light of
dawn and moonrise. Arise and come unto us! Be here now!

Encourage all to gesture and say:

Ancestors, come on this Samhain night,
Pass though the mists from shadow to light!

Move to the south, light the candle, and say:

Ancestors of the south, shades and spirits past, arise and come
unto us. Come by flame of passion and noonday sun; ancestors
of the south, arise and come unto us! Be here now!

Repeat the next gesture:

Ancestors, come on this Samhain night,
Pass though the mists from shadow to light!

Finally move to the west, light the candle, and say:

Ancestors of the west, shades and spirits past, arise now and come
unto us. Come by power of the ninth wave, by emotions and feeling.
Ancestors, blessed dead, arise now and come unto us! Be here now!

Repeat the next gesture as before:

Ancestors, come on this Samhain night,
Pass though the mists from shadow to light!

Move swiftly to the center of the space and encourage all present to raise their arms above their heads in a greeting gesture while all guests say:

We call to the spirits, we call to our kin,
We part now the veils and call them all in!
Come all ye dead, family and kin,
Come spirits of place and spirits within!
Be here now!

The host should now move swiftly to the ancestor altar/table and reach for one tealight candle; light this from the single lit candle that occupies the altar/table. Raise the candle up high and say words of this nature:

I call to my sister, (name); she died three years past (share a brief
biography of the deceased). Know that on this night you shall be
honored and remembered. Know that I will not forget you.

Now place the lit candle within the cauldron/bowl/coffin, the principle being that as the company continues this ritual gesture, an ethereal glow grows stronger within the receptacle. Now face the altar and tear off a small piece of bread from one half of the cut loaf. Hold it gently in your hand. All present should say:

Come, arise, O blessed dead. On Samhain night, come
share our bread! Long may you be remembered!

Eat the bread. Repeat the above with all present. This takes a little time; permit people to sit if they grow tired of standing. This ritual takes time, but in the dim candlelight and with words of memory and recollection, it is a rather moving, poignant, and somber ceremony.

When all participants have placed their candles, the host should approach the altar/table and raise the remaining half of the bread and say:

O blessed dead, accept this, our offering; remain with
us in this space and partake of our feast and know that
it is done in your memory. Blessed be the dead!

Encourage the mood to move from the somber to the celebratory. Share food and drinks within the space, and tell tales and stories of your ancestors. Direct people to the ancestors' altar/table and bring the dead alive; tell folk who they are and what they mean to you.

When the evening draws to a close, attend to the four candles and extinguish each one in turn while saying:

Spirits, return to distant shores,
This rite is done, we close the doors!
Long may you be remembered.

If the ritual commenced with ceremonial elements from your own tradition, conclude the ritual in your preferred manner. Leave the loaf outdoors as a gift to the spirits or offer your guests a piece for placement on their family graves. The ritual is complete.

TRINOXTION SAMONII DAY 3
(CIRCA NOVEMBER 1)
HONORING THE ANCIENT AND FALLEN DEAD

THE ANCIENTS

We stand today as the sum totality of our species; within our blood, heritage, and ancestry swim the memories of every single human being who has ever lived. Honoring the ancient dead requires a different frame of mind; we can easily conceptualize recent ancestors, even if some died over a hundred years ago. Photographs and records of their lives may still be available to view, so we have something to connect to. The ancient dead may not be as apparent. Tales of their lives have faded into the mists of time. Certain areas of the world have monuments erected by the ancient dead. In the British Isles we are fortunate that we can readily visit Neolithic and Bronze Age tombs and chambers. Within these places we can feel the songs of the ancestors, yet the ability to pinpoint actual personalities from the distant past is not so easy. The ability to visit these ancient places of the dead certainly makes connecting to them en masse a little easier, but not everybody has that luxury. If you can visit an actual ancient burial chamber for this contemplative ritual, by all means do so; if not, it is equally as effective on the inner planes.

Spend a few hours on the third day of Samhain researching the ancient dead of your lands. Cast your mind back to the periods before the coming of the church if you can—to the time when your lands were occupied by pre-Christian civilizations. Who were they? Do you know what they looked like, how they dressed, what their customs and traditions were? How did they honor their dead?

Take to sitting comfortably and close your eyes, breathe deeply, and imagine a dark landscape. The skies are pitch-black; not a single star illuminates the inky blackness. There is seemingly nothing in this landscape. Think these words or speak them out loud:

Ancestors, ancient and blessed dead
My feet upon your halls to tread.
Ancestors, come by ancient lore
Permit me entry, open the door.

Imagine a faint light in the darkness; it grows brighter and brighter, and as it does it illuminates the entrance to an ancient burial mound. A pair of mighty standing stones guard the entrance to the mound. The pulsating light within continues to shine, and within its glow shapes and forms of the ancient dead appear. They are faceless shadows of the past. Sit within this vision and consider the lives of the ancient dead.

As the vision nears its conclusion, imagine that the ancestral light emits a beam; it is directed at the center of your chest. Sense the light glowing within you. You carry the songs of the ancestors within you. Nothing is truly lost. The light within the mound grows faint and eventually vanishes. Within the inky blackness you sense a remnant of that light within you. Say these words or similar:

Ancestors, ancient dead, I breathe the air that you breathed, walk the land that you walked. I honor your living and dying. I carry a part of your song within me. Blessed be the ancient dead.

Return to your normal state. If you are at an actual ancient site, you may wish to leave an offering of flowers if appropriate.

THE FALLEN

Who understands the true nature of sacrifice? It is a conundrum that has plagued us from the dawn of humanity, yet sacrifice remains a real and visceral aspect of our lives. Each year countless human lives are offered in sacrifice through war and conflict. We may have lost loved ones in active service and descended into the pits of grief, but even if we have not lost a relative or loved one, we are all touched by those who fall in service. There is scarcely a community in the Western world and beyond that does not have a memorial to its fallen in service. They are silent places, somber and humbling. And yet the fallen are not necessarily those who were in active service; the collateral damage from war and conflict causes the deaths of innocents. Women, men, and children also fall.

On the third day of Samhain, if able, take yourself to your local memorial park or monument to the fallen. Stand in quiet contemplation; they did this for you. You stand as a part of the story, however detached we may think we are from conflict. Lives intertwine.

What is the true nature of sacrifice?

Close your eyes and imagine the fallen appearing behind you as if from a mist. Sense their sacrifice and project thoughts of gratitude and honor towards them. Whisper the following three times:

> *Blessed fallen, mighty dead*
> *Sacred fallen in death's bed.*
> *Blood that spilled beyond this place*
> *I honor you within this space.*
> *Your life as gift to those that live*
> *My thanks, my blessings, to you I give.*
> *Blessed fallen, O mighty dead*
> *Honored is the life you led.*

Leave a floral tribute imbued with your blessings.

POSTMORTEM

O Druids...to you alone it is given to know the gods
And spirits of the sky or perhaps not to know them at all.
You dwell in the distant, dark, and concealed groves.
And you say that shades of the dead do not seek
The silent lands of Erebus or the pallid kingdom of Dis,
But that the same spirit controls the limbs in another realm.
Death if what you say is true is but the midpoint of a long existence.

LUCAN, *PHARSALIA*

We are constantly being told what to believe, who to believe in, what belief is right and what is not. How about being radical and actually believing in ourselves to listen to the ebb and flow of spirit and soul that whisper to us from the edge of being? Spiritual teachers, religions, and traditions can only take us so far down the path of knowing. There comes a point when we are inevitably confronted with a gaping chasm, and we are faced with a choice—turn around, ignore it, and reach out for words of wisdom that may soothe the mind or take a few steps back, run like crazy towards it, and leap into the unknown. Sometimes we just have to trust that if we leap, the universe will catch us; it must, we are it, and this is what happens when we trust in ourselves to find truth for ourselves. Of course, we can be guided, inspired, and led to the edges of the chasm of mystery, but nobody can actually teach us to sense the spirit and soul; that must come from within.

Do not fear. Do not be fearful, for you truly have nothing to fear but fear itself. You are a child of the universe, and your life is unique; it is never denigrated or negated, for it is of immense value and worth. By your living the universe experiences the magic of life and the wonder of being human. All the relationships that you form are magical beyond words; they are the manner by which you bring color into the world that you live in.

Yes, you will die, and all those you love will die; our human bodies will fail and succumb to the dissolution of matter. But you carry the tales of those who have gone before you—you become their sum totality. The ancestors and their memories exist as a part of the great song of this world, and we should honor them as such. Never forget your dead or those who have long since passed; recall their stories and tell their tales, for their lives mattered too. Reach for their memories and for the echo that their spirits sense in that place beyond the veil of living. Never fear; cast aside your fears and know that you will carry this experience as spirit.

Death is not the end but the midpoint of a long and wondrous existence. Knowing that we continue cannot entirely alleviate the pain of loss, and it cannot remove our grief, for grieving is essential to the experience of being human. When death strikes, we do lose something—we lose that human relationship and the physical presence of someone we loved. Do not dishonor them by dismissing your grief; their life mattered, and it mattered to you. The message of death is to live, to experience the wonders of this world and this life in all its glory.

The meaning of life is to live, to love, to share through relationship the beauty and magic of this world. Let your body sing to the lyrics of life and find the music of the soul that hides deep within your being. Raise your voice in laughter; cry when tears well from the fountains of emotion. Listen to the rhythms of your body and to the emotions that make you so human.

LIVE! Take this life and be it, run with it through pain and joy, and bring every ounce of color and brightness you can to the song of the universe. This is your story; make it a good one. Do not approach the grave with regret and mediocrity but skid towards it on your back, with the brakes off, and slam into it sideways, crying "What a ride!"

GLOSSARY

Abred (AH-bred)—The apparent material world. Also known as the realm of necessity.

Akasha—Sanskrit word meaning "ether," the essence of all things.

Annwn (ANN-oon)—The indigenous Celtic otherworld, believed to be a parallel universe.

Autopsy—A term for the examination of a corpse after death; literally means "to see oneself."

Awen (AH-wen)—Welsh Celtic word that describes the flowing spirit of inspiration.

Beli Mawr (BELLee MAUR)—Welsh/Celtic god of the sky, sun, and fire.

Branwen (BRAN-wen)—Welsh/Celtic goddess of birds and the sea.

Cabbalistic—Referring to the system called the Cabala, a mystical system of Judaism.

Calan Gaeaf (KAL-ann GAY-av)—Welsh for Samhain/Halloween.

Ceugant (KAY-gant)—The realm of infinity, a place that is beyond accurate articulation and description.

Dwynwen (doo-INN-wen)—Welsh patron saint of lovers.

Dylan (DULL-ann)—Welsh/Celtic personification of the sea.

Ein Sof—One of the unapparent realms in the Cabbalistic system that exists prior to manifestation.

Gwynvyd (goo-IN-vid)—The world of spirit or energy; the unseen world known as the realm of spirit.

Hel bwyd cennad y meirw (HEL boo-id KENN-ad UH MAY-rue)—Welsh tradition of gathering food for the messengers or embassy of the dead.

Llyr (LL-ir)—Welsh/Celtic primary god of the sea.

Malkuth—Upon the Cabbalistic Tree of Life, this is the earthly material plane.

Nwyfre (NOOEE-vray)—A Welsh Celtic word that means "energy" and "sky."

Postmortem—A term that means "after death"; in the United Kingdom it is used to mean "autopsy."

Samonios (SAH-mon-ee-os)—Gaulish word meaning "summer's end."

Trinoxtion Samonii (TREE-nosh-TEE-on SAH-moni)—Gaulish phrase meaning "the three nights of Samhain."

Wyrd—An Anglo-Saxon word that equates to "fate" or "personal destiny."

Yesod—Upon the Cabbalistic Tree of Life, this is the realm directly above the earthly material plane. It is the seat of the emotions.

BIBLIOGRAPHY

Ab Ithel, Williams J., ed. *The Barddas of Iolo Morganwg.* Red Wheel/ Weiser, 2004.

Andrews, Ted. *Simplified Qabala Magic.* Llewellyn, 2003.

Ashcroft-Nowicki, Dolores. *The New Book of the Dead.* Aquarian Press, 1992.

Belanger, Michelle. *Walking the Twilight Path: A Gothic Book of the Dead.* Llewellyn, 2008.

Bonanno, George, A. *The Other Side of Sadness.* Basic Books, 2009.

Brown, Ray. *In Unexpected Places.* O Books/John Hunt, 2010.

Butler, Katy. *Knocking on Heaven's Door: The Path to a Better Way of Death.* Scribner, 2013.

Chopra, Deepak. *The Book of Secrets.* Rider-Random House, 2004.

———. *Life After Death.* Rider-Random House, 2008.

Conway, David. *The Magic of Herbs.* Panther Books, 1973.

Day, Christian. *The Witches' Book of the Dead.* Red Wheel/Weiser, 2011.

Doody, Mark, and Kristoffer Hughes. *Halloween: The Quintessential British Guide to Treats and Frights.* Thoth Publications, 2011.

Evans, Hugh. *Cwm Eithin.* Gwasg Y Brython, 1950.

Ford, Patrick K. *Ystoria Taliesin.* University of Wales Press, 1992.

Fortune, Dion. *Dion Fortune's Book of the Dead*. Red Wheel/Weiser, 2005.

———. *The Mystical Qabalah*. Aziloth Books, Milton Keynes, 2011.

———. *Through the Gates of Death*. Aquarian Press, 1968.

Green, Miranda. *Exploring the World of the Druids*. Thames and Hudson, 2005.

Greene, Brian. *The Fabric of the Cosmos*. Penguin, 2004.

Haycock, Marged. *Legendary Poems from the Book of Taliesin*. CMCS, 2007.

Hey, Tony, and Patrick Walters. *The New Quantum Universe*. Cambridge University Press, 2003.

Hughes, Kristoffer. *The Book of Celtic Magic: Transformative Teachings from the Cauldron of Awen*. Llewellyn, 2014.

———. *From the Cauldron Born: Exploring the Magic of Welsh Legend and Lore*. Llewellyn, 2012.

Kastenbaum, Robert. *The Psychology of Death*, 3rd ed. Free Association Books, 2000.

Kerrigan, Michael. *The History of Death*. Lions Press, 2007.

Koch, John T. *The Celtic Heroic Age*. Celtic Studies Publications, 1994.

Kübler-Ross, Elisabeth. *Death: The Final Stage of Growth*. Simon and Schuster, 1986.

———. *On Death and Dying*. Tavistock Publications, 1970.

Laszlo, Ervin. *Science and the Akashic Field: An Integral Theory of Everything*. Inner Traditions, 2004/2007.

Leming, Michael R., and George E. Dickinson. *Understanding Dying, Death & Bereavement*. Harcourt Brace College Publishers, 1998.

Lewis, C. S. *A Grief Observed*. Faber and Faber, 1961.

Lipton. Bruce H. *The Biology of Belief.* Hay House, 2005.

Markale, Jean. *The Druids: Celtic Priests of Nature.* Inner Traditions, 1999.

Morton, Lisa. *Trick or Treat: A History of Halloween.* Reaktion Books, 2012.

Moss, Robert. *The Dreamer's Book of the Dead.* Destiny, 2005.

Nichols, Ross. *The Book of Druidry.* Thorsons, 1975.

Parker, Will. *The Four Branches of the Mabinogi.* The Bardic Press, 2005.

Parkes, Colin Murray, and Holly G. Prigerson. *Bereavement: Studies of Grief in Adult Life.* Penguin, 2010.

Partington, Angela, ed. *The Oxford Dictionary of Quotations.* Oxford, 1996.

Rasberry, Sally, and Carole Rae Watanabe. *The Art of Dying.* Celestial Arts, 2001.

Regardie, Israel. *A Garden of Pomegranates.* Llewellyn, 1970.

Roach, Mary. *Six Feet Over: Adventures in the Afterlife.* Canongate, 2007.

Rogers, Nicholas. *Halloween: From Pagan Ritual to Party Night.* Oxford University Press, 2002.

Romanyshyn, Robert D. *The Soul in Grief: Love, Death and Transformation.* North Atlantic Books, 1999.

Starhawk. *The Pagan Book of Living and Dying.* Harper Collins, 1997.

Strogatz, Steven. *Sync: Rhythms of Nature, Rhythms of Ourselves.* Penguin, 2003.

Taylor, Timothy. *The Buried Soul: How Humans Invented Death.* Fourth Estate, 2002.

Underwood, Peter. *Ghosts and How to See Them.* Anaya, 1993.

Warden, J. William. *Grief Counseling and Grief Therapy: A Handbook for the Mental Health Practitioner*, 4th ed. Springer Publishing Company, 2009.

Whitaker, Agnes, ed. *All in the End Is Harvest*. Dartman, Longman, and Todd, 1984.

Wright, Philip, and Carrie West. *Death and the Pagan*. BCM, 2004.

ACKNOWLEDGMENTS

There have been a number of people who have contributed in one way or another to the writing of this book: colleagues, friends, and the bereaved whom I have dealt with along the way. However, none of this would have come about without the assistance and patience of a handful of individuals.

My first teacher, Pamela Thomas, took me by the hand and led me into the kingdom of the dead; I doubt that you could ever imagine the impact, effect, and influence you have had on the course of my life. Your wisdom, professionalism, and humor stood me in good ground for growth, and even in the youthfulness of the early '90s we would not have predicted this future; I am forever in your debt. None of these words would have ever come into being had it not been for the years I spent with you. Thank you.

Tracy Dent has been my longest and most faithful companion in the halls of the dead. Thank you for having endured my endless blabbing and musings over the years and for just being so uniquely fabulous and wonderful. Your constant encouragement and support have not gone unnoticed or unacknowledged.

Barrie Jenks, as usual, is a font of Bardic inspiration; thank you for continuously coming to my rescue with a verse or a nudge of just plain old encouragement. Christopher Hickman for his continuous support and inspiration and lending his ear to my musings. Thanks also to those who read the early version of this manuscript.

To my editorial team at Llewellyn Worldwide, Elysia Gallo and Rebecca Zins, an enormous debt of thanks for steering the book in the right direction and for your continuous encouragement and hard work. Thank you.

Finally, to all the thousands of dead who have influenced my journey, know that I honor you also.

GET MORE AT LLEWELLYN.COM

Visit us online to browse hundreds of our books and decks, plus sign up to receive our e-newsletters and exclusive online offers.

- **Free tarot readings • Spell-a-Day • Moon phases**
- **Recipes, spells, and tips • Blogs • Encyclopedia**
- **Author interviews, articles, and upcoming events**

GET SOCIAL WITH LLEWELLYN

 **Find us on Facebook**
www.Facebook.com/LlewellynBooks

Follow us on
www.Twitter.com/Llewellynbooks

GET BOOKS AT LLEWELLYN

LLEWELLYN ORDERING INFORMATION

 Order online: Visit our website at www.llewellyn.com to select your books and place an order on our secure server.

 Order by phone:
- Call toll free within the U.S. at 1-877-NEW-WRLD (1-877-639-9753)
- Call toll free within Canada at 1-866-NEW-WRLD (1-866-639-9753)
- We accept VISA, MasterCard, and American Express

 Order by mail:
Send the full price of your order (MN residents add 6.875% sales tax) in U.S. funds, plus postage and handling to: Llewellyn Worldwide, 2143 Wooddale Drive Woodbury, MN 55125-2989

POSTAGE AND HANDLING

STANDARD (U.S. & Canada):
(Please allow 12 business days)
$25.00 and under, add $4.00.
$25.01 and over, FREE SHIPPING.

INTERNATIONAL ORDERS (airmail only):
$16.00 for one book, plus $3.00 for each additional book.

Visit us online for more shipping options. Prices subject to change.

FREE CATALOG!

To order, call
1-877-
NEW-WRLD
ext. 8236
or visit our
website

from the

Cauldron Born

Exploring the Magic
of Welsh Legend & Lore

Kristoffer Hughes

FROM THE CAULDRON BORN

Exploring the Magic of Welsh Legend & Lore

Kristoffer Hughes

This exploration of the Welsh-Celtic myth of the prophet/poet Taliesin and the witch/goddess Cerridwen takes the reader on a transformative journey. It introduces them to core Celtic philosophy and magic, then embarks on a powerful, experiential foray into one of Wales' most profound legends. Readers will gain a deep understanding of the myth that is the heart of Celtic mystery and become well-versed in a magical ritual for successfully working with one of Celtica's most esteemed goddesses: Cerridwen.

Author Kristoffer Hughes, a practicing Druid and scholar, examines the historical development of the Taliesin myth, provides an engaging in-depth analysis of each character's archetypal role in the story, and presents practical applications, including a year-long magic ritual. As lyrical as it is practical, this unique guide offers readers the tools and understanding to fully immerse themselves into the mysteries of Celtic magic.

978-0-7387-3349-4 • 6 x 9 • 360 pp.

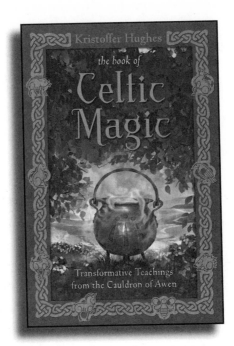

Kristoffer Hughes

the book of

Celtic Magic

Transformative Teachings
from the Cauldron of Awen

THE BOOK OF CELTIC MAGIC

Transformative Teachings from the Cauldron of Awen

Kristoffer Hughes

Delve into the depths of a magical current that spans over three thousand years. *The Book of Celtic Magic* provides its readers with the unsurpassed power of practical magic and the transformative forces of ancient Celtica.

Chief of the Anglesey Druid Order, Kristoffer Hughes invites you to explore the pantheon, myths, and magic of his native Wales. Discover the magical allies, the gods and goddesses, and the spirits of place that form the foundation of this vibrant tradition. Practice rituals that draw you closer to the divine energy of the plants and animals that surround you. Work with spells, conjurations, invocations, and magical tools that have been developed and refined from authentic Celtic sources. Complete with contemplative exercises and a glossary of terms, this step-by-step guide is a definitive source of real Celtic magic.

978-0-7387-3705-8 · 6 x 9 · 360 pp.

TO WRITE TO THE AUTHOR

If you wish to contact the author or would like more information about this book, please write to the author in care of Llewellyn Worldwide and we will forward your request. Both the author and the publisher appreciate hearing from you and learning of your enjoyment of this book and how it has helped you. Llewellyn Worldwide cannot guarantee that every letter written to the author can be answered, but all will be forwarded. Please write to:

Kristoffer Hughes
c/o Llewellyn Worldwide
2143 Wooddale Drive
Woodbury, MN 55125-2989

Please enclose a self-addressed stamped envelope for reply
or $1.00 to cover costs. If outside the USA, enclose
an international postal reply coupon.

Many of Llewellyn's authors have websites with additional information and resources. For more information, please visit our website:
WWW.LLEWELLYN.COM